CHASTITY IN EARLY STUART
LITERATURE AND CULTURE

In this book, Bonnie Lander Johnson explores early modern ideas about chastity. Drawing on a range of materials, from prose to theatre, moral controversy to legal trials, and court ceremonies – including royal birthing rituals – Lander Johnson demonstrates how crucial chastity was in the early Stuart decades. She argues that the virtue informed political, theological, and medical debates, and governed the construction of different literary genres. The book reveals that theatrical and court ceremonies were part of the same political debate as prose pamphlets and religious sermons. It offers new readings of Milton's *Comus*, Shakespeare's *The Winter's Tale*, Henrietta Maria's queenship and John Ford's plays and will appeal to scholars of early modern literature, theatre, political, medical and cultural history, and gender studies.

BONNIE LANDER JOHNSON is Fellow and Lecturer at Selwyn College, Cambridge. She has published articles in journals, including *Bulletin of the Society of Renaissance Studies*, *Shakespeare Quarterly*, and *Parergon: Journal of the Australian and New Zealand Association for Medieval and Early Modern Studies*.

CHASTITY IN EARLY STUART LITERATURE AND CULTURE

BONNIE LANDER JOHNSON

CAMBRIDGE
UNIVERSITY PRESS

CAMBRIDGE
UNIVERSITY PRESS

University Printing House, Cambridge CB2 8BS, United Kingdom

Cambridge University Press is part of the University of Cambridge.

It furthers the University's mission by disseminating knowledge in the pursuit of
education, learning and research at the highest international levels of excellence.

www.cambridge.org
Information on this title: www.cambridge.org/9781107130128

© Bonnie Lander Johnson 2015

This publication is in copyright. Subject to statutory exception
and to the provisions of relevant collective licensing agreements,
no reproduction of any part may take place without the written
permission of Cambridge University Press.

First published 2015

Printed in the United Kingdom by Clays, St Ives plc

A catalogue record for this publication is available from the British Library

Library of Congress Cataloguing in Publication Data
Lander, Bonnie, 1977–
Chastity in early Stuart literature and culture / Bonnie Lander Johnson.
pages cm
Includes bibliographical references and index.
ISBN 978-1-107-13012-8 (Hardback)
1. English literature–Early modern, 1500–1700–History and criticism. 2. Chastity in literature.
3. Sex in literature. 4. Literature and society–Great Britain–History–16th century.
5. Literature and society–Great Britain–History–17th century. I. Title.
PR428.S48L36 2015
820.9′353809031–dc23   2015019714
ISBN 978-1-107-13012-8 Hardback

Cambridge University Press has no responsibility for the persistence or accuracy
of URLs for external or third-party internet websites referred to in this publication,
and does not guarantee that any content on such websites is, or will remain,
accurate or appropriate.

Contents

List of illustrations — *page* vi
Acknowledgements — vii

Introduction — 1

1 Unchastity in Shakespeare's *The Winter's Tale*, Caroline court performance and theological dispute — 10

2 Chastity, medical controversy and the theatre of John Ford — 46

3 Chastity, William Harvey's demonstrations and court ceremony — 82

4 Marian chastity: Caroline masques and Henrietta Maria's chaste births — 103

5 Protestant chastity: the language of resistance in Milton's 'A Maske' and *A Maske* — 138

Conclusion — 172

Bibliography — 175
Index — 193

List of illustrations

1 and 2 Interiorum corporis humani partium viva delineatio. Perutilis anatomes interiorum muliebris partium cognitio ac earundem situs, figura, numerus, positio, hand [sic] iniucounda cognitu (1559). *page* 65
3 William Harvey, Exercitatio anatomica de motu cordis et sanguinis in animalibus (G. FitzerFrankfurt, 1628). 98

Acknowledgements

I have been working on early modern chastity in one form or another for more years than I ought to admit and in this time have accrued more debts than I can remember. My interest in the subject began with an honours-year essay on Milton's *Comus* at Sydney University in 2005 and has dogged me ever since: it became the focus of a masters thesis at Melbourne and then a DPhil at Oxford. I therefore have numerous supervisors, advisors, and assessors whose careful and generous advice has helped to shape my thinking from a very developmental stage: Barry Spurr, Penny Gay, Deirdre Coleman, Beverley Sherry, Louise D'Arcens, Marion J. Campbell, Laurie Maguire, Sharon Achinstein, Margaret Kean, and Alison Shell.

The work has also been read by or discussed with friends and colleagues more recently: Hester Lees-Jeffries (special thanks for such careful reading!), Eleanor Decamp, Jean Chothia, Elizabeth Scott-Baumann, Phillip Connell, Sophia Connell, Sarah Meer, Lucy Razzall, Julia Meszaros, Sophie Carney, Emily Ballou, Roger Dawson, Helen Barr, Henrietta Leyser, Heather Webb, Charlotte Woodford, Michael Tilby, Mina Gorji, Helen Thaventhiran, and David Hillman. Sarah Stanton at Cambridge University Press has supported this project through the final stages of its development and it has been a pleasure to see the work emerge under her careful guidance and that of the manuscript's anonymous readers. My colleagues at Selwyn College have generously enabled the leave that has meant I could finish this book while also juggling the arrival of two babies. And it is to the broader community at Selwyn College and the Cambridge English Faculty that I owe my gratitude for such intellectual stimulation and fellowship. My students have been a constant inspiration and my colleagues a delight.

My parents will, I hope, find this book tangible proof of my efforts over the too-numerous years of my education; I offer it as a gesture of gratitude for their encouragement and help. And if it were not for my own personal resolution to be chaste I would have no cause to thank with such sweetness my husband and children. Before them there was only writing and thinking, which are wonderful endeavours in themselves, but with them life is a supreme joy. My final, and perhaps surprising, thanks go to Henrietta Maria herself, who has come to be something of this project's patron saint. I hope she approves.

Introduction

What is chastity? For those contemporary westerners who do not observe the virtue for religious reasons, chastity usually means very little. It is perhaps considered an archaic form of social and sexual restriction, demarcation, or even control; a first-wave feminist act of sexual and social autonomy; a Petrarchan love-object's refusal to 'pity' her petitioner; or the cornerstone of Elizabeth I's statecraft. To most readers of English literature – both specialist and lay – chastity is perhaps a virtue or behaviour with an inherently literary nature. And with good reason: female assertions of chastity, as much as male attacks upon female chastity, have for centuries been a condition of English literary production. The gendered dynamic of Petrarchan desire underpinned the sonnet and romance traditions up to and well beyond their prodigious flowering in Renaissance England. Romance literature's long-standing concern with chastity also evolved into a theatrical interest when Shakespeare re-modelled the genre for the stage: his late plays all investigate the means by which women might defend their chastity against threats of sexual violence or wrongful accusations of adultery and fornication. And when in Richardson's extraordinarily popular *Pamela*, a serving girl unexpectedly defended her chastity against her master's advances, the novel form exploded into England's literary history.

In the early modern period, the relationship between chastity and literary production was especially insistent. A new generation of poets, who began to print and circulate their work more widely than their predecessors did, utilised chastity figuratively as a means of excusing their desire to make money from their wits. In *The Imprint of Gender*, Wendy Wall details the early modern culture of 'prefatorial disclosures' in which authors justified their decision to depart from the gentlemanly tradition of manuscript circulation by prefacing their works with elaborate disclaimers. Denying any consent in the unseemly act of 'pressing' and 'circulating' (bawdy puns introduced into the English language by the printing press), these prefaces figure the text as an unruly, wanton, or reluctantly debased daughter/lover who willingly or forcibly goes into the arms of another man (the reader) against the author's wishes.[1]

However, the period's figurative and literary concern with chastity was matched by a non-literary and very serious interest in the virtue as a moral imperative for men and women of all ages and stations. 'More than our brother is our chastity': Isabella's fraught attempt to preserve herself from the infectious and dissolute society closing in around her would have seemed rather valiant to many theatre-goers on the Bankside – an area of London as corrupt as *Measure for Measure*'s Vienna. For early moderns, chastity was not only one of the most important Christian virtues, both doctrinally and culturally, but one of the key conceptual frameworks through which individual men and women understood their relationship to their own bodies, to their community, to the wider Christian world, and to God. Importantly, chastity was not the same as virginity. Virginity was an anatomical state that preceded sexual activity; chastity was a state, both spiritual and physiological, of sexual integrity that could be observed through all stages of a person's adult life. When Leontes condemns Hermione in *The Winter's Tale* for the adultery he wrongfully believes she has committed with Polixenes, he is accusing her of unchastity.

Shakespeare's late plays initiated the flourishing of tragicomic drama which spanned the 1620s, 1630s and 1640s, when Beaumont and Fletcher, Massinger, Shirley, Brome, Ford, and others were all producing plays concerned with women's chastity at the thematic level. One of the aims of this book is to begin to explain why tragicomedy and the culture from which the genre emerged were so preoccupied with chastity, but it approaches this question from an oblique angle. In seeking reasons for chastity's importance in early Stuart England, I have looked to other disciplines and discourses beyond the theatre: medicine, theology, and politics. A definite interest in chastity can be traced in each of these areas, but only by first acknowledging the period's investment in figurative renderings of the virtue.

As this book will argue, the period of England's history which saw the greatest and most varied deployment of chastity figures was that spanning the reigns of Elizabeth I to Charles I. While much has been written on Elizabethan chastity, the importance of chastity to English public life in the period between the Virgin Queen's death and the Civil Wars remains

---

[1] Wendy Wall, *The Imprint of Gender: Authorship and Publication in the English Renaissance* (Ithaca and London: Cornell University Press, 1993), p. 169.

under-explored. Amid the political and doctrinal revolutions of the early seventeenth century, chastity came to occupy a special place in the figurative language through which poets and dramatists depicted a range of human experiences, from personal adornment to penitence and from participation in the Eucharist to the operations of legal justice. In the hands of polemical prose writers – especially those circulating pamphlets in the 1630s and 1640s – the figurative language of chastity became crucial to arguments about England's surest road to prosperity and salvation. To a large extent, this book explores chastity at the linguistic, figurative, and discursive levels because it is only by acknowledging the breadth of chastity's presence in the various forms of written language left to us that we are able to appreciate how influential the virtue must have been for the individuals who wrote and read them.

To recognise the full scope of chastity's significance as a moral imperative in both the rhetoric of public discourse and the consciousness of individuals in the early modern period requires acknowledging those instances when the virtue is evoked but not necessarily mentioned by name. Such evocations are usually barely recognisable to the modern eye as references to chastity. Often when the body was used figuratively to describe an organisation or institution, chastity was also evoked. This is because figurative descriptions of social or political organisations were rarely deployed without reference to some moral imperative and chastity was the virtue governing the moral state of bodies. When Elizabeth I's body was used as a figure for the emerging nation (as it was in a number of her portraits for instance), her chastity in turn figured the impenetrability of England's borders. Early modern descriptions of incorporated institutions – city, state, nation, Parliament, Crown, Church, family – made full use of their bodily figuration to assert the importance of maintaining the integrity (or chastity) of bodily boundaries against outside assault or inside corruption or schism. To this end, chastity was evoked either positively (as in the case of Elizabeth I's body as a figure for chaste England) or negatively (as in descriptions of the Roman Church, the Whore of Babylon, as that corrupted body from which the chaste Protestant English Church must be protected). In the early decades of the seventeenth century, reformed theologians were preoccupied with theorising the relationship between the English and Roman Churches. But under Charles I, when tension grew more fierce within the English Church between Laudian and Puritan approaches to doctrine and worship, churchmen were debating the relationship between the monarch's two bodies (his body natural and body politic), the relationship between the monarch and the church, between the monarch and Parliament, Parliament and the church, and between the visible church and the invisible church. These debates often thought through the relationships between the various figurative bodies in terms of marital or extra-marital unions, chaste or unchaste bodies.

One of the main inconsistencies in this kind of metaphorical thinking is the fact that ensuring the chastity or integrity of institutions by policing their borders denies a fundamental reality of institutional organisation: people must be able to come and go. For a 'body' to be totally sound, its infected parts must be either rejected or healed and re-absorbed, but this kind of maintenance means that the institution's chastity is actually only secured through a continual process of change. Such 'bodies' are therefore never truly contained. However, where one vision of chastity broke down, another – opposing – vision of chastity could be deployed. The conceptual and linguistic correlation between chastity and containment could also be reversed in descriptions of purging as chastisement. The pre-Reformation Church had a long history of ensuring that the sins of individual members were absolved before they could infect the whole. A similar model of 'purging' communal bodies became one of the defining features of the English Civil Wars, both rhetorically and actually. The final scenes of early Stuart drama routinely staged similar purging and purification of the families and states whose lives they depicted: from the tearful penitence of sinners to the punishment of transgressors who are 'removed' from the communal body by death. Indeed, it is on this point that tragicomedy often diverged from tragedy. Tragicomedies staged the purification of a community through the penitence and cleansing of its unchaste transgressors and their re-absorption into the collective body, while tragedies saw the communal body purged through death. Tragicomedy's interest in the restoration of familial, dynastic, or state unity through the punishment, reform, and healing of erroneous members is one of the areas in which the genre's thematic interest in chastity coincides with its structural interest in chastity: those sinners who are chastened and re-absorbed into the communal body in the plays' final scenes are so after being healed of their crimes against chastity (*The Winter's Tale*'s Leontes, *Cymbeline*'s Iachimo and Posthumus, *The Broken Heart*'s Bassanes).

It is not only in descriptions of bodies and boundaries that chastity was utilised but also in the many figurative descriptions of coupling and issue that flourished in early modern English. The period saw a range of parental tropes emerging as descriptions for all sorts of human endeavour. This linguistic field offered opportunities to compare legitimate with illegitimate 'issue', such as the true and erroneous copies produced by the printing press; true and false currency; the good (English) and 'bastard' (Spanish) wine in increasing commercial circulation; the good and bad blood purged by one's barber-surgeon; or virtuous and erroneous endeavour of any kind. Shakespeare often utilised this kind of comparison to describe the relative legitimacy of thoughts, such as Leontes' long and anxious meditation over which 'coupling' between his fantasy and his mind have produced the true 'issue' or true thought about the relative chastity of Polixenes' and Hermione's relationship. Early modern writing (both moral and medical) on the whole range of bodily processes involved in human reproduction was concerned with chastity. Procreation, pregnancy, childbirth, breast-feeding, weaning: each stage attracted writing on the importance of men's and (primarily) women's chastity as a defence against polluting the physiological and spiritual health of infants. Infants were themselves signs of their parents' chastity: a chaste union produced a healthy baby; an unchaste union produced a sickly or monstrous baby. The Puritan pamphleteers who wrote extensively on monstrous births as signs of God's disapproval of English orthodoxy were to a large extent making figurative use of this commonplace. Their analysis of the reasons behind monstrous births do not emphasise the unchastity of the infants' parents but rather that of the institutional body whose illness and error found its pathological sign in unhealthy issue.

In opposition to these claims, the court announced its capacity to ensure the chastity of nation and Church and, by pointing to Henrietta Maria's body, was able to exploit the correlation between chastity and healthy fertility. The Queen's masques celebrated her cultural and religious influence on the chastity of the court by placing her prodigiously fertile body centre-stage. Little scholarly attention has been paid to the ceremonial elements of Henrietta Maria's many births and their coincidence with court masques, or to the possibility that these two forms of ceremony referenced each other symbolically – most especially in their use of the Throne of State and the canopied birthing bed. My own analysis of Henrietta Maria's births begins with the child she lost (her first son, who was baptised Charles and buried with full state ceremony) and the speculation surrounding his still-birth. With an almost tragicomic insistence on the return of her lost and mourned baby, Henrietta Maria went on to give her next, healthy, child the same name as the one she buried. The ritual circumstances of the Queen's first, and most anxiously observed, healthy birth (that of King Charles II) have much to say about Henrietta Maria's swift rise to popularity in the 1630s and her increased cultural influence at court. At a time when the Queen's French courtiers and religious were fighting to remain in England, the success of this birth (and the likelihood that it was overseen by French, Catholic midwives, and nuns) marks a crucial turning point in the court's acceptance of Henrietta Maria's cultural and spiritual tastes. Those elements of the Queen's birthing rituals that were not publicly visible did leave their symbolic trace in the very public image of the Throne of State, in which, and beside which, Henrietta Maria's fertile body became an increasingly celebrated presence in the 1630s.

In the early seventeenth century, the Throne of State emerged as an important means of thinking about the relative chastity of the royal body it represented and contained, but also of the various chaste relationships which that body needed to maintain – with its subjects and with God. The Caroline masques, together with the full range of court ceremony, asserted a particular vision of the Throne of State as an object that not only exemplified the court's chastity but made the virtue available to those subjects who beheld the throne at court. Critics of the court instead claimed that under Charles I, the Throne of State was increasingly infected by the unchaste alliances it was forced to contain. By the late-1630s, criticism of Charles' religiously 'unchaste' marriage to Henrietta Maria found expression in images of the Throne stained, liquified, and prostituted. But these images of a debased throne were also used to accuse Charles of tyranny. In early Stuart writing, tyranny and pride were often described as an unchastening of the monarch's relationship with his people or with God. These two opposing views of the Throne can be found in the Earl of Castlehaven's trial (1631), a legal performance designed to assert the Crown's chastity and authority over a wayward and apparently grossly unchaste peer. Satirical commentary on the trial instead described the Throne of State as so unchastened, so stained by pride, as to undermine its claims to chaste authority. Castlehaven's complete lack of remorse ensured that the trial ultimately failed to communicate its intended statement about the court's ability to police chastity. For this reason, Cynthia Herrup has suggested the trial contributed to the growing distrust of the King's ability to properly possess the Crown.[2]

This debate about the relative chastity of the Throne of State formed the backdrop for Milton's intervention into the genre of the royal masque. Milton's own developing understanding of what constituted a chaste

[2] Cynthia B. Herrup, *A House in Gross Disorder: Sex, Law, and the 2nd Earl of Castlehaven* (Oxford: Oxford University Press, 2001).

subject, a chaste throne, and the genre through which chastity was best realised, was a central concern of his masque. But his awareness of the very different generic demands of a performed and printed text, and how these differences could be mapped along local debates about thrones as single and reverenced or individual and dispersed, means that the two versions of *A Masque Performed at Ludlow Castle* emerge as subtle but definite contributions to Civil War debates about chastity.

Milton's masque enjoyed the unique status of being both a courtly, occasional performance text and a printed and widely circulated text for private reading: it therefore offers a perfect opportunity to explore how the two genres shaped those distinct versions of chastity emerging in the Caroline period. A central concern of this book is how the court's cult of chastity built its vision of the virtue out of (and in conversation with) the formal and thematic concerns of tragicomedy and masquing, and how critics of the court similarly built their own interpretation of chastity out of the genre and technologies most available to them and most suited to their agenda: the sermon and printed pamphlet. In this way, a fuller understanding of chastity's role in the rhetorical and moral struggles of the Caroline period reveals how much the revolutionary years that were to follow were shaped by textual phenomena: by those forms of communication that best realised and articulated the oppositional voices that were in the 1620s, 1630s, and 1640s competing to claim chastity as their own.

This book traces figurative references to unchastity – sluices, illegitimate couplings, tyrannical thrones – in texts from the early Stuart period in order to demonstrate how powerfully persuasive the threat of unchastity was to readers and audiences in the politically-fraught environment that emerged in the 1640s. By doing so, it demonstrates that certain images that had come to signal unchastity could still function as signs of danger in texts that were not explicitly concerned with the problem of unchastity as such. Writers, dramatists, and masquers on both sides of the court/commonwealth divide subtly drew upon the symbolic power of unchastity in order to strengthen their warnings against collusion with the wrong political organisation, participation in the wrong religious observations, or enjoyment of the wrong dramatic or poetic texts.

The most persistent early modern medical view of unchastity drew on the Galenic theory of the unchaste body as a broken or leaky container that cannot hold onto its fluids. Chapter 1 traces the many instances in which this depiction of unchastity was used to describe real and figurative bodies and the increasingly revolutionary purpose of such uses. Focussing especially on the term 'sluice', the chapter examines Sir John Harington's bawdy detailing of his flushable privy in *The Metamorphosis of Ajax*, Shakespeare's *The Winter's Tale* (in which Leontes describes Hermione's apparently adulterous body as 'sluiced'), and the many anti-court sermons and pamphlets of the 1630s and 1640s that describe England and the English Church as sluiced by the unchaste influence of Rome, Charles I, his French Queen, and Archbishop Laud. The chapter concludes with a reading of anti-court commentary on Queen Henrietta Maria's movements around London and the royal palaces, which describe the Queen's unchaste (Catholic) body as the infection opening those moral sluices in the city through which the plague could circulate more freely.

Chapter 2 inverts the argument of Chapter 1, asking instead how early moderns thought about sluicing as a way of healing unchastity, of chastising the corrupted body. It examines the growing Caroline interest in discourses of penance as spiritual purging and the theatre's interest in both medical purging (phlebotomy) and spiritual purging (tears) as means of repairing unchaste relationships and healing communities. Through its analysis of the highly emblematic death scenes in Ford's *The Broken Heart* and *'Tis Pity She's a Whore*, the emblem tradition, and debates about new medical technologies, this chapter explores early modern interest in purging/chastising as a means of strengthening those communal bodies whose figurative chastity had been damaged either by the actual unchastity of individual members or by political/religious division. From early Stuart thought on the chastity of communal bodies comes that commonplace assertion that forms a crucial part of this book's analysis: unchastity as a form of pride or tyranny. This model of unchastity can be traced back to Shakespearean tragicomedy and went on to form a central part of the pre-revolutionary thought I trace through the 1630s and 1640s.

Drawing on Chapter 2's analysis of chastity's place in early Stuart thinking about communal bonds, Chapter 3 examines further chastity's role in discussions of pride and tyranny, focussing particularly on revolutionary depictions of the Throne of State. The Caroline court and its 'cult of chastity' used the many elaborate masques of the 1630s to claim that the chastity of Charles' and Henrietta Maria's marriage protected the nation as a spiritual community and confirmed the sanctity of the Throne. The success of this message can be inferred by the lengths to which court critics had to go in order to undermine it. Anti-court writers instead claimed that under Charles, the Throne of State was unchaste (sluiced, prostituted). Such images enabled writers to accuse the court of pride and tyranny – a form of erroneous and unchaste relationship with God and fellow-man that threatened the unity and stability of the nation. Chapter 3 concentrates on a range of anti-court depictions of the Throne of State as unchaste and in need of reform, found in commentary on the high ceremony at Charles' court, anti-Catholic images of the throned 'Purple Whore' in Rome, discussions of William Harvey's discovery of blood's circulation, and the Earl of Castlehaven's trial.

Chapter 4 focusses on the Caroline court's cult of chastity in the 1630s and how it was built from cultural practices that were also tragicomic devices: familial unity, female fertility, cloistered devotional piety, spectacle, and wonder. Exploring Henrietta Maria's devotional world, and the many royal birthing rituals that coincided with her court masques, this chapter outlines that form of chastity that was most threatening to the vision of the virtue articulated by court-critics.

John Milton's masque, with its chaste maiden trapped in Comus' unchaste throne, offered a particular argument about the need to overcome both the unchaste tyranny of princes and, within the individual heart, the tyranny of pride. Milton's vision of chastity saw spiritual combat enacted through the processes of textual production and a complex deployment of the classical humility topos that placed the submission of the self to authority within a framework of political opposition. Chapter 5 offers a comparative reading of the performed and printed versions of *A Maske Performed at Ludlow Castle* because in each text, Milton drew the line between chastity and tyranny very differently. This chapter argues that Milton's individualism is most apparent in his interrogation of the human heart's unchaste propensity to pride and that for Milton the heart was therefore not only the most superior site of moral and spiritual combat but the place of the greatest human achievement and the closest proximity to the divine will. As the breach which ruptures the bond between God and individual believers, the unchastity of pride was not only the greatest of all sins in Milton's theology of virtue but the hardest to overcome – much harder than the overthrowing of tyrannical princes.

Chapter 5's analysis of Milton's performed and printed masques demonstrates how morally intentioned was Milton's translation of the performed genre into the written word. Strengthened by those anti-court and anti-Laudian arguments laid out in previous chapters, Milton's adaptation explicitly denied the chastity most associated with the court's performed masques and re-inscribed it in the language and printed discourses of political rebellion and theological introspection. In this sense, his masque constitutes a major intervention in the Caroline cult of chastity and needs to be considered as a significant marker of change in the turning of public opinion against the King.

CHAPTER I

Unchastity in Shakespeare's The Winter's Tale, *Caroline court performance and theological dispute*

> *And many a man there is (even at this present,*
> *Now, while I speak this) holds his wife by th'arm,*
> *That little thinks she has been sluiced in's absence*
> *And his pond fished by his next neighbor (by*
> *Sir Smile, his neighbour). Nay, there's comfort in't,*
> *Whiles other men have gates and those gates open'd,*
> *(As mine), against their will . . .*
> *From east, west, north, and south; be it concluded,*
> *No barricado for a belly. Know't,*
> *It will let in and out the enemy*
> *With bag and baggage.*[1]

Leontes' remarkable diatribe against adultery describes women's unchastity as a body sluiced, a pond fished, a gate opened, and a belly penetrated – a cluster of images that all depict physical and moral openness and the illegitimate movement of fluids. The speech is typical of the antifeminist rants often expressed by those male lovers on the early modern stage who are violently consumed by sexual jealousy. Leontes, however, concentrates more than his peers on one commonplace perception of the unchaste, female body: its openness and its capacity to be 'sluiced'. Although it was in circulation before Shakespeare's use in *The Winter's Tale*, the popularity of the sluice as a sign of unchastity grew rapidly after 1611, and throughout the early Stuart period, it accrued a number of associated images, all operating within the schema of fluidity and openness. The *OED* does not list any meaning for sluice other than the most material and benign, but the figurative importance of sluicing to Leontes' fear of unchastity and his descent into madness has been noted by both Gail Kern Paster and David Hillman.[2] In this chapter, I want to trace some of the ways in which

---

[1] Shakespeare, *First Folio*, p. 279.
[2] Gail Kern Paster, *Humoring the Body* (Chicago: Chicago University Press, 2004), p. 71; David Hillman, 'Visceral Knowledge: Shakespeare, Skepticism, and the Interior of the Early Modern Body',

sluice imagery became more insistently associated with unchastity, both on and off the stage, and how the association took on the polemical force it possessed in the anticourt writing of the 1620s, 1630s and 1640s. During these decades, pamphlet writers and preachers thought through various forms of real and figurative unions – between married monarchs, between the King and Parliament, between Crown and Church – in terms that regularly utilised images of sluices, pipes, conduits, and gates. It was through such imagery that polemicists negotiated the difficult process of alliance-building and made their arguments convincing to readers and congregants. In the hands of anticourt writers, sluice imagery continued to bear the antifeminist slur so evident in Leontes' usage. It was applied most often to women's bodies and to figurative bodies gendered female; when it was applied to male bodies, it tended to have a feminising effect. Crucially, royalist and courtly deployment of sluice images also exploited their feminine implications, but in a far more celebratory manner.

The consistent presence of sluice imagery as a warning against figurative forms of unchastity can be found in a range of arguments about the state of English leadership, both royal and ecclesial. However, to fully trace the controversial role unchastity played in early Stuart political and religious dispute, I will also be exploring the possibility that sluice imagery was applied not only to bodies, both actual and figurative, but to architectural spaces. As Margaret Healy has demonstrated, plague writing was one area in which both buildings and cities were described as bodies whose leakiness threatened everyone in and around them.[3] Queen Henrietta Maria's arrival in England in 1625, a time of high plague deaths, meant that anxieties about her (sexually and religiously) unchaste body were caught up in anxieties about the movement of contagion around London and around the royal palaces. Court-observers expressed their desire to see the new Queen and her religious attendants more fully contained within the royal houses and, through conversion, within the Protestant faith, because they believed that this would halt the spread of disease. Tellingly, concern over Henrietta Maria's movement around London and her use of the royal buildings became more pronounced when she began to sponsor major architectural works which introduced into the city not only the public spectacles familiar to her in France but the religious spectacles – the Mass and all ritual observances of monastic life –

---

in David Hillman and Carla Mazzio (eds.), *The Body in Parts: Fantasies of Corporeality in Early Modern Europe* (London: Routledge, 1997), pp. 81–106, 95.

[3] Margaret Healy, *Fictions of Disease in Early Modern England: Bodies, Plagues, and Politics* (New York: Palgrave, 2001), p. 18.

that she hoped would again become commonplace in her adopted country. It was in this atmosphere that the Queen prepared her first court performances, including *The Shepherds' Paradise* (1633) which displays a particular interest in the containment of bodies within various buildings that are designated as either chaste or unchaste and either holy or unholy. In this performance, the Queen asserted the chastity of her own body, her own buildings, and the blessings that both might have on those who were near them.

My exploration of the early Stuart interest in sluicing as a figure for unchastity will also touch on Sir John Harington's *The Metamorphosis of Ajax* (1596), in order to assess some of the figurative (in this case, bawdy) means whereby sluicing was already becoming associated with unchastity in the late sixteenth century. Harington's Elizabethan tract landed its author in trouble because of its political allegory, and has received a good deal of critical attention for this reason. But Gail Kern Paster has noted the tract's uses of unchastity[4] and there is still a lot of work to be done in this direction, especially on Harington's bawdy awareness of the potential for privies and their system of pipes and sewers to metaphorically associate the opening of bodies with the openings of buildings and the circulation of chaste and unchaste matter around the city. It is the same correlation between these three forms of unchastity that, in a far less satirical manner, drove Leontes mad.

Having witnessed a conversation between his wife and best friend, Leontes accuses Hermione of 'never but once' having spoken as well as she does to Polixenes. That once was 'when / Three crabbèd months had soured themselves to death / Ere I could make thee open thy white hand / And clap thyself my love; then didst thou utter, / "I am yours for ever".[5] For Leontes, Hermione's willingness to unclasp her heart in her words to Polixenes (when she had been so unwilling to offer her 'yes' to Leontes himself) means she will most certainly unclasp her entire person to him. Even Hermione's hand, which when closed had once felt to Leontes as cold as death, becomes too open, 'too hot', when extended to his friend (1.2.108).[6] He imagines that by so 'open[ing]' herself to Polixenes, Hermione has breached the enclosure which their marriage ought to have placed around their shared blood, allowing it instead to 'mingle':

---

[4] Gail Kern Paster, 'The Epistemology of the Water Closet: John Harington's *Metamorphosis of Ajax* and Elizabethan Technologies of Shame', in Curtis Perry (ed.), *Material Culture and Cultural Materialisms* (Turnhout: Brepols, 2001), pp. 139–58.
[5] 1.2.88–104. All references are to Stephen Orgel's 1996 Oxford edition of *The Winter's Tale*.
[6] For an analysis of the culture of female speech and gesture in early modern courts, see Martine Van Elk, '"Our Praises are Our Wages": Courtly Exchange, Social Mobility, and Female Speech in *The Winter's Tale*,' *Philological Quarterly* 79.4 (2000), pp. 429–58.

> To mingle friendship far is mingling bloods.
> I have *tremor cordis* on me: my heart dances,
> But not for joy, not joy.
>   (1.2.108–10)

Leontes' 'fear of mingling',[7] and his concomitant obsession with enclosure, becomes the pattern of his madness. The vision which is increasingly fixed in his mind is of the Galenic body, and women's bodies in particular, as leaky and unsound containers.[8] He is disarmed by the presence of his son, in whose body his own blood is mingled with Hermione's. Taking Mamillius from his mother, Leontes announces: 'I am glad you did not / nurse him . . . / Though he does bear signs of me, yet you / Have too much blood in him' (2.1.56–8). Leontes' fear of his wife's unchaste fluids causes him to retreat fully into a self-protective enclosure and also into those conventional modes of early modern gendered hatred most associated with the fear of women's porousness. Having ejected Hermione and his new 'bastard' daughter from the court, Leontes surrounds himself with only his male attendants and is violently dismissive of Paulina's attempts to enter with the baby and argue on Hermione's behalf. 'Out', he cries repeatedly. Calling Paulina a 'mankind witch' and an 'intelligencing bawd' (2.3.67–8), Leontes tells Antigonus that his wife is 'Lady Margery, your midwife' (2.3.159). 'Lady Margery', both a midwife and 'margery-prater' (a hen), is heavily loaded with connotations of bawdry, corruption, and secrecy. The insult collapses all of Leontes' most conventional fears about women's porousness and deceit into one formulation: women talk, give birth, are licentious, lascivious, they lie, steal, and keep from men the truth of their sexual activity and the paternity of their babies. The watery threat of women's unchastity completely overwhelms him: 'inch thick, knee-deep, o'er head and ears a forked one!' (1.2.184).

Laurie Maguire has detailed one of the most common early modern methods of testing virginity, which involved giving a woman a diuretic in order to see if she could hold her urine. 'The chaste woman was sealed, impermeable; the unchaste woman was porous, incontinent'.[9] This understanding of how the female body is altered after intercourse informs the 'sieve' portraits of Queen Elizabeth. Like Chastity in Cesare Ripa's

---

[7] Huston Diehl, '"Does not the Stone Rebuke Me?": The Pauline Rebuke and Paulina's Lawful Magic in *The Winter's Tale*' in Patricia Badir and Paul Yachnin (eds.), *Shakespeare and the Cultures of Performance* (Aldershot: Ashgate, 2008), pp. 69–82, 69.
[8] Paster, *The Body Embarrassed*, pp. 23–63.
[9] Laurie Maguire, 'Virginity tests', in Colin Blakemore and Sheila Jennett (eds.), *The Oxford Companion to the Body* (Oxford: Oxford University Press, 2001), pp. 713–4.

Iconologia (1611) and following the legend of the Vestal Virgin, Tuccia (who proved her chastity by carrying a sieve filled with water from the Tiber to the Temple), Elizabeth holds a sieve in her hand in a series of portraits from 1579–83. Testing a woman's capacity to hold liquid in a sieve is another early modern virginity test documented by Maguire. In order to pass this test, women would cover the sieve with fat to stop water falling through it: a 'cheat' which contributed to commonplaces about the secrecy, dishonesty, and unchastity of midwives, to whom the technique was attributed. This same attribution informs the legend of Agnes Sampson, one of the 'Berwick witches' charged with plotting against the life of James I, and her dramatic counterpart in *Macbeth*. Sampson was said to take to the ocean in a sieve, her ability to stay afloat – while also drunk and in a storm – was taken as a sign of her diabolical powers but also of her unchastity.[10]

But Leontes' fixation on Hermione's porousness moves beyond descriptions of her body. His repeated reference in the barricado speech to his neighbour suggests the possibility that he is thinking about Christ's commandment against adultery – the crime of coveting a neighbour's wife. Whether or not 'neighbour' in itself implies also the architectural dwelling that ought to separate Leontes' neighbour from his wife, the speech as a whole certainly evidences this slippage between houses and bodies. All men, Leontes consoles himself, have 'gates' that are opened against their will. Hermione's body is itself something of a gate – where a barricado ought to be – and 'the enemy' moves in and out of it 'with bag and baggage'. Leontes describes his neighbour as a thief who steals fish from his pond and goods from his house. His desperate attempts at border control extend beyond his and Hermione's bodies to his estate. When he hears of Camillo's and Polixenes' escape, his first concern is how the 'posterns' came 'so easily open'. The Lord Leontes is interrogating reminds him that Camillo has always enjoyed that 'great authority / Which often hath no less prevailed than so / On your command'. 'I know't too well' is Leontes' reply (2.1.52–5). He now doubts everyone: his wife and friend and his most loyal servant have all breached the barriers which, in his extreme anxiety, he has worked so rigidly to maintain around both his body and his buildings.

In Leontes' imagination, the need to police the borders of both his wife's body and his buildings is a defence against disease. Although he asserts in his barricado speech that there is 'no physic' for a bawdy planet, he does seek to avoid further contamination. Crucially, he imagines unchastity itself as a

---

[10] See John Dover Wilson, *Life in Shakespeare's England: A Book of Elizabethan Prose* (New York: Cosimo, 2008), p. 34; and Laurie Maguire, 'Virginity tests'.

Unchastity, court performance and theological dispute

disease. That is, unchastity is both the means by which disease spreads and the disease itself. He diagnoses unchastity as the source of an infection moving from Polixenes to Hermione and then himself. 'Who does infect her? / Why... Bohemia' (1.2.303–5). Polixenes himself describes unchastity as a disease: he asserts his innocence by claiming that he is untouched by 'the great'st infection / That e'er was heard or read' (1.2.375–418). Through Leontes' distortions, Hermione's pregnant body ceases to signify the robust health of both their marriage and their court and becomes instead a grotesque sign of sexual, moral, and political inversion and contamination. The openness of her body and her manners (her 'yes'), which were previously enjoyed and desired by Leontes, become instead excessive, too sensual, too hot, too open, and too capable of letting in and out fluids and disease. He perceives such unchastity as a condition not just of her body but of the space within their home, which, like her body, ought to be contained and protected against 'sir smile', his neighbour.

In her account of early modern plague narratives, Margaret Healy argues that 'a recurring motif from medieval and early modern writings is the human body as a fortified (materially and/or spiritually) yet vulnerable enclosure – castle, ship, city or temple – threatened constantly by "enimie" incursions which can only be averted through sound and vigilant regimen'.[11] A number of critics have noted the early modern tendency, both on and off the stage, to figure houses which ought properly to contain health, material goods, and virtue as the chaste bodies of the women contained within them, or, conversely, unchaste houses as the unchaste bodies of the gossips who spill out of their doors, finding themselves in court defamation cases.[12] 'The physical boundaries of property' were, Diane Purkiss notes, 'identified with the social boundaries of property'.[13] Such an analogical relationship between house and body did, under ordinary circumstances, present problems. Frances Dolan argues that were a woman to be 'truly sealed within her household', she would be 'unable to perform such functions as going to market to sell and buy, attending church, or engaging in the life of the

---

[11] Healy, *Fictions of Disease in Early Modern England*, p. 18.
[12] Lena Cowen Orlin, 'Women on the Threshold', *Shakespeare Studies* 25 (1997), pp. 50–58; Alice T. Friedman, 'Inside/Out: Women, Domesticity, and the Pleasures of the City', in Lena Cowen Orlin (ed.), *Material London ca. 1600* (Philadelphia: University of Pennsylvania Press, 2000), pp. 232–50; Lisa Jardine, *Still Harping on Daughters: Women and Drama in the Age of Shakespeare* (Brighton: Harvester, 1983), Chapter 4; Frances Dolan, 'Gender and the "Lost" Spaces of Catholicism', *Journal of Interdisciplinary History* 32:4 (2002), pp. 641–65, 660.
[13] Diane Purkiss, 'Women's Stories of Witchcraft in Early Modern England: the House, the Body, the Child', *Gender and History* 7:3 (1995), pp. 408–32, 415.

community'.[14] The necessity for women to wander abroad ensured that those anxious commonplaces that collapsed unchastity and disease with the threat of female mobility and the necessary openness of architectural spaces (windows, doors) remained in circulation. Such commonplaces certainly informed popular gendered thinking about the spread of evil. A common talisman against a witch was a bottle containing pins and urine which was designed to block the urinary tract of the witch and thus stop up the 'poysonous matter' thought to proceed from her body. These objects were then placed at the thresholds of houses. In fact, most charms, both protective and execrative, were buried at the doors of houses because doors were the passages through which curses might penetrate to where they could do the most damage or good: the interior of homes. Charms were also buried at the boundaries of Parishes and the thresholds of towns.[15]

Leontes' impassioned description of unchastity as something at once fluid (involving sluices and ponds) and architectural (made up of walls, gates, and private spaces that ought to be protected) may seem surprising, certainly inventive, but it was in fact commonplace. If it had not been, Sir John Harington's *The Metamorphosis of Ajax* (1596) would have been a far more serious piece of writing than it is, or is supposed to be.[16] Harington builds humour into his design for a flushable privy (and into his justification for treating of such 'homely' matter) by playing on the semantic and conceptual convergence between private architectural spaces, the movement of fluid (around bodies, buildings, cities), and fornication.

Gail Kern Paster has detailed the early modern association between sexual pleasure and evacuation of all kinds, and the more specific association between defecation and ejaculation.[17] Harington treats this convergence at length when he claims that a comfortable jakes is the solution to man's natural tendency towards the 'chiefest of all our sensual pleasures ... the sweet sinne of letchery'.[18] Only in 'a good easie close stoole' can a man find a more honourable solace than lechery 'when he hath had a lust

---

[14] Dolan, 'Gender and the "Lost" Spaces of Catholicism', p. 660.
[15] See Chris Laoutaris, *Shakespearean Maternities* (Edinburgh: Edinburgh University Press, 2008), chapter 3.
[16] *The Metamorphosis of Ajax* has received increased attention in the last few decades. Key studies include: John Leland, 'A Joyful Noise: *The Metamorphosis of Ajax* as Spiritual Tract', *South Atlantic Review* 47 (1982), pp. 53–62; Jason Scott-Warren, 'The Privy Politics of Sir John Harington's *New Discourse of a Stale Subject, Called the Metamorphosis of Ajax*'. *Studies in Philology* 93 (1996), pp. 412–442; Paster, 'The Epistemology of the Water Closet'.
[17] Paster, 'The Epistemology of the Water Closet, p. 151; Paster, *Humoring the Body* (Chicago: Chicago University Press, 2004).
[18] Elizabeth Story Donno (ed.), *Sir John Harington's A New Discourse of a Stale Subject, Called The Metamorphosis of Ajax* (London: Routledge, 1962).

Unchastity, court performance and theological dispute

thereto' (84). Harington repeatedly plays with the bawdy implications of privies as enclosed, private spaces from which water is sluiced and in which the body sluices itself. It is into these private places that he wishes his book (and himself) to enter so that he may improve, reform, 'sweeten', and make chaste the privies of great women throughout the country (including the Queen), even while he is himself allowed full access to them.

Harington's exploitation of the commonplace convergence between jakes and brothels is extensive but nowhere more elaborate than in the dictionary episode. In it, he narrates himself reading one of Pliny's letters, which gives instructions on sanitisation and the need to cover the city's open sewers with vaults. Harington then describes his search, through a number of dictionaries, to find the English for Pliny's *confornicari*.

> F, fa, fe, fi, fo, for, for, foramen, forfex, forica, forma, fornicator, (now I think I am near it) fornix, fornicor, aris, are. There, there what says he of that? A vault or Arche, to vault or arch anything with a compass. (135–6)

Harington's search – which runs counter to alphabetical order – enables him to collapse the passive *fornicor, fornicaris* (to commit fornication) with the active *fornicare* (to make an arch or a vault). Having elsewhere in *The Metamorphosis* already described the role of vaults, arches, sluices and sinks in the building of privies, Harington is here able to make more explicit use of 'vaulting house' as a bawdy term for a brothel. He develops the conceit further by having his companion look for *confornicari* under 'con' in the French dictionary:

> Looke it sirra there in the dictionarie. Con, con. Tush what dost thou looke in the French? thou wilt make a sweete peece of looking, to looke for confornicar in the French. (135)

By looking in a book for a 'con', Harington's hypothetical companion (who is, perhaps, also his reader) makes a 'sweet peece' of looking. Playing on 'sweet' as both cleansing and making fit for sexual purpose, the joke draws on Harington's repeated suggestion that his book is not only a guide to reforming privies (and thus chastening the parlours of great ladies) but also that the book itself belongs inside the privy – that it is the kind of trash only fit to be used for toilet paper. Were it to be so used, the book itself would make a 'sweet piece' of looking at the 'cons' of great ladies.

Crucially, the *confornicari* letter from Pliny which begins the dictionary episode instructs Trajan to build vaults over the city's open sewers in order to stop the spread of disease around the city. In Pliny's argument for covering waters and sewers – which is also Harington's argument – the construction of the vaulting house contains the circulation of waters and prevents the spread of disease (both actions being figures for the curtailing of sexual license). The building of the vault is thus a form of chastity. But in the cant term for brothel – a vaulting house – it signifies it's opposite. Harington later applies Pliny's concerns for enclosing sewers more specifically to Elizabethan London when he talks of the gates of the city from which filth is washed away (146–7). In doing so, he finds means, via word play, to suggest that although this part of the city (called Hornsey) may be filthy (with both excrement and the unchastity implied by the horns of its name), it is by far cleaner than those 'most glorious and gracious' of London streets which have more 'horns' in them (both 'visible and invisible') than any other. Harington also exploits the image, later used by Leontes, of unchastity as a fished pond. Before offering his view that a good close stool is a more honourable way of managing lust and bodily ejaculation than acts of lechery, Harington describes the human condition as a hopeless searching for passing pleasures: 'so short & momentary the contentments that we fish for, in this Ocean of miseries, which either we misse, (fishing before the net, as the proverb is) or if we catch them, they prove but like Eeles, sleight & slipperie' (83–4).

Harington's tract describes his new flushable toilet as a system of vaults and sluices that enclose, channel, and reform the movement of fluids and disease within bodies and around buildings and cities. While his new device promises to reform a space heavily associated with unchastity, his text's bawdy humour does little to lessen the association. That unchastity should itself signify the spread of disease is not surprising, since illness is precisely what sexual licence caused in a pre-contraceptive age. But the more subtle point to be grasped from Harington and Leontes is that unchastity and disease already figured each other reciprocally via the cluster of sluicing images I am describing here as both architectural and fluid. Just as women's (unchaste) bodies cannot contain the fluids they ought to, so the buildings that ought to contain, or properly dispose of, those fluids that cause disease cannot always do so.

There is one further implication bound up in this cluster of images which, although it is not prominent in *The Winter's Tale*, certainly features in Harington's text and would go on to prove critical to religious polemicists in subsequent decades. While Harington does not use unchastity to describe confessional difference or incite confessional dispute, he does use it in more general terms as a figure for irreligion. When at the end of his text, Harington narrates an imagined trial against him for the indecency of *The Metamorphosis*, he predicts that he will be accused of irreligion (not atheism but rather both Puritanism and Catholicism), unchastity, and treason. Throughout the tract, he repeatedly compares the houses he would see cleansed and sweetened of their filth with the bodies of Christians whose souls require cleansing. Indeed, for John Leland, *The Metamorphosis* operates entirely as a Christian moral parable.[19] Harington regularly equates the 'soul' with the 'sinke'. Yet even before Harington's direct equation of the two entities, sinks already figured corrupted souls: 'sink' was a term for the gathering of vice and corruption. In *The Actes of the Englysh Votaryes* (1546–50), John Bale used 'sink' to describe Rome as 'so synnefull a syncke & pernicious puddell'.[20]

While Harington did not develop the potential for chastity's liquid imagery to signify confessional difference, Middleton's use of 'sluice' to figure unchastity in *The Ghost of Lucrece* (1600) could be seen as emerging out of changes to eucharistic doctrine and the stigmatisation of belief in transubstantiation. Lucrece laments:

> Now is my tyde of bloud: Come, quench thy soule,
> The sluces of my spirit now runs againe:
> Come, I haue made my breast an Ivorie bowle,
> To hold the bloud that streameth from my veyne,
> Drinke to my chastitie which thou hast slaine:
> But (woe the while) that labour is in vaine.
> To drinke to that which cannot pledge againe.[21]

Lucrece's chastity runs out of her along with the blood and spirit that is sluiced from her body as much through rape as though her grievous remembrance of rape. Figured eucharistically, her rape (a sacrifice on which the nation was founded) is equated to the sacrifice of Christ and his passionate suffering. Yet, unlike Christ's redemptive bloodshed, Lucrece's blood is merely a human 'pledge', one which fails to bring back her chastity. Where Christ's death is chaste and continues to bring life to those who partake of it, Lucrece's rape and suicide secure only her perpetual unchastity – 'To seale my soule with Rape and Murders stampe'[22] – and to pledge to it would be in 'vaine' since, unlike Christ's chaste blood, it cannot pledge anything in return. Lucrece interprets the permanent sluicing of her body as an inverse eucharistic feast.

---

[19] Leland, 'A Joyful Noise: *The Metamorphosis of Ajax* as Spiritual Tract'.
[20] John Bale, *The first two partes of the actes or vnchast examples of the Englysh votaryes gathered out of their owne legenades and chronycles by Johan Bale* ... (London, 1551), ii.
[21] Thomas Middleton, *The Ghost of Lucrece* (London, 1600), p. 6.
[22] Middleton, *The Ghost of Lucrece*, p. 4.

The potential for unchastity's sluice imagery to converge with eucharistic controversy was taken much further in Phineas Fletcher's anti-Catholic *The Locusts, or Appolyonists* (1627). In Fletcher's verse, the Jesuit Cardinal Bellarmine speaks of the unchaste influence which spreads in liquid form from members of the Society of Jesus to women and from women to Protestant men:

> ... women sooner drinke our lore,
> Men sooner sippe it from their lippes, than ours:
> Sweetly they learne, and sweetly teach: with store
>   Of teares, smiles, kisses, and ten thousand arts
>   They lay close batt'ry to mens frayler parts:
> So finely steale themselves, and us into their hearts.
>   (Canto IV, st. 21–2)

For Fletcher, Catholicism is a sexualised and liquid force that travels via unchaste women to the bodies of those they speak to/seduce, thereby infecting Protestant men with Jesuit unchastity. For anti-Catholics like Fletcher, the Jesuit desire to share in the cup of Christ's transfigured blood is already a sign of unchastity (erroneous religion, physical despoliation) even before it is embedded in the more elaborated picture of liquified and unchaste kisses and whispers.

Why was unchastity in particular the virtue around which fears of dissolution and infection gathered? Above all virtues, chastity oversaw the integrity of bodies. It protected against the unseen and unacknowledged spread of adulterers' blood into illegitimate veins. That is, chastity protected against the loss of the self. As Leontes and the controversialists with whom this chapter is concerned all suggest, early modern identity existed very much in the blood and depended for its safety and purity on the sharing of blood only through legitimate unions. However, chastity also played a more figurative, and I think more powerful, role as a virtue capable of protecting against all forms of broken bonds and dissolved boundaries. In a period so beset by schism at various institutional levels, concern for the integrity of boundaries emerged as a pervasive anxiety. The same fears about unchaste human bodies applied to thinking about unchaste institutional or collective, figurative bodies such as the Church or nation. In turn, many elements of early modern English society that were deemed threatening to the integrity of individual and collective bodies were identified as unchaste: women, Catholics, foreigners, theatrical performance and spectacle, heretics, traitors, tyrants. Consequently, images of unchastity, when applied to any one of these threats, summoned by an associative logic many or all of the others.

Importantly, the 'baggage' which Leontes fears will be carried freely by his 'neighbour' in and out of his property (his wife's body, his house) already implied all those elements of early modern society which I am arguing were associated with and identified as unchastity. The *OED* cites numerous usages from the late sixteenth to the early seventeenth century of 'baggage' as rotten and decayed matter, diseased matter, immoral and contaminated states of being, fallen women, but also as Catholic ritual, ornaments, and objects of 'idolatrous' worship. It was this last association – between unchastity and idolatry – that enabled depictions of the vice as openness, fluidity and contamination to take on the polemical and ultimately revolutionary function which they served in the years of Charles I and Henrietta Maria's reign.

Doors, gates, pipes: chaste and unchaste unions in Caroline religious dispute

When members of the Long Parliament met for their first public fast in 1640, they did so on 17 November, the day on which the nation had for decades celebrated the Accession of Queen Elizabeth I. The sermon was preached by the staunchly Puritan Cornelius Burgess, who argued that God's covenant with his people was a marital bond, a 'fervent, intire, loyall, chaste love'. He did not speak on politics, but his argument for the total fidelity between believers and God sent a powerful message about the unnecessary place of a monarch in the covenant. For Burgess, the best and perhaps the only monarch was one who simply enabled and protected the marital bond between God and his people. Elizabeth's memory hovered over the proceedings: not only was she on the day of his sermon being celebrated across the country in the ringing of bells and lighting of fires, but Burgess spoke passionately of her triumph over the Whore of Babylon. Elizabeth, he argued, was the door by which God's chosen first entered into the 'nuptial knot' with God because she led them away from the adultery and prostitution of idolatry.[23] He stipulated that the Church which sets up pictures and ornaments has allowed itself to be 'exposed and prostituted to all manner of whoredomes and filthiness' (26).

> A wise man will never marry a strumpet, nor with any woman that hath another husband; his wife shall bee onely his owne, none else shall have interest in her. Much lesse then, will the Holy and jealous God admit of any Spouse that is wedded to any lust . . . purge out and cast away (as a *Menstrous*

[23] Cornelius Burgess, *A Sermon preached to the honourable house of commons . . . at the publique fast* (London, 1641), pp. 43, 18.

cloth) all *Idols* and *Idolatry* in particular. All our lusts are lothsome to his stomack, but nothing is so abominable to his Soule, as Idolatry. (47)

To demonstrate the determination with which the godly must overcome unchastity and idolatry, Burgess invoked the story of King Asa who did not spare even his mother, Queen Macha, when he found she had erected an idol in a grove and worshipped it. 'So obscene' was the act that the Queen lost her crown because 'shee was not onely a grosse Idolatresse, but abominable strumpet: for ordinarily, idolatry and adultery, spiritual and bodily fornication goe together.' Not shy of controversy, Burgess builds from Deuteronomy a picture of Charles' marriage to Henrietta Maria: 'for though shee had beene neerer than a Mother, even the *Wife of his bosome*, yet if shee were an Idolater, and should *entice him secretly, saying let us goe and serve other Gods,* shee must have *been put to death,* and *his owne hand must have been first upon her'* (6–7). Unlike the Catholic Henrietta Maria (whose religious practices are the 'lothsome' 'menstrous cloth' which must be purged from England's Church), Elizabeth I was in Burgess's formulation, the chaste 'door' or 'pipe' connecting the bodies of English men and women to God: 'If you would indeed honour Her precious memory; yea, honour God and your selves, and . . . continue the possession of what shee (as a most glorious Conduit pipe) hath transmitted to us' (46).

A good deal of Burgess's rhetorical power can be located in the fact that he refers at times to actual unchaste women (Queen Macha and, less explicitly, Henrietta Maria) but also to figurative unchaste women (the Whore of Babylon) and to figurative chaste bodies (England and the English Church). He shifts between these modes constantly, ensuring that the fear his audience feels for the unchastening of the figurative and communal bodies in which they are members feeds and is fed by the threat posed by the actual (unchaste) bodies in their midst. While Burgess made consummate use of this conceit, it was a technique already common among his peers. When arguing for the legitimacy of the Reformed Church and its claims to be the true visible Church of Christ, English theologians and divines described the nature of their separateness from Rome through various theories of unity, division and difference. I will return to this literature in my next chapter. Relevant here is one aspect of the language with which many of the arguments were constructed. Christ's parable of the Kingdom of Heaven as a field containing both wheat and darnel, true and erroneous Christians, was sometimes invoked.[24]

---

[24] Matthew 13: 24–43.

However, the trope dominating discussions of the visible Church was the Pauline image of the body. In the early modern period, the Church was still almost universally understood as both the body of Christ and as his bride: discussion of it was therefore understandably dominated by descriptions of both health and chastity. Indeed, because the Church was both body and bride, bodily health and chastity were in these debates mutually dependent concepts. Early seventeenth century arguments about the nature of the visible Church abound with descriptions of it as a body whole and dismembered, healthy and diseased, chaste and unchaste. Also routine amid these descriptions were references to the sluices, doors, and gates which either enabled the illegitimate passage of unchaste fluid or contained the right and good passage of chaste fluids.

By the end of the 1630s, 'sluice' was in especially frequent use among Puritan critics of the court who believed Charles' promotion of Laud was a backsliding in religion. The anonymous *Novembris Monstrum, or, Rome brovght to bed in England with the whores miscarying*, written in the year of the Irish uprising, describes the corrupt sexual relationship between Phocas and Pope Gregory I. It argues that 'Phocas will ope a sluce, from which shall flee / Supremacy to swell the Bishops See'.[25] Here the sluice in the body of the Emperor (or Charles) releases that fluid which impregnates Rome. The punning correlation between semen running into a feminised body and a broken bank letting water out to sea is in keeping with the etymology of 'sluice'. But it also plays into early modern English fears that the corruption of the King's body by his tolerance of Catholics equated to a breach of English shores.

Prynne used the term, and its suggestion that the King's body, like English shores, could be opened and drained, when criticising the court of popery in *The Soveraigne Power of Parliaments and Kingdomes* (1643). He complained that the King gave his word in a solemn oath and in two printed declarations not to abandon his 'Loving Subjects' or the Petition of Right, nor to violate the purity or perfection of 'Lawes, Liberties, Properties, Religion' by 'back-sliding to Popery'. Prynne accused the King of breaching his fidelity to Parliament through 'severall inundations of oppressions, Taxes, grievances, Innovations and relapses to Popery (which have flowed in upon them ever since as if there had bene no bankes to keepe them out, but sluces onely to let them in the faster')'.[26] Elsewhere Prynne argues that in Ezekiel, the vision of the temple was perfectly

---

[25] Anon., *Novembris Monstrum* (London, 1641), p. 90.
[26] William Prynne, *The Soveraigne Power of Parliaments and Kingdomes* (London, 1643), p. 34.

described so that its 'exact rule' could be maintained 'Else a sluce would be opened to drowne the whole world in superstition and error'.[27] Henry Burton also used the term in *Conformity's Deformity* (1646) when he said of the new orthodoxy under Archbishop Laud: 'Conformity the sluice, or inlet of all superstition and slavery'. He goes on:

> And in truth, this was that very sluice, which when first opened, did let in that inundation and deluge not only of will-worship, in all kinde of ceremonies and superstitions, but also of humane forms and frames of Church-government, and in all of them such a tyrannicall power over all consciences and Churches, as hath wholly drowned all; so as Christs Dove can no where finde, where to set her foot.[28]

In Burton's account, the unchastity of growing ritualism and clericalism is a watery deluge, pouring from the sluice Laud opened in the body of the Church, Christ's body, until it so covered the land as to alienate the Paraclete. John Bastwicke used the same image for the body of Laud himself, when arguing that the Archbishop's interest in ritual and ceremony only corrupted the body hiding beneath his fine vestments until it was corroded and full of holes. 'Coming daily from the starchamber ... see what pompe grandeur and magnificence he goeth in; the whole multitude standing bare wherever he passeth, having also a great number of Gentlemen, and other servants waiting on him, al uncovered, some of them cariying his tayle, for the better breaking and venting of his wind & easing of his holy body (for it is full of holes)'.[29]

When Burgess delivered his sermon before the Long Parliament in 1640, he made full use of the watery imagery so associated with unchastity to delineate the true Church from the false. Drawing on the commonplace depiction of the Catholic Church as the Whore of Babylon, he argued that 'Babylon the Great, the Mother of harlots and abominations of the earth' was a *'woman drunken with the bloud of the Saints, and with the bloud of the Martyrs of Jesus* ... She is never in her element, but when she is swimming in bloud. So insatiable is she, that like the *horse-leeches* daughter, *she never saith, it is enough'*.[30] Casting Mary Tudor as the murderous midwife who sluiced the Church of its chastity, Burgess argued that Henry VIII began the first deliverance of the Church from Babylon when he 'threw out the *Pope*', but that this good work was soon 'abort[ed]' by his

---

[27] William Prynne, *Truth Triumphing over Falsehood* (London, 1645), p. 129.
[28] Henry Burton, *Conformitie's Deformity* (London, 1646), p. 12.
[29] John Bastwicke, *The Letany of John Bastwicke* (Leiden, 1637), p. 6.
[30] Burgess, *A Sermon preached to the honourable house of commons* (1641), p. 24.

daughter who 'quickly turn'd the Tide, before it was halfe high water: and she set all the Gates wide open againe both for Pope, and Popery to reenter with triumph, and to drinke drunk of the bloud of our Ancestors'. God, however, 'discharged her, and released his people from her cruelty'. Burgess argued that although Elizabeth rescued her people from the contagion of her predecessor, she did not do nearly enough to purge the Church of its error. Yet he lays the blame for this at Mary's feet. Unlike Mary, who aborted and sluiced the true Church, letting out chastity and letting in Idolatry, Elizabeth opened the '*doore of hope*'.

The language of chastity provided controversialists with a powerfully effective way of navigating the complex process of political alliance-building. Depicting a certain alliance as chaste and all others as unchaste was a persuasive method by which to promote one's view of the country's surest road to prosperity and salvation, while undermining the view proposed by opponents. In 1624, the Puritan Thomas Scott warned against the match between Charles I and the Spanish Infanta by arguing that the bonds between King and Parliament were marital. He claimed that one's own mother is a preferable guardian to someone else's mother since she can nourish her children with her own breast, while another cannot:

> Princes are maried to the commonwealth; & the wife hath power of the husbands body, as he the husband of hers. The Common-wealth then hath power of the Prince in this point. Their wives ought to be as Mothers to every Subject. And were not he a Foole, that would not desire a Naturall Mother, rather than a Step-Mother? Queenes ought to be nursing Mothers to the Church: Who then would seeke a dry-Nurse, that might have another.[31]

However much he worried the distinction between the two kinds of queenly mother, Scott is very clear that the most chaste relationship ought to be between the King and Parliament. This is the only relationship he describes as spousal, one in which both parties have a total claim to each other's body. The Queen, however, is only depicted in relation to her children or subjects. Where Parliament is the King's 'wife', his queen is merely a 'naturall' mother, preferable only to a step-mother. The implication of adultery between the King and the 'natural' mother of his children reveals Scott's real claim: all queens, whether Protestant or Catholic, enjoy the King outside the true, legal and chaste bond that exists between him and his Parliament. All queens, therefore, threaten to breach the integrity

---

[31] *Vox Regis* (1642), pp. 13–4.

of the nation. A Protestant queen merely poses a lesser risk than a Catholic. Where a Catholic queen is a daughter of the Whore of Babylon, a Protestant queen (when compared to Parliament as a chaste spouse) might at worst be only a whore.

Bastwick made inventive use of the Whore of Babylon figure when he accused Archbishop Laud of ruining his reputation. When in prison, he wrote an ironic letter requesting his jailer to ask the Archbishop and William Juxon, Bishop of London, if they might consider being godparents to the child his wife was about to deliver. Bastwick explained that after the persecution he had suffered, neither he nor his wife had any friends remaining to take on the role, but if the two Church leaders would accept the task, his child was sure to be well provided for since 'the WHORE OF BABYLON, their old mistris . . . with whom they have so long committed fornication' would also be his child's godmother.[32]

When the Whore of Babylon was evoked, it was often followed closely by arguments for the King's susceptibility to a variety of diseased influences. In early Stuart England, popery was consistently associated with a nexus of courtly sins, including the 'notion of evil counsel'.[33] The figure was highly evocative, not just of evil councillors as unchaste bedfellows but of their council itself as a diseased poison which undermined the bodily integrity of the King and thus of the Crown and the Nation. Once the King ceased to call Parliament, the image of a diabolical advisor pouring poison into the King's ear and infecting him bodily became central to arguments that Charles was vulnerable, 'fallible', and in need of Parliament to save him from the influence of those who, themselves fornicating with the Whore of Babylon, infected the King and corrupted his previously chaste fidelity to Parliament.[34]

It is no surprise that in this atmosphere, Parliamentary nostalgia for the reign of Elizabeth I escalated. Her rule was recalled as a time when the commons enjoyed the rightful fruits of their sovereign's love and the Virgin Queen herself was celebrated for the very virtues which Charles lacked. For Peter Smart and many other divines, she was the chaste embodiment of true religion; for Prynne, she was free from any corrupting desire to participate in theatrical performance; for Nathaniel Bacon, she

---

[32] Basticke, *Letany* (Leiden, 1637), p. 11.
[33] A. Bellany, *The Politics of Court Scandal in Early Modern England: News Culture and the Overbury Affair, 1603–1660* (Cambridge and New York: Cambridge University Press, 2002). p. 176.
[34] Andrew McRae, 'Stigmatising Prynne' in Ian Atherton and Julie Sanders (eds.), *The 1630s: Interdisciplinary Essays on Culture and Politics in the Caroline Period* (Manchester: Manchester University Press, 2006), pp. 171–88, 177–8.

knew the limits of her power and submitted to the will of her Parliament. Where at the beginning of Charles' reign, Henrietta Maria's wifely devotion and fecundity had been a standard trope not only in court art and literature but in popular prints sold in London stationers,[35] the end of his reign and the interregnum years saw a rise, at least among pro-Parliamentarians, of interest in Elizabeth's virginity. Elizabeth's famous and final 'Golden Speech', celebrated by Parliamentarians who read in it a tone of loving submission to their predecessors, was reprinted continually throughout Charles' reign and was reportedly presented to him during the Parliament of 1628 to urge him to sign the Petition of Right.[36] Pro-Parliamentary interest in criticising those who could lay claim to the sovereign can be seen as an attempt to both police the sovereign's bodily boundaries and to argue that no union, other than the institutional union being proposed by the writer, was legitimate.

In *The Continuation of an Historicall Discourse of the Government of England* (1650/51), Nathaniel Bacon argued that a 'Queen Regent is doubtless a dangerous condition for England ... unless she be married onely to her People'.[37] He describes Elizabeth's virtues by comparing her to her predecessor. Unlike Mary, Elizabeth was not married and was thus able to marry herself to her people. Bacon argued that Mary's loyalty to her people was compromised by her loyalty to her husband and to a foreign Catholic power whose counsel she preferred over that of her Parliament. 'She thought nothing too dear for the King'. The more she loved her husband and rejected Parliament, the more she erred: 'where a Forraine mighty King is so nigh the Helme, its dangerous to trust the same to his Wife without the joynt concurrence of the Lords. The matter in fact declared no less, for many times She had steered quite wide, had not the Lords been more stiff to their principles then She'. Mary forgot that the title of Supremacy only gave the monarch power to 'visit, correct, repress, redress, Offences and Enormities: This Power and no other did Queen Elizabeth claime'. For Bacon, it was Elizabeth's 'infirmity' as an unmarried woman that made her a successful ruler because she trusted herself to Parliament, whereas Mary, like Charles I, thought too much of her own

---

[35] Malcolm Smuts, 'Religion, European Politics and Henrietta Maria's Circle, 1625–41' in *Henrietta Maria: Piety, Politics and Patronage*, pp. 13–38, 20.

[36] Thomas Birch (ed.), *The Court and Times of Charles I*. 2 Vols. (London: Henry Colburn, 1848), pp. 1, 378. I will be referring in the body of the text to the letters collected in these two volumes, citing volume and page numbers.

[37] Nathaniel Bacon, *The Continuation of an Historicall Discourse of the Government of England* (London, 1650). p. 281.

abilities: 'when the Throne is full of a King, and he as full of opinion of his own sufficiency and Power, a Parliament is looked upon as an old fashion out of fashion'. However, 'where the Crown is too heavy for the wearer by reason of infirmity, the Parliament is looked upon as the chief supporters in the maintaining both the Honour and Power of that Authority, that otherwise would fall under contempt'.[38] Elizabeth's memory became a touchstone for those zealous Reformists who did not shy away from advocating the violent separation of the unchaste from the body of the Church when they committed idolatry, a sin that by the 1640s was so routinely figured as an act of adultery that the two were almost interchangeable terms. By the beginning of the decade, such claims were being made with greater confidence about the King and Queen themselves, who were, in the eyes of many, idolators.

The religious polemicists described here were borrowing more than a word when they developed and utilised Leontes' 'sluice' and its concomitant images of breaching and breaking the integrity of those bodies, both actual and figurative, whose chastity ought rightly to be maintained. They were also claiming for their own cause a set of figures which spoke to the early modern popular desire to maintain the moral and physiological security of individuals and institutions through just and true unions and allegiances. However, anticourt polemicists were not the only voices claiming chastity for their own cause and accusing their opponents of vice and infection. At the Caroline court, the monarchs were claiming that their own chaste union was in fact the 'door of hope' between earth and heaven. Directly countering arguments to the contrary, Caroline masques presented the monarchs' union as that source of providential love which could protect England's communal integrity against the sluice or breach which in the court's formulation was caused by court-detractors and schismatics.

Rather than a 'door' or 'gate', the figure first used at court for the chaste connection between heaven and earth was of 'pipes'. In the 1633 court pastoral, *The Shepherds' Paradise*, Henrietta Maria, playing the Queen

---

[38] Bacon, *The Continuation of an Historicall Discourse of the Government of England*, pp. 274–77. As John Watkins has argued, Caroline Royalists also recalled the Virgin Queen when claiming the chastity of their cause. They remembered Elizabeth as a sovereign 'who chastised outspoken members of Commons for raising impertinent questions about her marriage and the succession'. Where Elizabeth's body was for advocates of commonwealth the image of gracious giving and chaste submission, for Royalists, it was a divine site of chaste authority, an image of queenship that strengthened their loyalty to Henrietta Maria. John Watkins, *Representing Elizabeth in Stuart England: Literature, History, Sovereignty* (Cambridge: Cambridge University Press, 2002), p. 88.

of Chastity, remarked that true and chaste love 'is a spiritt extracted out of the whole Masse of vertue, & twoe hearts soe equall in it, as they are measur'd by one another; they are the vessels wherein ioyn'd by Pipes as subtile as our thoughts, by wch it runnes soe fast from one into another, as the exchange & the returne, are but one instant.'[39] The chaste influence running between the 'pipes' of the monarchs' chastely-united 'vessells' was celebrated at court in all aspects of the Carlomaria tradition, which saw the glorious chastity of the monarchs' conjoined bodies as a powerful force for good. The tradition was expressed as much in Van Dyck's double portraits of the monarchs as in the conjoined heraldry and tableaux which emerged in all the royal palaces and masques, but it was articulated most explicitly in Thomas Carew's 1634 *Coelum Britannicum*.

Staged under an arch depicting the Queen's fertility and virtue and the King's strength and valour, *Coelum Britannicum* was a celebration of the monarchs' capacity to spread their chaste influence to those around them. The 'exemplar life' of the 'Bright glorious Twins of Love and Majesty' has, the masque claims, not only 'transfus'd a zealous heat / Of imitation through [their] virtuous Court' but caused all the classical deities to convert to a chaste life. Inspired by the monarchs' 'matrimoniall union', Jupiter inscribes over his 'bedchamber dore' 'CARLOMARIA' and vows to forever live by their chaste example.[40] Momentarily threatened by the anti-masque (which is led by an upstart from the 'adulterate Sphere'), the perfect union of the monarchs is ultimately confirmed through the celebration of their 'pure Soules entwin'd'. The monarchs' spiritual and bodily unity brings about the same condition in their 'subjects', who are drawn through admiration and imitation – 'their melting hearts / That flow with cheerefull loyall reverence' – into one body of 'hearts combin'd'. Through this perfect union and unity, the wonder of heaven enters the earthly sphere: 'Mortality cannot with more / Religious zeale, the gods adore ... This Royall Payre, for whom Fate will / Make Motion cease, and Time stand still; / Since Good is here so perfect'. Of the Carlomaria tradition, with its unprecedented celebration of chaste and domesticated marital union, Graham Parry has noted that 'the platonic hermaphrodite of the two balanced souls mixed equally has reappeared as the controlling spirit of the blessed isles of Great Britain, and its name is CARLOMARIA'.[41]

---

[39] William Davenant, *Shepherds' Paradise* (London, 1633), p. 73.
[40] Rhodes Dunlop (ed.), *The Poems of Thomas Carew and his Masque Coelum Britannicum* (Oxford: Clarendon Press, 1964), pp. 151–85, 160.
[41] Graham Parry, *The Golden Age Restor'd: The Culture of the Stuart Court, 1603–42* (Manchester: Manchester University Press, 1981), p. 184.

The masque's claim for the monarchs' virtue through a depiction of perfect union, bodily integrity, and heavenly grace used the same set of imagery as Burgess would in his sermon six years later. Burgess, and many other pro-Parliamentarians, used the sluice figures for chastity to argue that in fact the best union, that between King and Parliament, was being eclipsed by the Queen. In opposition to the claims of Caroline masques, these tracts identified Henrietta Maria or Archbishop Laud (or both) as the source of unchastity and Parliament as the chaste influence that could release the King from his poisonous and unchaste enthrallment, thus opening up the real 'gate' between England and Heaven. As the 1630s drew on, anticourt commentators increasingly observed the proximity of the Queen's body to the King as a source of alarm and Henrietta Maria's body came to figure the cluster of unchaste influences which Parliamentarians feared were overwhelming the throne.[42] In *The Great Eclipse of the Sun, or Charles His Waine Over-clouded* (1644), Charles is eclipsed by the evil counsel of 'this Popish Plannet, the Queen'. The tract accuses Henrietta Maria of seducing Charles, 'under the Royall Curtaines' 'to advance the Plots of the Catholickes'. The tract narrates how the King, infected by the opinions of the Queen, along with the 'Popish', 'Cavalier', 'cring[ing]' and 'bow[ing]' bishops, and the King's counsellors and judges (by everyone except his neglected Parliament), began to 'pray unto the Lady *Mary* and be rul'd by his little *Queen Mary*, who had convinced him that to do so was not 'idolatry, but the way to increase his Royal Offspring'. Demonstrating how violent the effect of sluicing could be when the unchaste union in question held such earthly and divine authority, the tract exhorts the King to resist the carnal influence of the Queen and free his reason, which has, like the kingdom itself, been so drowned in a 'Deluge of blood' that '*Noahs* dove' cannot 'finde a place to rest' his foot.[43]

[42] For the discussion about the nature and perception of the Queen's influence on Charles, and of early modern wives on their prominent husbands more generally, see Robin Clifton, 'Fear of Popery', in C. Russell (ed.), *The Origins of the English Civil War* (London: Macmillan, 1973), pp. 144–67, 162; John Miller, *Popery and Politics in England, 1660–1688* (Cambridge: Cambridge University Press, 1973), p. 84; Caroline Hibbard, *Charles I and the Popish Plot* (Chapel Hill: University of North Carolina Press, 1983), p. 228; Martin Butler, *Theatre and Crisis 1632–1642* (Cambridge: Cambridge University Press, 1984); Kevin Sharpe, *Criticism and Compliment* (Cambridge: Cambridge University Press, 1987); Richard Cust and Ann Hughes, 'Introduction: After Revisionism', in *Conflict in Early Stuart England: Studies in Religion and Politics 1603–1642* (London: Longman, 1989), p. 20; Peter Lake, 'Anti-Popery: The Structure of a Prejudice', in *Conflict in Early Stuart England*, p. 88; Sharon Achinstein, 'Women on Top in the Pamphlet Literature of the English Revolution', *Women's Studies* 24 (1994), pp. 131–63; Frances Dolan, *Whores of Babylon*, p. 123; Malcolm Smuts, *Court Culture and the Origins of a Royalist Tradition* (Philadelphia: University of Pennsylvania Press, 1999), pp. 194–5.

[43] See also Britland's analysis of *Tyrannical-Government Anatomised*, the 1642 Parliamentary play in *Drama at the Courts of Henrietta Maria*, pp. 198–9.

Sometimes, pro-Parliamentarians did not specifically name those close to the King whom they accused of being the source of unchaste influence or infection. This was a highly effective rhetorical device that both protected the writers against the charge of treason while instilling in the tracts' many readers a generalised fear of corruption spreading freely and unseen from any or all of the King's advisors to the King himself and then to all his subjects: a powerful fear easily stirred in a plague-ridden century. Charles found this technique a difficult one to combat. Seeking to shift authority back into the official machinery of State, he requested in his answer to the petition which accompanied The Grand Remonstrance (1641), that its signatories identify those they accused and 'bring a particular charge and sufficient proof' so that the accused may be brought to a legal trial and to otherwise 'forbear such general aspersions as may reflect upon all our councel'.[44] But the non-specific charge of a corrupting influence, of 'evil counsels', was effective precisely because it laid general aspersions upon all those close to the King and (as the antidote for such a secretive, dispersed, and infecting influence) Parliament could offer itself as the identifiable, chaste, upright, just, and true partner to the Crown.[45]

The Grand Remonstrance, produced after the 1640 meeting of the Long Parliament, is both a series of commands (veiled as requests) to the King and a brilliant piece of narrative-making. The document records events from the beginning of Charles' reign, written entirely from a pro-Parliamentary and anti-Catholic, anti-Laudian stance. The central claim of the narrative is that, having neglected his Parliament, the King has allowed the country to fall into schism and chaos, thereby leaving it open to attack. 'The pressing dangers and distempers of the State' have caused the neglected Parliament 'with much earnestness to desire' the return of the King from Scotland so that they may enjoy 'the comfort of your gracious presence, and likewise the unity and justice of your royal authority, to give more life and power to the dutiful and loyal counsels and endeavours of your Parliament, for the prevention of that eminent ruin and destruction wherein your kingdoms of England and Scotland are threatened'. The tract goes on to argue that 'jealousies' between King and Parliament will result in 'violent distraction and interruption', 'insurrection', and 'danger and division' among the People. Their message is clear: when Parliament and King are separated, 'ruin and destruction' ensue; when they are together 'unity and justice', 'peace and safety' prevail.

---

[44] Charles I, *His Majesties Answer to the Petition which Accompanied the Declaration of the House of Commons* (London, 1641), p. 4.
[45] *A Remonstrance of the State of the Kingdome of England* (1641), p. 14.

The tract reports that 'with much earnestness and faithfulness of affection and zeal to the public good of his kingdom and his Majesty's honor and service', the commons have struggled without their King. Yet still the 'wicked', 'devilish' party, under the leadership of the Archbishop, having already 'corrupted and distempered the whole frame and Government of the Kingdome', 'labour[ed] to seduce' the King and to separate him from his Parliament. Arguing that the proper relationship is not between the Crown and Canterbury, but the Crown and Parliament, the tract aligns the popish Archbishop's party with the Catholic uprising in Ireland whose members have 'committed murders, rapes, and other villainies, and shaken off all bonds of obedience to his Majestie'. The 'malicious ... popish party ... foment jealousies between the king and Parliament' and they cannot take care of the King's needs as well as his Parliament can, for they have 'brought him to that want, that he could not supply his ordinarie, and necessary expenses'.[46]

When describing the dangers which continue to threaten the fidelity between the King and Commons, the tract's authors argued that those opposed to the reunion of the King and his Parliament sought a 'breach' from which will flow more 'injustice, oppression, and violence'. In a second image, even more reminiscent of Leontes' fears of dissolution, the tract depicts the King's initial dismissal of his Parliament as a separation from which disease *'broke in upon us* without any restraint or moderation'.[47] In his response to the tract, the King turned this image back on his petitioners. Warning them against any further rebellion, he reinterpreted their resistance to his authority as the truly unchaste act of separation. He instructed them that 'should any malignant party ... be willing to sacrifice the Peace and Happinesse of their Countrey to their own sinister ends and ambitions under what pretense of Religion and Conscience soever; If they shall endeavour to lessen our Reputation and interest, and to weaken Our Lawful Power and Authority with Our good Subjects ... that all disorder and confusion may *break in upon Us,* We doubt not, but God in his good time will discover them to Us'.[48] Charles' warning proved prescient. The question raised in both 1641 tracts over whose body (the King's or Parliament's) would be broken in upon was answered at the end of the decade with the breaching of the King's body

---

[46] *A Remonstrance of the State of the Kingdome of England* (1641), pp. 11, 3, 15, 23, 24.
[47] *A Remonstrance of the State of the Kingdome of England* (1641), p. 4.
[48] Charles Stuart. *His Majesties Declaration to all His Loving Subjects* (1641), emphasis mine.

on the very stage where his 'effeminate' masques had been performed before the enemies of the Commons.

Walls, shores, streets: the spread of disease and erroneous religion as unchastity

Leontes' obsession with chastity as a means of ensuring the integrity of somatic borders against dissolution and contamination was already in currency off-stage, not only in Galenic models for women's leaky bodies but in commonplace fears over the containment of disease and in the rich store of affective language through which anti-Catholicism had been expressed throughout Elizabeth I's reign. In times of high plague deaths, commonplace associations between unchastity, moral dissolution, and erroneous religion proliferated. As a means of ensuring the containment of infection, such errors (already marked as feminine) were often associated with women. One obvious reason for this is that women's activities could more easily be contained within the material enclosure of houses. The image of chastity as somatic integrity was in this way often applied figuratively to the architectural spaces in which bodies might be contained. One earlier example of this, which I have already touched on, can be found in *The Metamorphosis of Ajax*. Harington describes the unchaste body not only as the unflushable privy/unregulated parlour but also as the city whose open sewers circulate disease. By 1625, when Charles I married Henrietta Maria, the King was thought by many to be introducing into England precisely that unchaste infection which would not only sluice the nation and true Church of its moral and spiritual health but which could be mapped along the unseen movement of the plague and its real, visible, and very alarming spread of contamination.

If indeed the early modern perception of unchastity as an infection can be understood as applying to space, then in many respects England's soil was, like England's Church, figured as a body through which roads and rivers ran like veins which were as susceptible as veins to unchaste invasion and infection. This is certainly how plague tracts figured London.[49] As Margaret Healy has argued: 'Geographical location, then—inside and outside the city walls—articulated and reflected a growing social polarization and widespread fear about disorder and subversion in early modern

---

[49] Anon., *Lachrymae Londinenses: or, Londons lamentations and teares for Gods heauie visitation of the plague of pestilence* ... (London, 1626) contains a complaint by Mater Londinia which figures the city as her body.

London. The boundaries of the City body, like the boundaries of individual bodies *c.* 1600, were felt to be vulnerable sites, requiring especial policing to protect the inner body from pollution'.[50] Leontes feels this same fear when he interprets his estate as an extension of his own body, guarding its entrance and exits against that sluicing he believes has been caused by his wife's apparent unchastity. The same anxiety is evident in the language of Elizabeth's pursuivants, for whom the 'secret creeks and landing places' were those passages into and across the country through which Jesuits came and went. Feeding this same anxiety were early modern fears that recusants were infecting the country from within. Frances Dolan and Diana Barnes have noted the view that recusancy depended on female sub-cultures which spread unseen through communities, 'bypass[ing] the authority of husbands and priests' and causing 'a festering infection' to 'secretly tak[e] hold from within'.[51] The image of unchaste beliefs spreading unseen like a plague between bodies was certainly on the minds of Londoners when Henrietta Maria arrived in the capital in 1625. The young Queen's journey to London coincided with the spread of plague and the preparation of a naval fleet to depart for Spain. An awareness of the moral and divine significance of these convergent events – the arrival of the Queen and her Catholic entourage, the departure of healthy young Protestant Englishmen overseas to war, and the spread of infectious disease – is evident in letters from the period as it is in the agreement by the Lords and Commons that a general fast throughout the country must be kept in order to 'give God thanks for the happy succession of his majesty after his father', that 'the Divine Majesty will be pleased to cease the plague', and 'to the good success of the fleet'(I:34).

At the centre of reports relating to the events of 1625 is the body of the new Queen. Her arrival in London stalled by her illness, she was visited by Dr Meddus who reported that she is 'a brave lady', though touched a little by green sickness. The Doctor's reference to the Queen's need to commence a fully sexual marriage with the King is richly suggestive of anti-Catholic views that her body was a foreign and suspicious object in need of full possession by the King and, through him, full appropriation by Protestant England. The same letter then recounts that the Queen followed the Doctor's advice and ate something, despite the presence of

---

[50] Healy, *Fictions of Disease in Early Modern England*, pp. 93–4.
[51] Barnes, 'The Secretary of Ladies and Feminine Friendship at the Court of Henrietta Maria' in *Henrietta Maria: Piety, Politics and Patronage*, pp.39–56, 54, 56. See also Frances Dolan, '"The Wretched Subject the Whole Town Talks of": Representing Elizabeth Cellier' in *Catholicism and Anti-Catholicism in Early Modern English Texts*, pp. 157–211.

The spread of disease and erroneous religion as unchastity

her confessor who wished for her to maintain her fast as it was the feast of St. John the Baptist (I:31). Again ignoring her confessor's advice, Henrietta Maria spent the night alone with the King.[52] Dr Meddus recounts how hopeful are those who 'know best [the Queen's] disposition' that she will convert (I:17).[53]

The sexualisation of religious conversion was a popular Reformation trope, of which scholars have long been aware,[54] although, as Phineas Fletcher's anti-Jesuit poem demonstrates,[55] it was usually used in a pejorative way to describe the unchaste exchanges between Catholic priests and the women to whom they ministered or between Catholic wives and their Protestant husbands. In the 1625 accounts of the Queen's arrival, observers were more confident of the King's capacity to convert Henrietta Maria. Dr Meddus' letter reveals that he, and presumably his reader also, actually thought the Queen might convert immediately upon her arrival – a view in keeping with the assumption that a night alone with the King might sort her out. Crucially, the correspondents noted that in those first days, when the Queen's conversion did not come, the number of plague deaths in London almost doubled (I:32). This narrative, told collectively by a group of correspondents, tells the story of unchaste infections entering English shores in the person of the Queen and of the power of the King's Protestant body to overcome the threat posed by her and her entourage. However, despite the correspondents' initial hopes, the King's chastening of the Queen did not come quickly or easily and the correlation between the spread of plague and the Queen's movement towards the centre of London was reported with increasing alarm.

Anxiety over the pathological effect which the Queen's unchaste resistance to conversion had on London reached its climax when Henrietta Maria and her entourage took up residence in the royal palaces. The

---

[52] She promised her Confessor she would not 'give scandal' on her first night with the King.
[53] Corroborating this image of Henrietta Maria's readiness to choose the King and his Church over that of her homeland, Mead reports rumours that the Queen's slow progress from France to Dover, initially attributed to Marie de Medici's illness, was rather due to the Pope's legate instructing Henrietta Maria to spend sixteen ('some say twenty-six') days in penance for consenting to marry Charles before the papal dispensation was issued. The letter concludes by suggesting that the King triumphed over Rome when he demanded the Queen come to him immediately. She apparently consented, leaving the Papal legate at Amiens, and departing for England even before her confession could be heard. *Court and Times of Charles I*, I, p. 32.
[54] Dolan, *Whores of Babylon*, pp. 45–94, especially 76 and 90–91; Claire McEachern, '"A whore at the first blush seemeth only a woman": John Bale's *Image of Both Churches* and the Terms of Religious Difference in the Early English Reformation', *Journal of Medieval and Renaissance Studies* 25 (1995), pp. 245–69.
[55] See page 20.

correspondents soon reported that 'the friars so frequent the Queen's private chamber that the King is much offended'. Observers feared the degree to which the new Catholic party had penetrated the court and presented their intimacy with the Queen as a disease moving ever inward to the heart of the palace and realm: to the King himself. The friars' regular presence inside the most inner chambers of the royal palace was reported alongside the discovery that the plague had penetrated right into the King's kitchen, killing the son of Charles' baker (I:39–40). In the same week, Mead reported the number of plague deaths rose so steeply, they were thought to be caused not only by the spread of initial disease but by the eruption of new infections across the city. In response, Parliament announced their intention of withholding all further funds for the King's war until he agreed to tax recusants more heavily and disinherit his Catholic peers. Over the following weeks, the number of plague deaths continued to rise, far surpassing the number of the 1603 plague. Then in September, they began to abate. Joseph Mead wrote that 'we have some here make an observation, that the first abatement of the plague was the week following that wherein came out the proclamation against the papists' (I:46). He wondered how the plague was progressing in France and Spain, because he has heard no report. He had, however, heard it was very bad in Constantinople, 'where it is no wonder' (I:49).

The association between plague and Catholicism was as well-established in Protestant countries as the association between Catholicism and unchastity.[56] It had been cemented in English thought during the 1603 plague which coincided with the death of Protestantism's chaste exemplar,

[56] Dolan, 'Gender and the "Lost" Spaces of Catholicism'. Nicole Greenspan notes the seventeenth century awareness that Catholicism was a particularly dangerous form of contagion because it was pleasurable, physically intoxicating and offered Protestants a sensual enjoyment. It could also be caught abroad and brought back to England where the carrier might infect others: 'Religious Contagion in Mid-Seventeenth-Century England', in Claire L. Carlin (ed.) *Imagining Contagion in Early Modern Europe* (Basingstoke: Palgrave Macmillan, 2005), pp. 212–42. See also Harris, *Foreign Bodies and the Body Politic*; Healy, *Fictions of Disease*. William G. Naphy treats some of the religious implications of plague in sixteenth-century Geneva, in *Plagues, Poisons and Potions: Plague-Spreading Conspiracies in the Western Alps 1530–1640* (Manchester: Manchester University Press, 2002). See also Margaret Pelling, 'Skirting the City? Disease, Social Change and Divided Households in the Seventeenth-Century Metropolis', in Paul Griffiths and Mark S. R. Jenner (eds.) *Londinopolis: Essays in the Cultural and Social History of Early Modern London* (Manchester: Manchester University Press, 2000), pp. 154–75; Marie B. Rowlands, 'Recusant Women, 1560–1640', in Mary Prior (ed.), *Women in English Society, 1500–1800* (New York: Methuen & Co, 1985), pp. 149–80; Diane Willen, 'Women in the Public Sphere in Early Modern England: The Case of the Urban Working Poor', in Dorothy O. Helly and Susan M. Reverby (eds.), *Gendered Domains: Re-thinking Public and Private in Women's History* (Ithaca: Cornell University Press, 1992), p. 183–198. For an analysis of the eyes as the window through which lust is transmitted or 'caught', see Donald Beecher, 'Windows on Contagion', *Imagining Contagion in Early Modern Europe*, pp. 32–46.

Elizabeth I.[57] Throughout the Reformation in England, fear of plague was expressed in descriptions of the City, and of England as a whole, as a body around which disease moved, emanating from sites of moral infection such as theatres, the houses of Catholics, and ale houses. In arguments of this kind, chastity was particularly important because it was a virtue which policed borders. In Healy's words: 'the boundaries of the City body, like the boundaries of individual bodies ... were felt to be vulnerable sites, requiring especial policing to protect' the interiors from pollution.[58] Elizabeth I's chastity was used in exactly this way in early conceptualisations of nationhood. Her impenetrable body figured the impenetrable borders of the English maps on which she was depicted. By not marrying the Continent, Elizabeth and her chaste body were the perfect tropes for the safety of the island's borders.[59]

The problem of policing borders becomes particularly interesting when we turn to architectural spaces. Chastity often surfaced in plays, pamphlets, and letters wherever vulnerable architectural thresholds were at stake. Following Laura Gowing, Martin Ingram, Loreen Giese, and Sara Mendelson, Lena Orlin has written about the significance of doorsteps and windows in early modern defamation cases and the concomitant theatrical representations of gossips and unruly housewives who loiter at their doors and windows when they should be inside. Alice Friedman's work takes a similar materialist approach to the gendering of early modern London spaces.[60] In times of crisis, like plague, when the movement of moral and material infection through the city put a premium on containment, houses were far more insistently perceived as bodies which, like a woman's naturally leaky body, required quarantine. As I have noted, Henrietta Maria's arrival in the Royal palaces was interpreted by Parliament as a potential threat to the palaces themselves. And in Dr Meddus' first 1625 report of Henrietta Maria's green sickness, he assures his reader that the King took charge of the situation: 'that same night, having supped at Canterbury, her majesty went to bed, and, some time after, his majesty followed her; but, being entered her bed-chamber, the first thing he did,

---

[57] Richelle Munkhoff, 'Contagious Figuration: Plague and the Impenetrable Nation after the Death of Elizabeth' in Rebecca Totaro and Ernest B. Gilman (eds.), *Representing the Plague in Early Modern England* (London: Routledge, 2011), pp. 97–112.
[58] Healy, *Fictions of Disease*, pp. 93–4.
[59] For a lively analysis of Elizabethan border chastity, see Linda Woodbridge, 'Palisading the Elizabethan Body Politics', *Texas Studies in Literature and Language* 33:3 (1991), pp. 327–54.
[60] Lena Cowen Orlin, 'Women on the Threshold'; Alice T. Friedman, 'Inside/Out: Women, Domesticity, and the Pleasures of the City', in *Material London c. 1600*.

he bolted all the doors round about'. It was the material structure of the palace rooms which enabled the King to lock himself in with his religiously wayward wife and to close out her confessor.

This image of a building as a kind of chastity belt – something which encloses 'round about' the chastity within – brings new light to urban geographers' 'flow' theory, a theory whose relevance to the early modern theatre Julie Sanders has already noted.[61] In his chapter in *Patterned Ground*, Tim Ingold writes that in our lived experience, the self is not locked in the body but open to its surroundings ... the mind overflows into the environment just as the environment flows into the mind. In the same way, he argues, 'the environment pours into ... building[s], giving rise to ... echoes of reverberation and patterns of light and shade. The significant division, then, is not so much between inside and outside, as between the movement 'from the inside going out', and 'from the outside going in'.[62] The point of doors and windows is to let in and out those elements which a building requires to make it a functioning interior, but such structural openness also renders interiors vulnerable. A point worth considering here is the fact that it was light through stained glass windows which penetrated the interior of devotional spaces, transforming and beautifying their interiors, and that this particular openness between inside and outside came to be interpreted as an unchaste adornment whose violation was given official sanction at various moments throughout the Civil Wars.

In the 1620s and 1630s, anxieties over the vulnerability of architectural openness only grew more pronounced when Henrietta Maria began to open Catholic chapels and monastic spaces throughout London. Father Cyprian of Ganache reports that on their arrival, Henrietta Maria's Capuchin Friars settled in monastic quarters in London which both Catholics and curious Protestants visited. The Friars also maintained a constant presence in the chapel at Somerset House where the cycle of sung

---

[61] Julie Sanders, *The Cultural Geography of Early Modern Drama 1620–1650* (Cambridge: Cambridge University Press, 2011), p. 12.
[62] Tim Ingold, 'Buildings' in Stephan Harrison, Steve Pile and Nigel Thrift (eds.), *Patterned Ground: Entanglements of Nature and Culture* (London: Reaktion Books, 2004), p. 239. See also *Environment and Embodiment in Early Modern England*, edited by Mary Floyd-Wilson and Garett Sullivan (Basingstoke: Palgrave Macmillan, 2007); *Sensible Flesh: On Touch in Early Modern Culture*, edited by Elizabeth D. Harvey (Philadelphia: University of Pennsylvania Press, 2003); Cynthia Marshall, *Shattering the Self: Violence, Subjectivity, and Early Modern Texts* (Baltimore: Johns Hopkins University Press, 2002); Gail Kern Paster, *The Body Embarrassed: Drama and Disciplines of Shame in Early Modern England* (Ithaca: Cornell University Press, 1993); Timothy Reiss, *Mirages of the Self: Patterns of Personhood in Ancient and Early Modern Europe* (California: Stanford University Press, 2003); Nancy Selleck, *The Interpersonal Idiom in Shakespeare, Donne and Early Modern Culture* (Basingstoke: Palgrave Macmillan, 2008); John Sutton, *Philosophy and Memory Traces: Descartes to Connectionism* (Cambridge: Cambridge University Press, 1998).

The spread of disease and erroneous religion as unchastity 39

and silent prayer, Mass, lectures, preaching, catechism, meditation, and confession (all in both French and English) continued throughout the day and night. The daily routine at the chapel was as full as, if not more full than, that of a monastic house. It was the most significant, and certainly the largest and busiest, legal space of continual Catholic worship since the dissolution of the monasteries and it was right in the middle of London. Although Charles himself visited the chapel, as did a good number of his courtiers, he was routinely called to greater vigilance by the Commons, and he appears to have responded by occasionally strengthening his guard on the chapel door.[63] Shortly after the arrival of the Capuchins in 1629, Beaulieu reported that the 'hundreds and thousands' of Papists who once 'flocked openly' to the chapels of the Queen and the foreign ambassadors and who had greatly anticipated the new devotional space, were disappointed after the King announced that no subject of his would be allowed to go inside their buildings. The Queen and the ambassadors protested on the grounds that he was limiting their legal right to practice their religion freely, but Charles and his council retorted that no foreign Catholic would be prohibited from entering. Instead, the Crown's pursuivants were to wait outside on the street to deter Protestants from going inside (1:67).

It was at the threshold of these buildings that the drama of their threat to English society was played out. Cyprian recalls that the first English Catholics to attend a Mass said by the Capuchins in the Queen's temporary chapel in 1630 were dragged away by the King's officers and imprisoned (1:67). One of the women wishing to attend Mass was pregnant and, taken from the site by force, she apparently miscarried her child (1:67). Calls for the King to restrict access to Catholic chapels marked the sites as both clandestine and foreign. They were pockets of legal but suspect Popery, which to Catholics were some of the most thoroughly sanctified areas in the city and to anti-Catholics, sites of infection that were difficult to remove but which, like houses touched by plague, could be sealed off to protect the King's subjects from the spread of disease. Of course, in addition to these solely religious spaces, Henrietta Maria spent her years in London pursuing a remarkable number of building projects – projects which introduced into the English court architectural, artistic, and cultural innovations inspired by the foreign Catholic courts in which the Queen was raised. Of the dozen royal properties in use by the court in the years

---

[63] For scholarship on the conflict surrounding the chapels, see Gordon Albion, *Charles I and the Court of Rome: A Study in Seventeenth-Century Diplomacy* (London: Burns, Oates & Washbourne, 1935); Clifton, 'The Fear of Popery', pp. 144–67; and 'The Popular Fear of Catholics During the English Revolution', *Past & Present* 52 (1971), pp. 23–55; Walsham, '"The Fatall Vesper": Providentialism and Anti-Popery in Late Jacobean London', *Past & Present* 144 (1994), pp. 36–87.

40   Unchastity, court performance and theological dispute

of Charles' reign, six were in Henrietta Maria's jointure by 1630, and Wimbledon was added in 1639. Only three palaces were used by the King, who pursued no building despite elaborate plans for Whitehall. Throughout the years of her reign, both during her husband's life and in the years after Charles II reclaimed the throne, Henrietta Maria was building and developing Somerset House, Greenwich, and Wimbledon.[64]

While these palaces may not have immediately posed the same threats as the religious spaces Henrietta Maria sponsored, reports did quickly circulate that she was reshaping the inner chambers of the royal palaces into rooms in which she and her ladies could retreat and observe the full office in a monastic manner: where they could 'live like nuns' and observe those unchaste and excessive penitential practices which so worried court observers on her first arrival.[65] William Prynne condemned the monastic cycle of prayers and penance maintained by the Queen and her women as 'unnaturall', 'unchristian', and 'shamefull'.[66] His criticisms of the 'unholy orders' are not dissimilar to those which the King himself directed at the young Queen's devotional life and the effect it had on the royal palaces. H. Haynes records that the official explanation for the 1626 expulsion of Henrietta Maria's French retinue was because the priests had 'wrought the Queen's person, as it were to a kind of rule of monastic obedience, so far as to make her do things base and servile'.[67] The French ambassador was requested by the King:

> to wean the queen from certain degrading ceremonies ... and especially from betaking herself on solemn festivals to some small rooms built like a monastery at the top of her palace, where she remains without decorum, as she did lately on All Saints' Day.[68]

The Ambassador does not elaborate on the base and servile acts, but John Pory reports in 1626 that the Queen's penitential acts of self-mortification included going barefoot, waiting on her own servants at table and being careful of how much she kissed the King. In Pory's report, these acts are

---

[64] Hibbard, 'Henrietta Maria in the 1630s: Perspectives on the Role of Consort Queens in *Ancien Régime* courts' in *The 1630s*, p. 97. Hibbard also describes the extraordinary degree to which Henrietta Maria attended to the building and furnishing of her chapels, p. 125.
[65] Salvetti, whom Caroline Hibbard notes is a detached observer, reported that at Easter in 1626, Henrietta Maria and her ladies retired to Somerset House where cells, a refectory and an oratory had been set up 'in the manner of a monastery' and there they 'sang the hours of the Virgin and lived together like nuns'. Salvetti, quoted in Hibbard, 'Henrietta Maria', *Court Historian*, p. 20.
[66] William Prynne, *Histriomastix The Player's Scourge, or, Actor's Tragaedie, Divided into Two Parts* ... (London, 1633), pp. 201–2.
[67] H. Haynes, *Henrietta Maria* (London, 1912), pp. 321–2.   [68] Hibbard, 'Henrietta Maria', p. 24.

forced on her by her priests and he hopes that after they have been dismissed, 'the queen will by degrees find the sweetness of liberty, in being exempted from those beggarly rudiments of popish penance' (I:122). Underlining these criticisms is the knowledge of how often the Queen abstained from sexual intercourse on feast days: how often she preferred the company of her Catholic confessors over that of the King. From the anti-Catholic perspective of court critics, the Queen's religious observances were not only unchaste because they were idolatrous but because they diminished the degree to which the King (and by extension, the nation and the English church) had proper (chaste) access to her body and proper control over her use of the architectural spaces of the court.

One of the benefits of understanding the association made by the Queen's critics between unchastity, erroneous religion, and the movement of disease around London, is that to do so opens up important possibilities for reading the response by Henrietta Maria and her supporters. Crucially, it enables us to see that the conviction behind the Queen's building projects contributed to the message being delivered in her masques and performances. *The Shepherds' Paradise* of 1633 and *The Temple of Love* in 1635 are key examples of this. Both performances were staged around the time of construction at Somerset House – the first shortly after the building of the temporary chapel and the second after the opening of the permanent chapel. In both performances, the Queen reveals to the court those special topographical and architectural spaces in which can be found right religion, chastity, and moral health. When these court performances are read with reference to suggestions by the Queen's detractors that her body was an unchaste and infecting influence on the collective body of England, we can interpret their claims for the Queen's chaste influence as explicit denials of anti-Catholic propaganda.

The Shepherds' Paradise is a pastoral in which the King pours praises on the chaste Fidamira, elevating her to the level of a saint and offering her any of his palaces and temples that she may wish to claim as her own devotional spaces. The King promises to secure the buildings from any 'impure breath' by placing a guard outside each one. He tells her to

> Choose what place agrees best with your intent, if you will accept this Palace, I'll leave it to you, and your privacy shall be secured to you by a guard … Choose what temple you like best and the entrance shall be forbid to all but you, that no impure breath may mix with yours. But Fidamira, these your devotions perfected, I shall expect you will accept our Court for sanctuary to that saintlike innocence that shines about you. It were impiety to let you live in the crowd of common persons and

your own piety will enjoin you to allow my daughter your company, as a pattern for virtuous youth.[69]

In declining his offer, Fidamira rejects an architectural space within the King's palace and enclosed by the King's guard, choosing instead a space a little further apart, still guarded by the King's garrison, but ruled by Henrietta Maria herself. She resists one version of a chaste life, in which she is enclosed, policed and the appointed educator of the King's daughter, for a life of communal and monastic chastity under the Queen's rule. This 'heavenly institution' as it is called in *The Shepherds' Paradise* is established in an area not far from the court but enclosed on all sides by 'impregnable' walls in which stands a single passage. The passage is guarded by the King's garrison in order to 'deliver to [the community] suitors not invaders'.[70]

Against charges that the Queen's devotional spaces were unchaste sites of infection from which Londoners required protection, Montagu's pastoral argues that they are instead places in which courtiers can find solace away from the moral turpitude of public life, where they can live communally with other men and women who strive for moral perfection and who value the same style of devotion and social etiquette as the Queen: one marked by chastity, beauty, passionate prayer, and female authority. The pastoral stipulates that by virtue of its central place within the architecture of the court, the community continues, despite its guarded enclosure, to heal and influence those outside its walls. The play's courtiers are never hostile towards the enclosed community and receive comfort from the knowledge that it exists even when they have not yet discovered the narrow passage by which to enter. All 'foreign Nations', the pastoral argues, though they have not seen the 'heavenly' and 'peaceful harbour', know of it, 'admire' its 'privileged laws and ceremonies' and are consoled by the many reports they hear of its 'strange repaire of wrack't & hopeles fortunes' and 'blessings' it brings to those in 'distresse' (1.6.470–496).

The message of *The Shepherds' Paradise* clearly took root. The peace and stability of the 1630s may have been short-lived but the decade was marked by a significantly increased desire, in and around the court, for precisely the spiritual and cultural practices promoted by the Queen. Henrietta Maria's popularity can be traced to a number of other factors, but among those factors must be counted the fact that in the decade after her arrival, the number of plague deaths dropped to some of the century's lowest.

---

[69] Walter Montagu, *The Shepherds' Paradise*. Malone Society Reprints, vol. 159 edited by Sarah Poynting (Oxford: Oxford University Press, 1997), pp. 19, 612–24.
[70] Montagu, *The Shepherds' Paradise*, pp. 27, 2.1.847–57.

The spread of disease and erroneous religion as unchastity 43

To Father Cyprian of Ganache, this was no surprise. From his perspective, England was the lost and corrupted land into which the Queen and her co-religionists had poured their sanctifying and healing truth. When Cyprian described the Queen's laying of the temporary chapel's first stone, he compared the action to the laying of the cross on Christ's shoulders, thus interpreting the land on which the chapel would be built as a new Calvary, a site of redemption. On 'the mount' of Somerset House, she lay the cornerstone of the Church in the very 'first place' from which it had been 'hurled' by 'heresy ... when the religion was changed in this unhappy kingdom' (2:308). The Capuchin Friars then took up their residence where the people of London came to see them in their austere living conditions and peculiar dress 'as one goes to see Indians, malays, Savages, and men from the extremities of the earth' (2:309). The Friars believed they were evangelising simply by making their quarters available, since few Londoners in the early 1630s had any memory or knowledge of monastic existence. When the Queen formed the Confraternities of the Holy Rosary and St Francis, the space of the chapel was clearly marked as a site of self-mortification and Marian veneration. Remarkably, even a statue of the Virgin Mary, the object most reviled throughout the Reformation, was sent to Henrietta Maria from her mother and was carried to and around the London Chapel by a priest in pontifical habit (2:432–33).

These explicitly Catholic devotions introduced into the public spaces of London precisely those unchaste, diseased, and idolatrous images, gestures, and beliefs which had for decades been described by anti-Catholic writers as dangerous in the extreme. Amid the violent religious opposition of Caroline London, fear of the unchastening of architectural space – expressed hysterically by Leontes and satirically by Harington – took on revolutionary dimensions in Protestant attempts to protect sacred spaces against the idolatrous devotions observed by the Queen and her circle. In 1642, a pro-Parliamentary news sheet complained about the Queen's influence on London's royal and ecclesial buildings. 'Since the King's departure from *London*, *Whitehall* is become an *Amazonian Castle*, *St. James* an hospital for Strangers, *Somerset House* a Catholicke College, *Westminster*, a receptacle for Seminary Priests and Jesuits'.[71]

Of course, by the early-1640s, anti-court suspicion of the relative chastity of the city's architectural space was being expressed not just rhetorically but also in material and violent ways. By the end of the decade, the new buildings through which Henrietta Maria had sought to beautify,

---

[71] Anon., *The Scots Scouts Discoveries* (London, 1642), p. 25.

sanctify and (as her pastorals and masques argued) to chasten her adopted court were themselves 'purified' by Parliamentary forces. In spring 1643, the House of Commons moved through London, cleansing it of popish symbols. Early in April, a group of MPs led by Sir John Clotworthy and Henry Marten pillaged and desecrated Henrietta Maria's chapel and the Capuchin monastery at Somerset House. Simon Thurley has argued that 'by 1640 the perception of court space had become a vital and explosive component of national politics'. By then, popular and controversialist attention had shifted from Whitehall to Somerset House: 'the queen's palace became iconographically the most significant court space in England'.[72] Anticourt tracts in 1640 argued that through the Capuchin friars at Somerset House 'the king was contaminated with popery'.[73] The City of London accused the friars and others at Somerset House of unchastity – of being 'seducers of the people' – and when the parliamentary ordinance was given for the seizure of the King's houses, Somerset House was quickly broken into and ransacked, its chapel whitewashed and turned into a preaching house fit for the Lord Protectorate.

Both royalists and parliamentarians made use of the metaphorical slippage between bodies and buildings, and between unchastity and disease or chastity and health: to do so was to deploy rhetorical figures that communicated either the alarm required to convince Londoners of the court's ill-health or the authority to assert the court's beneficence. The rhetorical struggle I have begun to detail here took as its target the relative virtue and integrity of not only those crucial institutions through which early Stuart life was organised and defined but the very material and substantial world of streets, buildings, and (as I will go on to detail) the objects of divine and worldly governance. Early modern thinking on the chastity of space evidences a medicalised and moral interpretation of geography and topography: one that figured London itself as a body around which unchastity moved like an infectious disease. As I have suggested, Charles I's leniency to Catholics was perceived by a number of anti-Catholic commentators as a cause of plague. This diagnosis appealed to the commonplace belief in divine retribution and it can be attributed to just such a vertical model of cause and effect, but it was also

---

[72] Simon Thurley, 'The Politics of Court Space in Early Stuart London' in Marcello Fantoni (ed.), *The Politics of Space: European Courts 1500–1750* (Roma: Balzoni, 2009), pp. 193–208, 294.
[73] Thurley, 'The Politics of Court Space in Early Stuart London', pp. 304–5. See also Keith Lindley, 'London and Popular Freedom in the 1640s' in R.C. Richardson and G. M. Ridden (eds.), *Freedom and the English Revolution: Essays in History and Literature* (Manchester: Manchester University Press, 1986), pp. 111–50; and Hibbard, *Charles I and the Popish Plot*, pp. 198–9.

an anxious mapping of the unseen spread of disease across London, a disease of which the Queen (and if not directly the Queen, then her Catholic entourage) were the cause. After initial hopes for Henrietta Maria's conversion were disappointed, the young Queen's unchaste body, and in time, her unchaste houses and chapels, were to anti-Catholic commentators a source of infection whose proximity to the King was particularly alarming. However, Henrietta Maria's early court performances made use of the same thinking about moral influence, arguing conversely that the monarchs' chaste marriage was a source of sanctity and grace. Their bodies radiated a chastity whose healing was available to all subjects, just as Henrietta Maria's ambitious building projects purified London and made the chastity so celebrated in masques directly available to the city's inhabitants through the very spaces in which they daily moved.

Arguably, the purging of the Chapels Royal, and other acts of political 'cleansing' such as the 1648 'Pride's Purge', were partly motivated by those polemical arguments (in the pamphlets, sermons, and court-commentary I have detailed) that described crucial ecclesial and royal spaces as unchaste and infected. This spatial cleansing of unchaste influences is not dissimilar to Leontes' hysterical impulse to eject from his house all the women and children he believes are associated with his wife's apparent unchastity. However, if such 'purges' are to be understood as reactions to a form of unchastity that was perceived as that which breaches the properly contained body, then the question that must be addressed is how such unchastity could be healed by further breaching and breaking, further opening and 'sluicing', of the 'body' already so contaminated. By following early Stuart descriptions of bodily purging, both medical and moral, it becomes evident that a popular understanding of physiological and spiritual chastisement saw the sluiced body as chaste, rather than unchaste. The potential for chastity to be represented by these seemingly opposing interpretations of the leaky body was of particular interest to John Ford; it is to Ford's plays that I will turn in my next chapter.

CHAPTER 2

Chastity, medical controversy and the theatre of John Ford

In his discussion of the first 'sieve' portrait of Elizabeth in 1579, Roy Strong notes that the motto written around the sieve (A terra il ben mal dimora insella: The good falls to the ground while the bad remains in the saddle) follows the emblem tradition's interpretation of the sieve as discernment. Referring to Elizabeth, Strong notes that 'the English Vestal is thus not only chaste but wise'.[1] I suggest instead that the dual signification of the sieve need not produce a reading of Elizabeth as chaste *and* wise. Rather, the sieve, in signifying chastity, already signifies the wise discernment and separation of good from bad. The Vestal Virgins, whose chaste sieve (through which no water flows) is referenced in Elizabeth's portrait, were themselves considered wise: because of their sexual purity and sanctity, they had a special monopoly on the truth. They were regularly sought to give legal testimonies (which they alone could provide without the customary oath), to oversee the care of state documents, and they could pardon or punish any civilian with merely a touch or glance. By virtue of their chastity, the Vestal Virgins oversaw the integrity of the Roman state: their special awareness of good and evil made them guardians not only of the moral integrity of individual Romans but of the state as one body: through their touch, individual bodies were punished or pardoned (removed or retained) and the figurative body of the state was kept sound. In this way, the chastity of the body politic was maintained by sluicing or purging the bad. This understanding of chastity runs counter to the one I explored in the last chapter but was as commonplace in early modern thought as the equation between unchastity and sluicing.

One explanation for this apparent inconsistency can be found in the early modern interpretation of chastity as a form of temperance. From a Galenic perspective, excessive indulgence would result in precisely that humoural imbalance, that plethora, for which medical purges were designed.

[1] Roy Strong. *Gloriana: The Portraits of Queen Elizabeth* (London: Thames and Hudson, 1987), p. 97.

The unchaste person was therefore restored to a state of chaste bodily containment through purging or sluicing (of blood, tears, urine, etc.). In the same way, by maintaining chastity, one avoided the medical need to open the body; one maintained the body's integrity through virtue. However, I am interested in the way chastity-as-sluicing functioned in the same religious and political language in which its reverse figure operated and how it produced in this writing and in the drama of the period a moral and pathological equation between unchastity and tyranny or pride. Whether used in a political formulation, such as the 1648 Pride's Purge, or the religious language of penance and communion with which this chapter is concerned, chastity-as-sluicing and unchastity-as-pride borrowed heavily from the Galenic medical language of purges, excess, and plethora.

The Winter's Tale is particularly sensitive to competing understandings of chastity and their pathological expression. Leontes' obsession with the integrity of his wife's chaste body and his subsequent desire to purge his house of any sign of her apparent unchastity in order to protect himself utilises both perceptions of chastity – as a sound body and a purged body. But both positions are clearly diseased, springing as they do from Leontes' misogynist distrust of female sexuality. In fact, both positions are simply two sides of the same anxious concern over boundary control; neither position allows for any possibility of healing and return. It falls to the play's women to initiate a deeper and more mature form of communal chastity by healing error and reuniting the Sicilian court: by purging sin, not just the sinner. *The Winter's Tale* requires that Leontes move out of his narrow vision of chastity as bodily integrity (both actual and figurative) and be converted to the women's understanding of the virtue as that which sustains communal relationships – not by removing any threatening bodies but by healing breaches. While Leontes thinks that he is at the centre of a diminished but healthy court, he is in fact the cause of the play's real unchastity and must undergo his own purging.

In the previous chapter, I detailed the anti-Catholic habit of depicting unchaste and tyrannical bodies as leaky. But, as Margaret Healy has noted, tyrannical bodies were also depicted as 'glutted, unvented' – or in need of purging.[2] Leontes' disease, his 'tremor cordis', is the pathological sign at the centre of *The Winter's Tale*'s question over who in the Sicilian court is unchaste. Leontes diagnoses unchastity as the source of an infection

---

[2] Margaret Healy, *Fictions of Disease in Early Modern England*, p. 214.

moving from Polixenes to Hermione and then himself ('who does infect her? / Why, he that wears her like a medal, hanging / About his neck, Bohemia' [1.2.303–5]). He believes his diagnosis of the court's disease is justified by his own symptoms: his blood thickening and struggling to pass through his chest is a pain that 'stabs the centre'; 'I have *tremor cordis* on me' (1.2.137/109). However, the very symptom he takes as proof that he has 'caught' in his blood the unchastity planted there by Hermione's and Polixenes' 'mingling' is to everyone else pathological evidence of the moral disease which infects first Leontes and then all those he abuses. When Camillo reports Leontes' suspicion of Polixenes' unchastity to Polixenes himself, his cautious language reveals his awareness that it is in fact Leontes who is not 'well'. 'There is a sickness / Which puts some of us in distemper, but / I cannot name the disease, and it is caught / Of you, that yet are well'. Like Camillo, Polixenes knows that his innocence is plain since his blood has not thickened, where Leontes' has. Were he guilty, he claims: 'O then my best blood turn / To an infected jelly ... Turn then my freshest reputation to / A savour that may strike the dullest nostril / Where I arrive, and my approach be shunned, / Nay, hated too, worse than the great'st infection / That e'er was heard or read' (1.2.375–418).

Paulina is the first to articulate explicitly that the symptoms Leontes exhibits are signs of his tyranny, a diagnosis which Hermione then takes up when defending herself on trial and which the oracle finally confirms. However, Paulina's first reference to tyranny describes both Leontes and his disease in one formulation: 'fear you his tyrannous passion, more, alas, / Than the Queen's life?' (2.3.27–8). Leontes' passion causes him to torment his wife and subjects tyrannically, but he is also himself subject to a tyrannical passion of pride – the physiological symptom of which is his 'tremor cordis' and his rigid obsession with self-enclosure and self-protection. Paulina offers Leontes and his tyrannous passion her own counsel as medicine and physic. Announcing herself Leontes' 'physician' and 'most obedient counsellor' (2.3.54–5), she promises to heal his 'rotten' and 'weak-hinged' opinions (2.3.88/17). By reminding Leontes that his wife is chaste, Paulina brings him 'cordial comfort' and 'words as medicinal as true, / Honest as either, to purge him of that humour / That presses him from sleep' (5.3.77/2.3.37). When on trial, Hermione defends her 'integrity' by pointing to the absence of any proof of her infidelity, save that which Leontes' 'jealousies awake' (3.2.111). His jealousy and her trial are, she says, 'rigour, not law' (3.2.11–2). Modern editors gloss the opposition in this phrase as tyranny versus justice or order. In modern staging, Hermione's speech is sometimes altered for clarity, and 'rigour' is replaced by 'tyranny'.[3] However, in losing rigour, we lose also the physical image of a tyrant's body rigid with fear, anger, and distress. That is, we lose the image of Leontes' body under the tyranny of his own distress. It is his rigid self-enclosure that enables Leontes to protect himself against his vision of contagious and uncontained fluids, even to the point of committing heresy against the oracle. Obsessively focussed on the chastity (the integrity and impenetrability) of bodies, Leontes becomes trapped in the rigour of his own body, subject to his own tyrannical fear of contamination and tyrannically unable to recognise any opinion or form of power other than his own: 'you're liars all' (2.3.145). By suspecting Hermione of unchastity, Leontes calls into question the integrity not only of her body but of all bodies: of his friends, and of the state. He even heretically refuses to recognise the institutional body of Delphi when he denies the truth of its assertion that Hermione is innocent. What Leontes cannot see in his rigidity is that the rot emanates from him alone.

The statue scene might seem to grant Leontes the precise fulfillment of his initial, diseased wishes: to see the leaky body of his apparently unchaste wife transformed into a 'perfect', contained, mute, and impenetrable statue. But by the time Leontes reaches the final scene, he is no longer diseased and his wishes have changed: he now seeks the 'open' hand he once feared and the bodily 'heat' he once suspected (1.2.90; 1.2.108). For his desires to have been so reformed, Leontes has had to pass over from his rigid and tyrannical self-enclosure into a state of solubility: one achieved by his sixteen years of penance, in which his 'tears' are his 'recreation' (3.2.237–8). Unless sufficient meaning is discovered in the inordinate length of Leontes' sixteen-year penance, it can seem little more than a convenient piece of plotting, allowing Perdita to grow up enough that she can return to court at a marriageable age. For the ultimate effect of the play's statue scene to work, Leontes is required to experience precisely that somatic solubility he once so feared: he must spend sixteen years weeping. In penance, he is also undergoing that moral change through which he can be absorbed back into the community he ruined: he cleaves to Paulina (whom he once spurned), mourns for his daughter, Polixenes, and Camillo (all of whom he wronged), and supplicates himself to Hermione, his son, and God, where once, in his blasphemy, he condemned all three. He passes each day in prayer at the chapel where 'the dead bodies' of his 'Queen and son' lie with the cause of their death written upon their grave 'to our perpetual shame'. Leontes' language is ultimately transformed from

---

[3] Most recently in the 2001 production at the National.

the bitterness and tyranny of the trial scene to the quiet resolve of religious commitment: he 'vow[s]' to 'daily' use his new 'exercise' of tears, and commits himself to be directed by his accuser, Paulina, 'come, and lead me / To these sorrows' (3.2.230–240).

The disease that infects the Sicilian court is unchastity, but by exploiting the contradictions in early modern thinking on the virtue, a conflict is generated between Leontes' location of the disease in his wife's leaky body and everyone else's location of it in Leontes' rigid and tyrannical body. The gendered structure of error and healing which the play constructs is something to which I will return. For now, I want to emphasise the distinct means by which community cohesion is sought in the play: where Leontes wishes to simply remove all diseased and unchaste parts, Paulina affects a moral purging that circumvents the violence central to Leontes' methods. Similar disagreements over the best form of institutional purging can be traced in reformation debates about the chastity of that institutional body that underwent a succession of purges and schisms: the Visible Church. Cornelius Burgess' spectacularly anti-feminist Accession Day sermon, quoted in the last chapter, recalls Elizabeth's reign with affection while denouncing all forms of sexual and spiritual unchastity as diseases emanating from female bodies. For Burgess, the properly chaste body and bride of Christ (the Visible Church) is one which is purged of any lusts for idolatry as though they were as polluted and polluting as 'a menstrous cloth'. His argument is as much indebted to early modern understandings of chastity as bodily integrity (he presents Elizabeth as that glorious body, the chaste Church, connected to God through one inviolate 'conduit pipe') as it is to thinking on the chaste body as purged or sluiced. Both formulations follow Leontes' thought: women (real and figurative) are chaste and beloved when intact but must be purged (of 'menstrous' poisons) to remain chaste.

Burgess' position is staunchly Puritan and was echoed by many others. Radical arguments for separation and purification were largely the province of reformers and often went hand-in-hand with the misogyny expressed by both Leontes and Burgess. In 1615, the Calvinist controversialist, Thomas Adams, described the early Church as a beautiful virgin to whom God pledged his chaste love and the Reformation as the expulsion of illness from her body. He refers specifically to humoural theory when offering the diseased body as a figure for both the erroneous souls of individuals and of the whole body of the Church in which each soul is corporate. As the natural body 'when it is over charged in the veines and parts with ranke and rotten humours', which it has 'gathered by misdiet, surfetting, or infect ayres' until it 'growes dangerously sicke' and requires 'some fit evacuation ... So the body of a Church being infected with humours, and swolne with tumours of unsound doctrine, of unsounder life, superstitious ceremonies, corrupting the vitall pores and powers therof: troubled with the colde shakings of indevotion, or taken with the numnesse of induration, or terrified with windy passions of turbulent spirits cannot be at ease, till due reformation hath cured it'. Adams later calls on surgical imagery for the treatment of corruption. 'Bee the errour small, yet the ache of a finger keepes the body from perfect health. The greater it is the more dangerous. Especially ... when it possesseth a vitall part, and affecteth, infecteth the Rulers, of the Church ... So the disease may prove a Gangrene, and then ... no meanes can saue the whole, but cutting off the incurable part'.[4]

These early arguments generally applied to the severance and purging of all remnants of Rome from the body of the English Church, but were applied just as frequently in later decades by those non-conformist Calvinists who felt the Reformation had not gone far enough and that the Visible Church in England remained diseased. In 1623, Oliver Almond warned against 'infectious and pestilent heresy' and in 1646, John Brinsley asserted that 'the whole is infected, because a part is so ... the incestuous person ... by his continuance in the Church of Corinth uncast out, indangered the whole Flock'.[5] However, there were voices that denounced schism as itself a form of unchastity, as a failure to cure the body of the Church or to keep her community intact and whole. 'Alas!' wrote John Brinsley in response to St. Paul's call for a perfectly unified Church, 'what multiplicity of divisions are here to be found?' Despite his sympathy for the views held by the Independents, the Puritan Brinsley was concerned for the schism he saw at the parish level: 'Tongues divided: Hearts divided: Heads divided: Hands divided: State divided: Church divided: Cities divided: Towns divided: Families divided'.[6] The Presbyterian Robert Baillie in 1645 described the Church beset by schism as the 'dangerously-diseased Spouse of Christ'. Among arguments against schism as a form of

---

[4] Thomas Adams, *Englands sicknes, comparatively conferred with Israels Diuided into two sermons* (1615), p. 15, p. 30, p. 33. In subsequent decades, John Bastwicke made full use of his experience as a doctor when describing the Church as a diseased body.
[5] Oliver Almond, *The vncasing of heresie, or, The anatomie of protestancie* (1623), p. 3; John Brinsley, *The araignment of the present schism of new separation in old England. Together with a serious recommendation of church-unity and uniformity* ... (1646), pp. 42–3.
[6] John Brinsley, *The araignment of the present schism of new separation in old England. Together with a serious recommendation of church-unity and uniformity* ... (1646), p. 2.

purging can be found positions whose gendered language is far more sympathetic to the Church as bride or mother. The Puritan Vicar, Robert Abbot, regretted that the various sects emerging in the 1630s were like 'undutiful' and 'unnatural' sons, acknowledging their father but denying their mother. Such ungrateful children are, in Abbott's account, implicating the chastity of the Church, since their behaviour gives the impression that their mother has not been constant to Christ, her spouse, but rather living in 'perpetuall adulteries'. 'Surely', he concludes, addressing the Church, 'thy love is to thy husband alone'.[7]

It was Roman Catholic arguments for Church unity that made the strongest claims for purging and schism as forms of unchastity, and were the most defensive of the Church as a mother. Such arguments usually urged that if corruption in the Church is discovered, believers ought to remain loyal and seek to heal and correct her errors rather than abandoning her in her distress for 'to leave [our] mother thus on her sick bed ... is but the part of unnatural children'.[8] The Separatist minister, Henry Ainsworth, who was terrified of the contagion to which such loyalty would subject him, articulated a common Calvinist reaction to the Catholic position. He has no time for 'those children that dwell with their adulterous mother', a 'whore ... which lyeth in a deadly sort swollen with waters of the dropsie, or with poison', and he denounces their belief that by continuing to love her while 'abhorr[ing] her syn', they will 'call her back from evil'. He wishes instead to see the infectious Church burned in a spectacular act of purification. 'The skirts of the whore of Rome have been discouered' and when 'compared with the chastitie of Christs spowse', true Christians must 'hate the whore and burne her with fire'.[9] 'And then shall we be so far from mourning at her funeral, as we shall rejoyce with the heavenly multitude, and sing Hallelujah, when God hath given Sodoms judgment on her, and we see her smoke rise up for evermore'.[10]

---

[7] Robert Baillie, *A dissuasive from the errours of the time wherein the tenets of the principall sects, especially of the Independents, are drawn together in one map, for the most part in the words of their own authours, and their maine principles are examined by the touch-stone of the Holy Scriptures* (1645), p. 4; Robert Abbot, *A triall of our church-forsakers. Or A meditation tending to still the passions of unquiet Brownists* ... (1639), pp. 3–4.

[8] Quoted in Henry Ainsworth, *Counterpoyson considerations touching the poynts in difference between the godly ministers and people of the Church of England, and the seduced brethren of the separation* ... (1642), pp. 3–4.

[9] Henry Ainsworth, *Counterpoyson considerations touching the poynts in difference between the godly ministers and people of the Church of England, and the seduced brethren of the separation* ... (1642), pp. 3–4.

[10] Henry Ainsworth, *An animadversion to Mr Richard Clyftons advertisement* ...(1613), p. 104.

These two opposing views of how to cure the Visible Church of her unchastity can be loosely mapped along the different views offered by Leontes and Paulina in *The Winter's Tale*: the one seeking chastity through penitential tears and the reunification of communal bonds and the other through purging of those (female) bodies deemed infectious. One key point that needs to be made about perceptions of chastity-as-sluicing has to do with the relationship between penance and pride or tyranny. In *The Winter's Tale*, Leontes is cured of his pathological tyranny (his 'rigour') by giving in to the solubility and bodily dissolution of tearful penance. Only then can he be healed and drawn back into the community. Just as there is an uncertainty over communal integrity in the writing of radical Puritans, so there is also an uncertainty over external forms of penitence. Compared to their opponents, plain-religionists were far less likely to represent tyranny as a failure to express contrition somatically. They were instead inclined towards the representation of tyrants as those liquified and unchaste bodies that, like *Novembris Monstrum*'s Phocas, cannot stay upright in their watery thrones. Despite Ainsworth's fear of retaining the sinner while purging the sin, he could not denounce penance as a practice. In the tract quoted earlier, he elsewhere calls for the sinner to 'be reproved' and either 'purge himselfe by repentance, or be excommunicate' (16). Although Puritan writers regularly called fellow Christians to penitence, they were generally uncomfortable with the external expression of penitential purging. Excessive solubility in the penitent tended to create an opportunity for representations of idolatrous devotion and of the leaky body as feminised and unchaste. That is, for radical Puritans, the tearful purging of a penitential heart tended to be a sign of unreformed theology, insincerity, or outright corruption. In 1648, Lancelot Andrewes' *Manual of Private Devotions and Meditations* was published anonymously and with the intention of exposing Andrewes as a fraud. It was prefaced with satyrical praise for the original document: 'had you seen the Original Manuscript, happie in the glorious deformitie thereof, being slubber'd with His pious hands, and water'd with His penitential tears, you would have been forced to confess That Book belonged to no other then pure and Primitive Devotion'.[11] And the anti-Catholic *Novembris Monstrum* represents Error as 'drunk with the wine / Of Fornication' and 'walking with naked feete

---

[11] R.D.B.D., *A manual of the private devotions and meditations of The Right Reverend Father in God Lancelot Andrewes, late Lord Bishop of Winchester translated out of a fair Greek MS. of his amanuensis by R.D.B.D.* (London, 1648), pp. 7–8.

all scurfy growen' from 'dirty penance: In one hand's a pardon, / Th' other a purse to pay for his salvation' (119).

While reformists routinely called for the purging of the Church in order to maintain her chastity, they shied from depictions of penance in those liquid forms that were, in Puritan rhetoric especially, becoming increasingly associated with unchastity. Were puritan writers to advocate tearful penitence, they may have left open the possibility of precisely that more inclusive form of communal integrity for which penance was designed. But some Puritan writers register their uneasy awareness that to advocate the purging of sinners, rather than the purging of sin through penitence, is to run the risk of suggesting that the body of Christ is divisible and something over which they themselves possess a potentially tyrannical control. In 1646, John Brinsley resorts to lengthy comparisons between Galenic and Paracelsian medicine (which either treat 'like with like' or contrarily) in order to justify the removal of diseased members of the Church as a legitimate response to members' own rebellion. Brinsley's tract continually urges readers to remember the 'holy mystery' of Christ's body in communion. The Church must not be 'prostituted' by the retention of unchaste members and yet it must not be torn apart: to do so is 'as much as Christ himself seemeth hereby to be parted, and torn in pieces'. Any such dismemberment of Christ's 'mystical body' is, though Brinsley himself urges it, 'dishonorable and monstrous'.[12]

At stake in these debates is the problem of pride: to separate oneself from God and his Church (or to cause another to be so separated) were acts of pride, the gravest of sins. Controversialists whose aim it was to promote their particular vision of the true Church had to engage with questions of communal integrity, with the chastity of the body of Christ. They needed to identify themselves as protectors of the true Church and avoid any suggestion of their own pride and tyranny by instead accusing their opponents of these errors. Puritan reformists for whom this rhetoric became commonplace were largely writing in prose pamphlets and sermons: a form well suited to the arraignment of opponents. However, drama (and especially the tragicomedies so interested in chastity) was formally structured around the healing of schism. Contrition, penitence, forgiveness, the restoration of families and communities, these are fundamental tragicomic devices: devices that extend directly from tragicomedy's thematic concern with chastity. The conservative, resurrective, and inclusive nature of tragicomedy, which seeks the chaste reunification of communities, had a

---

[12] John Brinsley, *The araignment of the present schism of new separation in old England*, p. 19.

theological sympathy with the anti-Calvinism emerging within the English Church in the first half of the seventeenth century. In this genre, tyranny and pride are the vices of those sinners who resist penitential tears and reincorporation into their communities and who in doing so fall into a form of moral unchastity. On the issue of pride as a form of unchastity, pamphlet writers and the theatre of tragicomedy were in opposing camps.

In her study of *The Winter's Tale*'s role in local debates about predestination, Alison Shell suggests that the 'displacement of tragedy by tragicomedy in the English dramatic mainstream over the 1620s and 1630s' may have occurred 'in tandem with the rise of Arminian thought' and that tragicomedy would have 'resonated with the pro-Catholic theological moods within the court' and with the tastes of Henrietta Maria.[13] My own analysis of Henrietta Maria's cult of chastity pushes Shell's suggestion considerably further. Henrietta Maria used her masques to celebrate her particular vision of virtuous life, her own religious and spiritual practices, and her reform of court culture. As I will go on to detail in subsequent chapters, the Queen's cult of chastity was grounded in precisely those qualities that so structure the thematic and formal elements of tragicomic theatre: the reunification of communities, the healing of illness and error, the celebration of (chaste) female procreative capacities and their role in the production of spiritual wonder. It should come as no surprise that James Shirley, who wrote predominantly in the tragicomic mode, was something of a company dramatist to the Queen's Men during Henrietta Maria's reign. Rebecca Bailey has charted the Catholic elements of Shirley's plays and how they spoke to the Queen's own religious and cultural tastes.[14] If we are looking for evidence to support the emergence of two opposing visions of chastity in the 1620s and 1630s (between Puritan pamphlet writers on the one hand and the court, its masques, and tragicomic theatre on the other hand), then reference to the popularity of Shirley's theatre with the Queen is essential. And yet in order to more fully articulate how unchastity was evoked as a form of pride in this period, I instead want to turn to the theatre of John Ford. Despite the clear dominance of Shirley's tragicomic vision in the Queen's theatre company, we must recognise that John Ford was also popular: he was one of the main tragedians writing for the Queen's Men. Further, more than any other tragic dramatist of the day, Ford's theatre articulated the failure of communities and individuals to adhere to that vision of chaste union so celebrated in tragicomedy.

[13] Alison Shell, *Shakespeare and Religion* (London: A & C Black, 2010), p. 202.
[14] Rebecca A. Bailey, *Staging the Old Faith* (Manchester: Manchester University Press, 2009).

That is, his tragedies essentially share the same vision that I am tracing through tragicomedy and the Caroline cult of chastity: Ford simply articulated the failure of that vision. More than any of his peers, Ford was keenly aware of the ways in which chastity was bound up with pride and communal integrity; he was particularly sensitive to pride as a form of unchastity that can only be cured by penitential purges and reunification. Ford's exploration of pride as unchastity drew on his evident interest in the intersection between medical and theological discourses; an examination of his works, therefore, enables my analysis of chastity's role in early Stuart thought to expand further into the medical controversies of the 1620s and 1630s.

I want to trace Ford's thinking on chastity through two of his late 1620s plays in order to explore some of the ways in which the correlation between unchastity and pride was operating in those medical disputes from which the increasingly fraught language of penitential purging borrowed its vocabulary. As Ford's plays evidence, the medical world's interest in chastity and pride also borrowed from religious discourses. This is true of popular concerns about the moral dangers of new medical technologies – concerns that were not, in the main, touched by confessional disagreement. But it is also true of those emerging areas of medical practice that did intersect with confessional disputes: primarily the issues of penance and community cohesion. Ford gives his lovers some of early modern drama's most emblematic death scenes. These scenes belong to either tragicomic or tragic theatrical conventions and therefore either return or fail to return the play's lovers and communities to their ideal state of chaste unity. By simultaneously drawing on the medical and confessional discourses of penance and pride, communion and disjunction, Ford's death scenes not only fulfill their generic requirements; they also enact those confessional disagreements raging outside the theatre.

At first glance, *The Broken Heart* and *'Tis Pity She's a Whore* place an extraordinary value on chaste nuptial union as an absolute truth. The characters in *The Broken Heart* especially are incapable of existing without their beloved and only death ensures the continuation of their thwarted unions. The play mourns the destruction of passionate, requited love in a world capable of throwing up innumerable obstacles to peaceful unions, and recognises the loss such destruction presents not just for individuals but for the institutional structures by which individuals are incorporated. Ford treats this vision of an absolute chaste union tragically in *The Broken Heart* and his treatment has prompted critics to read the play in the light of the generic demands of Greek tragedies, which clearly influenced Ford.¹⁵ Yet the language with which the play pursues its ideal of chaste union is also saturated with Christian images of nuptial union, loss, penitence, and passion. As such, the play offers a second vision of happiness, which acknowledges that human passion has the propensity to run to extremes: suicide, revenge, envy, possessive jealousy, and the greatest of errors, pride: the elevation and sanctification of human passion to such heights that it is experienced as divine. This second vision recognises that there is only one passion whose extremity increases the happiness of human beings: the passion of Christ. Earthly unions which detract from this knowledge and focus solely on their object prove dangerously misdirected and violently undermine the integrity of the lovers' broader community. The play asks such lovers to relinquish their possessive desire, suffer their losses with penitential integrity, and, in hope, seek individual and institutional reparation, unity, and continuity.

As critics have noted,¹⁶ this second vision owes a great deal to the language of stoicism, with which *The Broken Heart* is familiar. Yet the play is also steeped in the somatic and religious imagery of the seventeenth-century baroque and its sources in the Christian vocabulary of penance. When chastity is the lens through which we approach *The Broken Heart*'s two visions of happiness, it is possible to see how clearly the one is being asked to convert to the other. Only one character fully awakens from possessive desire to a knowledge of how imperative to the health of the whole community and to God is the just and pure orientation of his heart. His successful conversion is enough to secure the future stability and health of Sparta and through it, the play takes on a tragicomic dimension. It is one vision of chastity that propels *The Broken Heart*'s tragic trajectory; it is another which allows the play enough comic renewal that 'if words have cloth'd the subject right', the audience 'may partake a pity with delight'.¹⁷

Gilles D. Montsarrat has observed that Ford's contribution to the Renaissance project of exploring the compatibility of Christian and classical modes of thought, representation, and morality was his keen

---

¹⁵ Dorothy M. Farr, *John Ford and Caroline Theatre* (London: Macmillan, 1979); Michael Neill (ed.), *John Ford: Critical Re-Visions* (Cambridge: Cambridge University Press, 1988); Gilles D. Montsarrat, *Light from the Porch: Stoicism and English Renaissance Literature* (Paris: Didier-Érudition, 1984); Reid Barbour, 'John Ford and Resolve,' *Studies in Philology* 86 (1989), pp. 341–66.
¹⁶ Monsarrat, *Light from the Porch*; Barbour, 'John Ford and Resolve'.
¹⁷ Prologue, pp. 18–9. All subsequent references will be cited in text and refer to the Oxford edition of the plays: Marion Lomax (ed.),'*Tis Pity She's a Whore and Other Plays* (Oxford: Oxford University Press, 1995).

awareness of the differences between the two traditions. Ford published two non-dramatic works simultaneously in 1613: *Christes Bloodie Sweate* and *The Golden Meane*. The first was a purely Christian poem whose margins were 'studded with nothing but biblical references, while the prose pamphlet borrows silently from Seneca and never quotes the Bible'. Yet Ford deploys the two distinct traditions to similar ends: 'true repentance' in *Christes Bloodie Sweate* and 'self-reformation' in *The Golden Meane*.[18] Ford's plays were written considerably later but they bear the mark of both the moral and literary traditions he explored in his early non-dramatic work. While the classical roots of Ford's plays have received considerable attention, their debt to the Christian tradition remains under-explored.[19]

In his introduction to the Revels edition of the play, T.J.B. Spencer begins his own interpretation of *The Broken Heart* as though he were intending to investigate its Christian relevance. He notes that the modern interpretation of the phrase 'broken heart' – disappointment in love – occludes the seventeenth-century's 'more solemn meaning': 'utterly oppressed by grief'.[20] Spencer lists a number of biblical references to broken-heartedness, each of which describe both the human suffering that God relieves and the redemptive gift God gives to humans of his own broken heart. Both forms of suffering deepen the relationship between God and humans. Of course, the other form of broken-heartedness most prominent in the sermons of Arminian churchmen (especially Andrewes and Laud) is the broken and contrite heart of the penitent sinner. Ford makes an important distinction among the characters of *The Broken Heart*: those who suffer passionate sorrow in such a way that brings them closer to God and the heavenly realm, and those whose passion remains earth-bound and circumscribed within the limits of possessive and self-seeking desire. This distinction emerges most fully in *The Broken Heart* when we understand the crucial theological link between the play's exploration of desire (and its orientation) and the image to which its title refers. Counter-Reformation theologies of the Passion, which were systematised most fully in the iconographics of Jesuit spirituality and grew in popularity throughout the baroque seventeenth century, asserted that when Christ's heart burst

---

[18] Monsarrat, *Light from the Porch*, p. 236.
[19] Two studies of the Christian tradition in Ford are Lisa Hopkins, *John Ford's Political Theatre* (Manchester: Manchester University Press, 1994) and Bruce Boehrer, '"Nice Philosophy": *'Tis Pity She's a Whore* and the Two Books of God', *Studies in English Literature, 1500–1900*, 24 (1984), pp. 355–71.
[20] T.J.B. Spencer (ed.), *The Broken Heart* (Manchester: Manchester University Press, 1980), pp. 32–4.

for sorrow he sweat blood from his skin. This is, of course, the central image of John Ford's poem, *Christes Bloody Sweate*.

> The holy and inviolate decree,
> In his unchaunging wisdome had appointed,
> That true way to happines should bee
> Found out in bloud, and bloud of his annointed:
> Whose pure vermilion red, did fairely guild,
> Sinn's blacke as night, for whom this lambe was kild.
> ...
>
> *Christs bloody* sweate, was that distilling river,
> The comfortable *Jordan*, whose faire streames
> Did cleanse the *Syrian Naaman*, and deliver
> His body from the leprosies extreames:
> We all are Naamans leprous, but more foule,
> Till in his bloody sweate he purge our soule.[21]

The violation of Christ's body (both from without, by his accusers, and from within, by his own blood and sweat) produces a 'decree' which is 'inviolate'. This unchanging and indestructible truth is that happiness is 'found out' in Christ's blood. Christians are called to know that most internalised substance of Christ because it cleanses and beautifies ('fairely guild[s]') the same black sins by which he was killed: Christ's blood heals the very 'foule' error that sought to destroy him.

Ford's use of chastity-as-sluicing in the lines given here works through the mystical contradictions of the Crucifixion narrative and its doctrines of forgiveness: the sluicing of Christ's body enacts a chastening of the penitent's body; Christ's bodily destruction ensures the unity of his figurative body, the Church. Ford takes the contemporary medical vocabulary of dissection and Galenic therapeutics – which argue that to violate and inspect the interior of the body is to know the self – and embeds it within the Christian vocabulary of penance and salvation. In so doing, he argues that to truly know the self is to know 'Christ our physition' (1115). His reference to the Naaman story from 2 Kings 5 argues that the knowledge gained by searching Christ's blood and waters is greater than that found in the search of one's own bodily excretions because such knowledge brings more than health: it brings salvation. The Syrian Naaman is cured of his leprosy by Elisha, who tells Naaman to bathe in the Jordan. Refusing to

---

[21] *Christes Bloodie Sweate*, in Judith M. Kennedy et al. (eds.), *The Nondramatic Works of John Ford* (New York: Center for Medieval and Renaissance Studies, 1991), pp. 109–14, pp. 545–6. All subsequent references will be cited in text.

believe that the waters of Israel have a greater healing power than those of his own country, Naaman initially rejects the treatment. When he does eventually bathe in the Jordan, he is not only cured but converted. Believing our own waters – our own bodies and selves – to be the most important, we are all diseased like Naaman. Ford calls the disease 'leprous extreames' and the healing river 'distilling'. Naaman's pride, a disease even more 'foule' in us than in him, is an extreme that must be distilled, or tempered. Like Naaman, our conversion is a form of chastisement by which we must acknowledge how much greater are Christ's waters (his blood, sweat, tears) than our own, for though our own sweat may purge our bodies, it is Christ's 'bloody sweat' that will 'purge our soule' (369–74).[22] Ford's images are not controversial or partisan; they do not announce his confessional allegiance. But when he picks up the same images in his drama, it is in order to depict as proud and unchaste those characters who refuse tearful penitence, deny the grace of communion, and believe that their own unchaste romantic passions are more divine than Christ's divine passion. It does become difficult to read Ford's death scenes as anything but anti-Calvinist.

'Divorce betwixt my body and my heart': Divisive passion as unchastity in the medicalised body

In his meditation on Jesus' agony in *Christes Bloody Sweate*, Ford describes the Church in Pauline terms as one body which through Christ's suffering receives the greatest of all graces: forgiveness for sins. He asserts that Christ's agony takes away the agony of each communicant and that the destruction of his physical body creates in its place the sanctified body of his incorporated Church: the passions which 'dissolve[d] the frame / Of his mortality, the curse and scourge / He was to beare, from sinners sinne to purge'. Christ's death was a death 'of one' but its effect was to make him, '*all one with all*' (172–4 / 14–15, italics Ford's).

The Broken Heart does not at first appear to express this joyful vision of spiritual unity and purity extending from the suffering and dissolution of the physical body. For most of the play, Ford's characters are beset by fears of division. Lisa Hopkins has noted the anxiety with which the language of Ford's plays express somatic dismemberment and fragmentation, producing 'a terrifying vision of the human body, and indeed the

---

[22] Later in *Christes Bloodie Sweate*, Ford lists the sins of those 'searching the rules of Phisicke, to disclose / The treasure that the helpe of Art could yeeld ... Much mischiefe and abuse', line 369–73.

human personality, as no longer integrated but as a potential war zone, in which different parts of the body grapple for mastery ... a Ford character becomes little more than a field of conflict'.[23] In *The Broken Heart* and *'Tis Pity She's a Whore*, this terrifying vision is constantly expressed through highly emblematic images of the human heart and blood, whose separation from the body articulates the characters' dislocation from their world because of a rupture in the chastity of their relationships. The melancholy Penthea muses on the treachery of fashionable men:

> Have'ee seen
> A straying heart? All crannies! every drop
> Of blood is turnèd to an amethyst,
> Which married bachelors hang in their ears.
>   (4.2.128–31)

Contemplating the cause of her madness, Penthea sees the unchaste, straying heart as an object removed from the body, dried out and emptied of its life-giving, loving, and redemptive functions. From the crannies of such a heart, drops of blood harden so much that they turn to amethyst and are worn as trophies by unchaste 'married bachelors'. The most internal spaces of the human body – the deep, internal cavities of the heart – are, in this image, fragmented into jewels to be worn externally on the ear for all to see. The most secret place is displayed most publicly and gratuitously; the unchaste mode of adornment exacerbates the cold and hard betrayal of love which the jewel signifies. Ronald Huebert is right to point to the Jesuit influence in Ford's image-making: the heart and the ear are the only traces of the human body in Penthea's emblematic vision.[24] The dominance of sense organs functioning in this image without any reference to the body to which they are attached is striking.

In *'Tis Pity*, Soranzo imagines each drop of his wife's unchaste blood as an entire human body in order that he might kill her endlessly:

> Come, strumpet, famous whore! were every drop
> Of blood that runs in thy adulterous veins
> A life, this sword (dost see't?) should in one blow
> Confound them all.
>   (4.3.1)

---

[23] Hopkins, *John Ford's Political Theatre*, p. 125.
[24] Ronald Huebert, *John Ford: Baroque English Dramatist* (Montreal: McGill-Queen's University Press, 1977), p. 37.

In both of the figures quoted here the externalised blood is both evidence of a truth contained within the body (its unchastity) and a fantasy of destruction, in which the lover's body is punished for its unchastity. Noting Brian Morris' critically influential observation that the word 'blood' features so prominently in '*Tis Pity*, Lisa Hopkins points to the fact that the word 'knowledge' appears just as frequently. Hopkins rightly argues that the play equates blood with identity and presents the sharing or gaining of blood as knowledge of another. The play's characters express 'an overwhelming need to see the heart, and the conception of it as the repository of truth and identity'. However, 'as Giovanni discovers, to reveal the heart is simultaneously to destroy it'.[25] Hopkins is referring here to the play's final scene, when Giovanni enters with his sister's heart on his blade. But the claim holds true for the siblings' relationship more generally, since their knowledge of each other's blood is so destructive.

The correlation between unchaste knowledge of the body and its destruction is a truth of which early moderns had become more acutely aware since the development of dissection. Before the popularisation of dissection, one only ever glimpsed the interior of the body when violence had been done to it. To know the interior of the cadavers on dissecting tables only exacerbated this awareness, both because the act of dissection is itself an assault on the body and because, as cautious observers of the new medical spectacle argued,[26] the ogling by spectators is an assault that values their curiosity above the decorum of the body anatomised. Annabella equates knowledge of the body with its destruction in her wry refusal to believe Soranzo loves her:

SORANZO: Did you but see my heart, then would you swear
ANNABELLA: That you were dead. (3.2.23)

Soranzo later returns the image maliciously: 'Not know it, strumpet! I'll rip up thy heart, / And find it [the truth] there' (4.3.53). In fact it is Giovanni who removes his sister's heart and bears it on the tip of his dagger. Giovanni's final rape of Annabella's body exemplifies the extremes of unchastity which the siblings knew in life. His final and literal claim over her heart is both a statement that he knew and destroyed her best and a defence against any other man – especially her husband, Soranzo – knowing or killing her as he has done.

---

[25] *John Ford's Political Theatre*, p. 148. See also Lisa Hopkins, 'Knowing Their Loves: Knowledge, Ignorance, and Blindness in '*Tis Pity She's a Whore*', *Renaissance Forum* 3.1 (1998); John Ford, '*Tis Pity She's a Whore*, edited by Brian Morris (London: Ernest Benn, 1968), introduction, xxiv.
[26] Richard Sugg, *Murder After Death* (London and Ithaca: Cornell University Press, 2007), pp. 111–116.

The dismemberment of the female body had a powerful literary precedent in Petrarchan love poetry and in the gendered culture of dissection popularised by the anatomised woman on the *Fabrica* title page, but the cuckold's fixation on his wife's bodily boundaries as a sign of her adultery or chastity also has roots in the theology of vices and their early modern popularisation in the emblem tradition. When Soranzo first confesses his love to Annabella, Annabella's lover/brother, Giovanni, hovers above looking down at them. His gaze is one of possessive jealousy, a gaze Soranzo himself directs towards Annabella, and both Orgilus and Bassanes towards Penthea. In Ford, the cuckold's desire to know and to destroy his wife's or lover's body takes on a particular significance because it is so situated in his looking upon the woman he wants. The vice of envy, whose Latin root is *Invidia*, means 'to look upon maliciously'. Certainly, the cuckold's gaze is malicious, even murderous. And, as Orgilus himself observes, it 'waste[s]' him (1.3.38). The heart iconography in '*Tis Pity* links the play to envy in the emblem tradition: Ripa's personification of envy is a sallow old woman, looking out at the scene before her, while eating her own heart. Her leanness suggests she can take no other sustenance but feeds instead on her own malicious emotions, her desire for what is not hers. The theological link between looking and bitter self-consumption is one Milton would later articulate in his Satan. The 'devilish engine', through whom all God's good 'wrought but malice', 'back recoils upon himself' and looks maliciously upon the happiness Adam and Eve share in Paradise and the special favour God has shown them. Plotting his temptation 'aside the devil turned for envy ... Ey'd them askance, and to himself thus plaind. / Sight hateful, sight tormenting!'[27] Fittingly, the crime into which Satan drew Adam and Eve was excessive knowledge, making them commit his own error so that they, like him, will be self-consumed and envious of that good they can no longer know as entirely as they once did. In Milton, envy of God's greater knowledge led the first parents to pride, to the elevation of their own desires above God and his injunctions. In Ford, Giovanni's envious desire to know and destroy his sister leads him to a similar act of pride: he rejects God and elevates his passion and its object to divine heights. Incest fixes sexuality within a closed circulatory system: in wanting to possess his sister and to know her blood (both figuratively

---

[27] Book Four, lines 17, 49, 502–5. John Shawcross (ed.), *The Complete Poetry of John Milton* (New York: Anchor Books, 1971), p. 95, p. 111. All subsequent references to Milton's poetry will be cited in text and will refer to John Shawcross' edition.

through intercourse and literally through piercing her body), Giovanni is demonstrating the pride of self-orientated desire.[28]

The pride which leads to a belief that one knows that which only God can know was of particular relevance to the new fields of medical knowledge in which Ford's plays are interested. Envy led the first parents to desire erroneous knowledge; Grace led them to yearn for knowledge of God. Early modern defences of the new medical fields represented the greater knowledge of the human body as a means of increasing one's knowledge of God and his cosmic design and thus, basically virtuous.[29] Its critics, however, cited the theological link between looking, knowing, and self-consumption. Such criticism usually argued that the craze to know more about the body was dangerously excessive and too much turned towards the self, or rather: in paying excessive attention to the human body, one loses sight of the real and crucial self. The moral argument over the value of the new knowledge was built into its popular materials. Popularly known as Adam and Eve books, English anatomy broadsheets sometimes depicted male and female figures whose exterior torsos were drawn on a flap of paper which, when lifted, revealed their anatomised interiors. The figures sometimes bore in their hands a sign that read *Nosce Teipsum* (Know Thyself) [See Figures 1 and 2].[30]

Sir John Davies' *Nosce Teipsum* (1599), a poem deeply indebted to the emblem tradition and critical of new fields of knowledge, argued that God's hand had 'written in the hearts' of our first parents 'all the rules of good'.[31] This complete good was a 'skill infused' which 'did passe all arts' that man has developed since the fall. Davies continues with the heart imagery, drawing out the connections between the heart, seeing, and knowledge, when he describes Satan's influence on Adam and Eve:

> Even then to them the Spirit of Lyes suggests
>   That they were blind, because they saw not ill;
>   And breathes into their incorrupted brests
>   A curious wish, which did corrupt their will.
>
>   (1)

---

[28] The siblings perform a mock Christian marriage rite in which they vow to love each other faithfully or to die, but this totalising vision is particularly extreme for Giovanni. Bruce Boehrer has noted that he falls into a kind of totemism in which the universe is centered on his sister's body ('Nice Philosophy', p. 365).
[29] For a discussion of this body of work, see Chris Laoutaris, *Shakespearean Maternities*, (Edinburgh: Edinburgh University Press, 2008), p. 48.
[30] Laoutaris, *Shakespearean Maternities*, Chapter 1.
[31] John Davies, *Nosce teipsum this oracle expounded in two elegies, 1. Of humane knowledge, 2. Of the soule of man, and the immortalitie thereof* (London, 1599), p. 3. All subsequent references cited in text by page number.

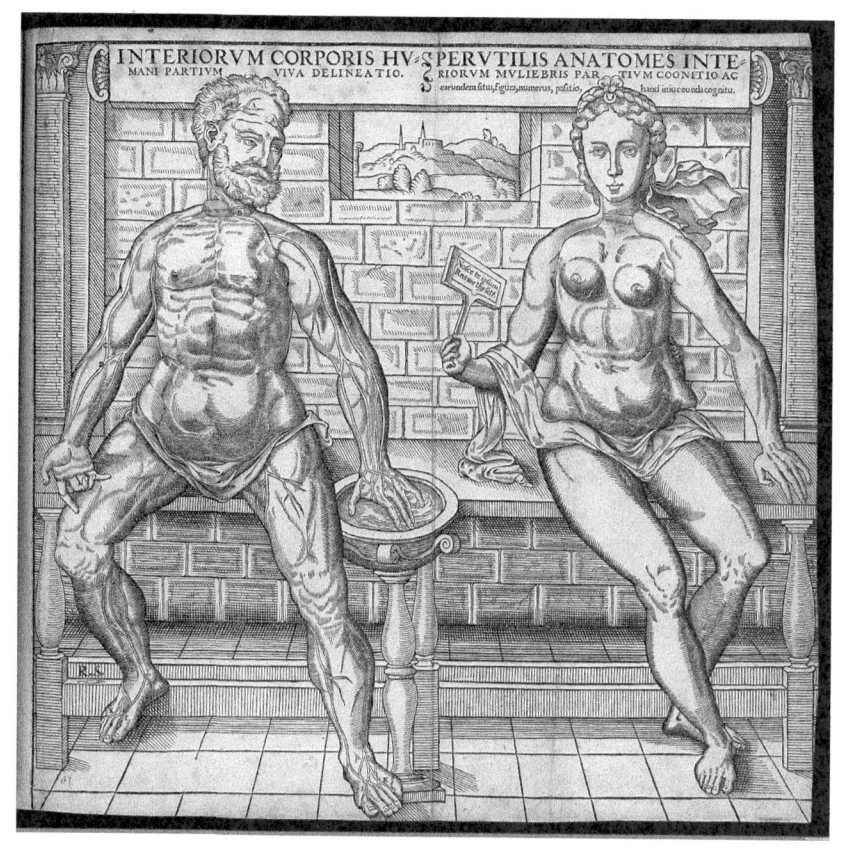

Divisive passion as unchastity in the medicalised body 65

Figures 1 and 2: Interiorum corporis humani partium viva delineatio. Perutilis anatomes interiorum muliebris partium cognitio ac earundem situs, figura, numerus, positio, hand [sic] iniucounda cognitu (1559). Wellcome Library, London.
https://creativecommons.org/licenses/by/4.0/

He then describes the mind's search for erroneous knowledge as self-oriented:

> No, doubtlesse; for the mind can backward cast
> Vpon her selfe, her vnderstanding light;
> But she is so corrupt, and so defac't,
> As her owne image doth her selfe affright.
>
> (5)

This horrifying encounter with the self in turn sends concupiscent man further out into the world in search of ever more erroneous knowledge:

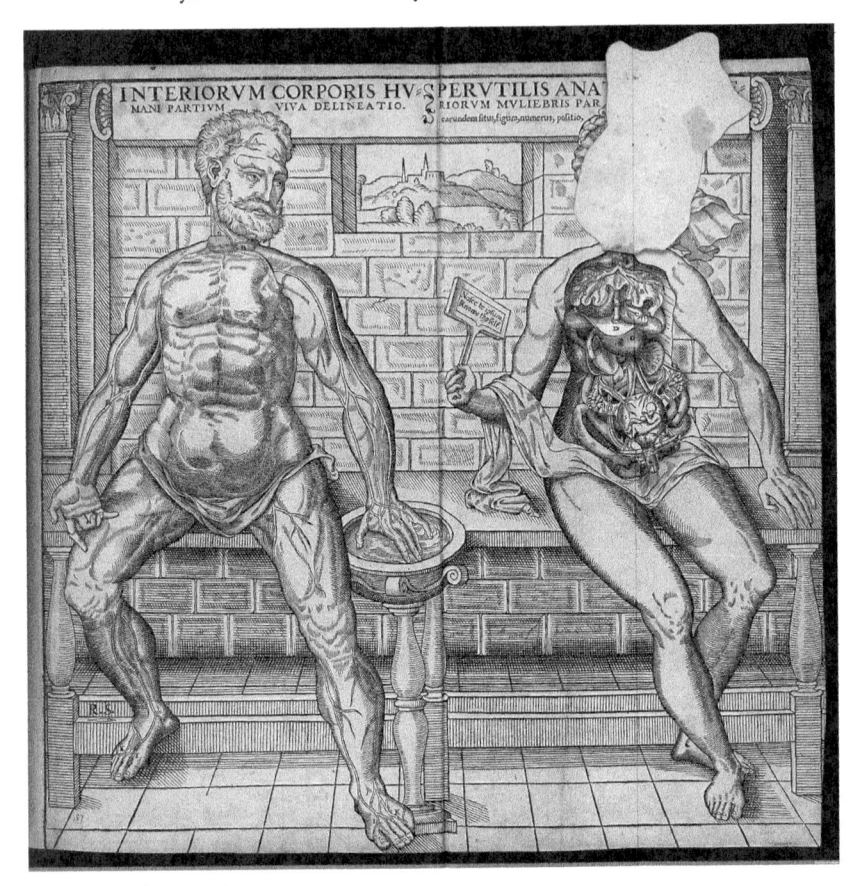

Figures 1 and 2: (*cont.*)

> And as the man loues least at home to bee,
> That hath a sluttish house haunted with spirits;
> So she, impatient her own faults to see,
> Turns from her selfe and in strange things delites.
> (6)

Here, an unchaste curiosity is a kind of envy for those delights which are longed for as a means of avoiding what is most ugly and unchaste in oneself. Such strange delights thus take one out of one's best self while at the same time continually affirming what is erroneous in one's desires. Davies' ambiguous construction, 'So she, impatient her own faults to see', captures the double pull which directs erroneous desires both away from and towards the self. Like Ripa's Envy, the man in Davies' passage eats out his own heart while looking fondly at, and seeking to know, what is not his. So caught between his worst self and all the good things he perceives in the world, he fails to know what is most good in himself: that best of inventions, which Davies refers to as the heart, the 'clocke within our breastes' (5):

> And while the face of outward things we find,
>   Pleasing and faire, agreeable and sweet;
> These things transport, and carry out the mind,
>   That with her selfe her selfe can never meet.
>
> (6)

The envious desire for excessive knowledge of another's (actual or figurative) heart, which ultimately devours the self, is epitomised by Ford's incestuous and anatomising lover, Giovanni. *'Tis Pity* opens with the Friar warning Giovanni that 'better'tis / To bless the sun than reason why it shines' (1.1.10), and ends with Giovanni collecting on his blade the hearts of his sister, his rival, and himself.

Giovanni had once been the Friar's best pupil, yet now he has 'left the schools / Of knowledge, to converse with lust and death' (1.1.57–8). Davies' understanding that the true self is located in the human heart is something *'Tis Pity* also knows well. The play's interest in knowledge and the body is such that, even more than *The Broken Heart*, it figures the disassembling of the body, the breaching of the body's boundaries, not just as a sign of unchastity but as a means of gaining knowledge more generally. Giovanni is shocked when the Friar condemns his incestuous lust, believing that his utter frankness should meet with greater sympathy. He complains that he has 'unclasped' himself and 'emptied the storehouse of my thought and heart' (1.1.14), a claim that Soranzo will later make to Annabella when he too does not receive the sympathy he expects (3.2.25). In their error, they believe that what they feel the most, their passion for erroneous knowledge, is the truth written on their hearts and therefore, is necessarily good. Having been exposed to the 'truth' of Giovanni's incestuous heart, the Friar instructs his pupil to engage in a different kind of self-assault:

> Hie to thy father's house, there lock thee fast
> Alone within thy chamber, then fall down
> On both thy knees, and grovel on the ground;
> Cry to thy heart, wash every word thou utter'st
> In tears, and, if't be possible, of blood;
> Beg heaven to cleanse the leprosy of lust
> That rots thy soul.
>
> (1.1.69–75)

68   Chastity, medical controversy and the theatre of John Ford

This penitential vision of opening the body in order to cleanse it of disease and to unlock its most fundamental and chaste knowledge relies on a belief in the salvation made possible by Christ's blood and tears. In the penitential vision of the body, its porousness – which in early modern commonplaces about women is a sign of their unchastity – becomes instead the means by which one purges sin and gains knowledge of God. That is, for the penitent, the body opened becomes a sign of chastity as a correctly orientated relationship with God rather than its opposite. When she comes to confess, the Friar gives Annabella the same instructions he gave her lover: 'I am glad to see this penance; for believe me, / You have unripped a soul so foul and guilty ... But weep, weep on; / These tears may do you good. Weep faster yet' (3.6.1–5).

We have seen in *Christes Bloody Sweate,* Ford's early vision of how erroneous the search for physical health through purgation can be when the greater healing of Christ's purged body is forgotten. Externalising the interior body through the study of one's fluids was particularly popular in England. Jonathan Sawday's *The Body Emblazoned* has in the last decades directed critics of early modern literature to the importance of what he terms the 'culture of dissection': developments in medical knowledge and technologies, the growing popularity of public dissection, the explicit renderings of the insides of the body by artists like Rembrandt, and anatomical texts filled with vivid illustrations of anatomised bodies.[32] Yet, as Deborah Harkness has pointed out, this culture was most pronounced in the city of Padua and there is little evidence to support the claim that a comparable culture of dissection existed in England.[33] Public anatomies did take place in Oxford, Cambridge, and in London at the College of Physicians and Barber-Surgeons' Hall, but they were not as regular or spectacular as those in Padua and did not attract Padua's staggering numbers. Harkness argues that the 'body curiosity' in Protestant England expressed itself through a culture of therapeutics 'that was centred on a subjective study of one's own body rather than a nominally objective eye-witnessing of the dismemberment of someone else's body'. Michael Schoenfeldt shares this view: 'Galenic medicine' he claims, 'led individuals to a kind of radical introspection'.[34]

---

[32] Sawday, *The Body Emblazoned: Dissection and the Human Body in Renaissance Culture,* (London: Routledge, 1996).
[33] Deborah Harkness, '*Nosce Teipsum*: Curiosity, the Humoural Body and the Culture of Therapeutics in Late Sixteenth- and Early Seventeenth-Century England', in R. J. W. Evans and Alexander Marr (eds.), *Curiosity and Wonder from the Renaissance to the Enlightenment* (Aldershot: Ashgate, 2006), pp. 171–192, 176.
[34] Schoenfeldt, *Bodies and Selves in Early Modern England,* pp. 1–22.

Both the culture of dissection and the culture of therapeutics involve opening the body, but the latter was practiced in the main by individuals themselves, under instruction from their physicians, administering at home the means by which to open the body through excretions of urine, vomit, blood, sweat, and excrement in order to observe the movement of humours. Purges were the study of the living body whose interior state was replicated in externalised signs – a very different form of physiological awareness to the scrutiny of bodies destroyed and opened. A supporter of therapeutics over anatomy, Bacon claimed that 'in the inquirie which is made by Anatomie, I finde much deficiencie: for they enquire of the Parts, and their Substances, Figures, and Collocations; But they enquire not of the Diversities of the Parts; the Secrecies of the Passages; and the seats or neastling of the humours'.[35] Jonathan Sawday argues that Bacon's claim is a sign of his ignorance about the continental culture of dissection, but Harkness suggests instead that it reflects Bacon's understanding of that culture and his dismissal of it on the grounds that it failed to sufficiently uncover the secrets of the body.[36] I find more productive here Harkness' findings that domestic therapeutic practices, which privileged the externalising signs of humoural movements around a living body as markers of its health, were certainly pervasive. Indeed, one of England's greatest and most controversial contributions to early modern knowledge of the body was William Harvey's discovery of the circulation of the blood through the heart and veins: a discovery achieved by observing the externalised movements of fluids in a living subject rather than the anatomising of a cadaver.

Ford arguably references this discovery explicitly in one of *The Broken Heart*'s emblematic death scenes.[37] Harvey's treatise was published in 1628, making it coincident with the years Ford was working on *The Broken Heart*, and although it was not translated into English until some years later, Harvey's Latin is grammar-school Latin, easily accessible to Ford. The treatise offers a description and a diagram of how to draw blood and Harvey's method is precisely that which Orgilus himself follows when he kills himself. Condemned to die for his murder of Ithocles, Orgilus selects phlebotomy, a fitting means by which to purge himself and his community of his crime. Seated in a chair centre-stage, he asks for a staff to clench in his hand so as to assist the passage of his blood from his open vein. This is,

---

[35] M. Kiernan (ed.), *The Advancement of Learning* (Oxford: Oxford University Press, 2000), p. 99.
[36] Harkness, '*Nosce Teipsum*', p. 191.
[37] Terri Clerico argues that Ford's treatment of the flow of blood within the contained circuit of incestuous love is indebted to his awareness of Harvey's discovery in 'The Politics of Blood: John Ford's *'Tis Pity She's a Whore'*, *English Literary Renaissance* 22:3 (1992), pp. 405–34.

of course, exactly how Harvey demonstrated his discovery of the circulation of blood in the anatomy theaters to which Beeston's Phoenix (in which Ford's play was performed) was architecturally allied. Harvey's popular print image (taken from Fabricius) with which he demonstrated the flow of blood depicts veins running along a flexed arm, extended away from the body and clutching a staff in its fist [See Figure 3].

Debates about the relative chastity of the two means by which early moderns could 'know' and 'see' the interior of the body hovered behind Ford's staging.[38] In *'Tis Pity*, the figure of a pierced heart is used to pose the play's questions about chaste and unchaste knowledge, or self-cleansing, penitential passion versus the envious passion that feeds on itself while seeking to anatomise another. Those characters in *'Tis Pity* who most influence Annabella's unchastity, Giovanni and Soranzo, deploy the figure of a pierced heart in order to do so, whereas the Friar, the only voice calling Annabella to contrition, uses the same image to chastise her and convince her of her crime. Both forms of the image assume that the heart is the source of truth and, when viewed together, constitute an argument about the nature of erroneous and chaste knowledge not dissimilar to early modern arguments about the value of new medical technologies.

Giovanni first imagines his heart pierced with a blade when he professes his love for his sister. Offering her his dagger and exposing his chest, he cries: 'strike home! / Rip up my bosom, there thou shalt behold / A heart, in which is writ the truth / I speak' (1.2.211). Where Eve led Adam into trespass, here Giovanni draws his sister into incestuous love, a knowledge and 'truth' that she too has felt but of which she dared not speak. Unlike her brother, Annabella is periodically repentant and in her first confession, the Friar confirms the unchastity of her deed by deploying the same figure Giovanni used in his 'marriage' proposal to his sister. Seeking to represent to Annabella the horrors of her damnation, the Friar argues that when in hell, she 'will wish each kiss [her] brother gave, / Had been a dagger's point'. It is the Friar's use of Giovanni's own passionate image that moves Annabella to contrition more than any of his gruesome and highly emblematic images of damnation. The Friar immediately reads the change in Annabella: 'But soft, methinks I see repentance work / New motions in your heart; say, how is't with you?' (3.7.27). Giovanni exposes his heart

[38] Harvey studied in Padua, in the anatomy theaters which Inigo Jones visited in the 1590s. For scholarship on the importance of architectural resonances between anatomy theaters and the English popular theatre, see Nunn, *Staging Anatomies*. For the theatricality of Padua's anatomies, see Cynthia Klestinec, 'Civility, Comportment, and the Anatomy Theater: Girolamo Fabrici and His Medical Students in Renaissance Padua', *Renaissance Quarterly* 60:2 (2007), pp. 434–63.

to be ravaged in order to press on Annabella how true his love is. In doing so, he is claiming that he must know her or die and Annabella's requital is therefore posited by him as an act of rescue. The Friar, however, reverses this argument. He uses the image of a pierced heart to rescue Annabella, arguing instead that it is her excessive knowledge of her brother that is the dagger to her heart.

The Friar's penitential use of the image affects Annabella so much that when the image next surfaces it has become in her mind a figure for her contrition. Here again, it is associated with differing kinds of knowledge. The dissembling Soranzo convinces her that his love plumbed her heart, 'and, as I thought, thy virtues', whereas her lover, he argues, only 'doated on the picture that hung out / Upon thy cheeks, to please his humorous eye'. Annabella reacts passionately to the suggestion that Soranzo read virtue in her heart, because she knows that in truth that is where her crime is written: 'O, my lord! / These words wound deeper than your sword could do' (4.3.125–9). When locked in Soranzo's 'prison' and unable to confess her sin, Annabella pierces her veins and writes her confession in her own blood. Her action has three purposes: it is an attempt to purge herself physically of her unchastity, to alert the Friar to her need for absolution, and to make known the truth of her contrition by writing it with the substance of her deepest self. Annabella writes her penitence in blood so as to announce that it is her true passion, thus aligning herself with the Friar's chaste rendering of the figure of the pierced heart and denying her complicity in the unchaste use with which Giovanni deploys it. Giovanni, of course, cannot accept such a rendering of the figure. He only understands pierced hearts as the suicidal alternative to the joy of their requited love. He refuses to acknowledge the verity of Annabella's confession, even while he reads it in her blood, because it signifies the greatest of arrows pointed at his heart:

> 'Tis her hand,
> I know't; and 'tis all written in her blood.
> She writes I know not what. Death ! I'll not fear
> An *armed thunderbolt aim'd at my heart.*
>   (5.3.31–3, italics mine)

Finally, the Friar offers Giovanni that chaste rendering of the image which so affected Annabella: 'thy blindness slays thee' he argues (5.3.22). And so it will.

It is Giovanni's rendering of the figure that ultimately triumphs when he stabs Annabella in the heart. Yet early in this decisive scene, the Friar's redemptive interpretation of the image struggles for a place.

Although Giovanni rejects the Church's moral teachings and his old tutor, he nonetheless tells his sister to pray when he comes upon her in her chamber. He does so because he means to kill her. But she, having associated herself with the Friar's understanding of pierced hearts as redemption, believes Giovanni has also been chastised. Annabella's 'I see your drift' is usually glossed as her recognition that her brother has come to kill her (5.5.66). But this reading makes no sense given that when Giovanni later says farewell to Annabella, she assumes he means to leave the room (5.5.81). 'I see your drift' immediately precedes Annabella's prayer for angelic protection, not because she realises she is about to be murdered but because, having spent so many long hours alone in penitence, she assumes her brother's desire for prayer is a sign that he has repented also. This moment sees each sibling interpreting oppositely Annabella's heart: blinded by his envious and unchaste passion, Giovanni believes her prayer is preparing her for the final act of their unchaste knowledge and destruction of each other; contrite and purged of her sin, Annabella assumes that her brother wishes her to pray because he too has experienced the chastity gained by repentant purging. But the moment passes, and Annabella is drawn definitively into Giovanni's reading of her pierced heart.

Giovanni violently actualises the play's most prominent image when he enters the banquet with his sister's heart on his blade. He then reads the final instance of the image as his doing rather than Christ's, and as the destruction of an erroneous, unrepentant, and envious lover, not the purging of a penitent soul. 'These hands have from her bosom ripped this heart,' he cries. 'Beh[old] the rape of life and beauty / Which I have acted'. ''Tis a heart, / A heart my Lords, in which is mine entombed', 'a love, for whose each drop of blood / I would have pawned my heart'. 'This dagger's point ploughed up / her fruitful womb, and left to me the fame / Of a most glorious executioner'. 'The glory of my deed / Darken'd the mid-day sun, made noon as night'. The final gruesome image of pierced hearts collecting on one blade literally joins all three characters in their unchastity and visually confirms the figure of the pierced heart as signifying envious and destructive knowledge (5.6.58;20;26–7;101–2;32–3;21–2). Annabella's spilt blood, Giovanni claims in a telling pun, has not purged her but has instead 'gilt' himself (5.6.67). All vestige of Annabella's and the Friar's understanding of pierced hearts as chaste, penitential passion have vanished, and are finally swept aside by the corrupt Cardinal's glib closing judgement that the entire tragedy has been caused by Annabella's unchastity alone: ''Tis pity she's a whore' (5.6.159).

'Excellent misery!': the chastity of Christ's broken heart

Ford's investigation of unchastity is crucially interested in the devastating effect of pride on collective bodies. Through the failures of his unchaste lovers, through their pride and their misplaced sense of heroism, Ford's plays assert the importance of community cohesion and mourn its loss. In *'Tis Pity*, such loss is total, but in *The Broken Heart*, one character embodies the wisdom Ford articulated in *Christes Bloody Sweate* and enables the play to reach a tragicomic dimension. When in the *Broken Heart*, Bassanes is separated from Penthea, he is reformed from a jealous husband and the play's most ridiculous figure to a penitent and wise man, who alone articulates the truths which the audience is left to digest after the play's four deaths. Bassanes' excessive, envious, and possessive behaviour motivates Ithocles to separate him from his wife and in his loneliness for Penthea, Bassanes begins to undergo a 'rare change' (4.2.6). Where once he harassed his servants with their duty to spy on and contain Penthea, he now instructs them to 'pray' and to use their 'recreations' well.

> All the service
> I will expect is quietness amongst'ee.
> Take liberty at home, abroad, at all times,
> And in your charities appease the gods,
> Whom I with my distractions have offended.
> (4.2.1–5)

Sensible of his great loss, Bassanes can no longer return to an ordinary life in which his staff perform their usual tasks. Instead, all is turned to his consideration of his crimes and how best to make amends for them. He knows that his crimes were not just against Penthea herself but against the entire community and the gods also, and that if there is to be any satisfaction for his fault, he must reorientate himself in relation to others on earth and to the heavens. The best assistance his staff can give him is to serve the gods and the wider community, not just himself. Indeed, the best task he can perform for those in his care, especially after his previous negligent influence on them, is to assist them in overcoming their own selfishness. The crime of self-interest is only satisfied by selflessness, just as the sorrows of the repentant sinner are only healed by drawing him into communion again with the heavenly and earthly body of which he is rightly a part. Grausis and Phulas, still ridiculous and comic figures, scoff at their master's changed state. Yet in so doing, they articulate the fundamental link between his prior envy, his new repentance, and chastity: 'My Lord, to cure the itch, is surely gelded. / The cuckold, in conceit, hath

74   Chastity, medical controversy and the theatre of John Ford

cast his horns' (4.27–8). While pointing out to Bassanes that any casting of his cuckold's horns is a function of his own fancy, or 'conceit', rather than a fact, Grausis and Phulas observe that to overcome his longing for Penthea, he has simply castrated himself. In their bawdry, they express a truth that is newly dawning on Bassanes: his desperate need to possess his wife was an act of unchastity, which demands the 'gelding' of his lust. His possessive desire requires chastening not just because it warps the truth, mutuality, and 'temple' of marital love, but because his marriage caused the unchaste separation of Penthea and Orgilus (4.2.32).

Bassanes acknowledges that in his desire to possess Penthea, he defiled her and their marriage. 'Of . . . beasts', he laments, 'the worst am I'. 'I, who was made a monarch / Of what a heart could wish for, — a chaste wife'. Such a wife, he feels in his penitence, is a 'temple built for adoration only', which he has 'level[ed] in the dust of causeless scandal'. He resolves that 'to redeem a sacrilege so impious', he will 'pour' his 'humility . . . before the deities / I have incenst'. This could be read as a statement of his conversion to the same cult as the many martyrs to love on the Jacobean and Caroline stage, in which romantic love is elevated to divine heights. But Bassanes' difference from them is evident in the nature of his resolve. Rather than pursue a life of devotion to the object of his love, or seek to take his own life because he cannot have her, he instead decides to seek reform because he realises his crime is against God, not against love. He resolves to cultivate 'a largess of more patience' than the displeased gods can require. 'No tempests of commotion shall disquiet / The calms of my composure' (4.2.28–39).

Bassanes is immediately tested in his vow to remain calm and humble: Orgilus enters the scene and presses home to him his destructiveness in an image that makes explicit the community-wide implications of Bassanes' crime:

> I have found thee,
> Thou patron of more horrors than the bulk
> Of manhood, hoop'd about with ribs of iron,
> Can cram within thy breast: Penthea, Bassanes
> Curst by thy jealousies, — more, by thy dotage, —
> Is left a prey to words.
>   (4.2.39–44)

Developing the play's use of the heart as a figure for the truth, Orgilus locates Bassanes' unchastity within his breast, where it has corrupted and replaced his heart. Bassanes' ribs are figured as a cage which have drawn into themselves the 'bulk of manhood'. This could be taken as a figure for the whole of one man's bulk contained within Bassanes' breast, but given the highly wrought and often grotesque somatic images used throughout the play, there is good reason to read Orgilus' image as one in which all of mankind is hooped together within Bassanes' breast. His crime is as big as all of mankind's crimes, and more literally, his crime implicates all of mankind.

Editors are not content with the description of Penthea in the earlier passage as 'left a prey to words'. There is no disputing that Orgilus is referring to her madness but the apparent illogic of the phrase has invited emendations. I see no problem with Penthea's madness being figured as an attack by language. Indeed, her mad scenes are confused soliloquies through which she is tormented by her own ever more elaborate descriptions of her desperate state. Moreover, the image of Penthea's madness as one in which she is disembodied is apt. Her self-starvation and her constant verbalised rumination on her misery literally remove her identity from the body she finds it impossible to inhabit (dedicated as that body is to two opposing loyalties) and casts her instead onto a plane of disembodied language. Orgilus' chastisement of Bassanes thus brings home the fact that his unchaste dotage on Penthea makes him a patron of all the horrors the entire body of mankind can produce while robbing Penthea of her place, not only in her own body but in the collective body. Bassanes' crime implicates all of humanity since it unjustly expels Penthea from humanity.

To begin to make amends, Bassanes must first locate himself among the lost. He tells Calantha that his 'reason is so clouded / With the thick darkness of my infinite woes' and asks to be given 'some corner of the world to wear out / The remnant of the minutes I must number'. He imagines this penitential space as one in which he:

>   ... may hear no sounds but sad complaints
>   Of virgins who have lost contracting partners;
>   Of husbands howling that their wives were ravisht
>   By some untimely fate; of friends divided
>   By churlish opposition; or of fathers
>   Weeping upon their children's slaughtered carcases;
>   Or daughters groaning o'er their fathers' hearses;
>   And I can dwell there, and with these keep consort
>   As musical as theirs.
>   (5.3.22–35)

Bassanes fittingly describes his penitence in the same terms with which Orgilus described Penthea's madness. Excluded by his own crimes from communion, he feels that he is in a darkened corner where he can only hear and know his own part in the 'music' of divided love and disembodied suffering. Bassanes is the only broken-hearted lover who does not participate in the elaborate performance of his own death. His life continues because his intent concentration on his crimes and his efforts to make amends through charity and selflessness are rewarded, justly, by his reunion with the Spartan community. In one of her final instructions before her death, Calantha makes Bassanes 'Sparta's marshal', incorporating him back into the body politic. She tells him that 'the multitudes of high employments could not / But set a peace to private griefs' (5.346–8). Orgilus and Bassanes both saw Bassanes' crime against Penthea as one that damaged the entire community. In her forgiveness of Bassanes, Calantha makes a division between his new public duties and his 'private griefs'. She re-embodies him from his own imagined dark corner by distinguishing his new stately self from the 'music' of his grief, which she relegates to a private place.

When Bassanes was still envious and possessive, Ithocles was well placed to chastise him and separate him from Penthea since Ithocles had himself become penitent for his crime against his sister. But Ithocles is only made sensible of his crime by the 'extremities' of his love for Calantha: 'Twas a fault, / A capital fault. For then I could not dive / Into the secrets of commanding love; / Since then, experience, by the extremities ... hath forced me to collect' (2.2.43–53). He has been chastened by 'extreme' love and has allowed that love to 'command' him. There are alarming contradictions in this language, which should alert us to the fact that Ithocles' conversion away from selfishness is incomplete, since he has simply moved from his desire for heroic glory on the battlefield to his desire for heroic glory in love. Like Bassanes, Ithocles uses religious language, but Ford is asking us to pay attention to the motivations behind such language. Ithocles requests 'satisfaction' for his crimes from Crotolon just as he later begs his sister to put him 'to any penance' for his 'tyranny'. Yet, in begging of them a sentiment which should rightly spring from his own heart, Ithocles can be understood as simply asking Crotolon and Penthea to forgive him and by so doing, relieve his guilt. He evidences no desire to be changed by his crime but rather merely to have it removed.

When we compare Ithocles' penitence to that of Bassanes, it appears luke-warm, especially since his contrition is always coupled with his aspirational love for Calantha. His passion for Calantha enables him to enter into his sister's and Orgilus' suffering, but it is not the passion of a contrite heart, which brings a penitent to detest his or her crimes in such a way that he or she pines for God's love and mercy. Ithocles' regret for his separation of the young lovers makes him pine instead for Calantha. The most striking evidence of this can be found in Ithocles' response to Penthea's prescription of her own murder as her brother's penance:

> After my victories abroad, at home
> I meet despair. Ingratitude of nature
> Hath made my actions monstrous. Thou shalt stand
> A deity, my sister, and be worshipped
> For thy resolvèd martyrdom—wronged maids
> And married wives shall to thy hallowed shrine
> Offer their orisons and sacrifice
> Pure turtles crowned with myrtle—if thy pity
> Unto a yielding brother's pressure lend
> One finger but to ease it.
>
> (3.2.80–89)

Ithocles praises her resolution to die for love. There is only so far his martyrology can be read metaphorically, especially since Ithocles develops the trope so elaborately. His references to 'pure' turtle doves and myrtle figure Penthea's desire to die for love as something pure and faithful and, ultimately, sacred and worthy of veneration. His detestation of his own 'monstrous' crime leads directly to excessive reverence for her as a goddess of thwarted love. Compared to the penitence of Bassanes, which seeks quietness and humility, acceptance, and a wish to consider his faults so as to better understand them, Ithocles' language is infused with the exact passions for which he praises his sister. He adopts the language of repentance only to silence his sister and to ward off the truth of his crime: 'Trouble not / The fountains of mine eyes with thine own story; / I sweat in blood for't' (3.2.109–11). Ithocles may cast himself as a penitent, but he is in fact an unfulfilled lover bearing sacrifices to Penthea's altar in the hope that she will bring him Calantha (which she does). His final remarks in the passage above are coercive to say the least: his elevation of Penthea to the status of a 'deity' and a martyr to love is dependent on her relief of his pain. By petitioning for his sister's pity, Ithocles indicates that he is in the realm of Platonic adoration. Begging for release from his suffering, he is speaking both to Calantha, the distant lady he adores, and to the deity he imagines Penthea to be – a deity he would worship were she to ease the pain of his lovesickness. Penthea stops him abruptly: 'O no more'. She reads his language clearly. Ithocles has kept his love for Calantha a secret, yet it is clear in this scene to Penthea that her brother is in love and transferring his passion onto his sister's grief. She asks: 'who is the saint you serve?' (3.2.89, 93).

Like Penthea and Orgilus who starve for each other because they cannot see beyond the earthly sphere in which their love reigns supreme, Ithocles mistakes romantic love for love of God. In a phrase that reveals his search for a Real Presence not found in the valour of battle victories or the power of statesmen, Ithocles snatches up the ring Calantha tosses to him, calling it 'a real, visible, material happiness' (5.1.50). Ithocles' reference to the ring as sacramental is idolatrous: Calantha's ring is merely a token of her love. It is not part of a wedding ceremony properly performed to all of Sparta, yet Ithocles has exaggerated it into a sign of divine grace. His raptures over the ring signal Ithocles' mistaken belief that Calantha's love will cure him of the sorrow he feels for his crime against his sister. By seeking human love, particularly the love of a woman far his superior, Ithocles has not moved beyond the scope of his initial act of proud unchastity against Penthea and Orgilus but rather remains enclosed by his wish to cure a selfish action with a self-orientated desire.

Only Bassanes expresses his penitential sorrow in terms which actually redress the unchaste pride of his own prior actions and those of his community. Unlike Ithocles, his loss has placed him in correct relationship with God; it has not propelled him towards a greater ambition and hunger for earthly satisfaction. Only Bassanes' expressions of pain are like those of Christ's own broken heart and bloody sweat. He recognises that a rupture has occurred in the divine presence which keeps the body of the community incorporated, causing chaos, and that healing can only occur through the re-establishment of connections between the earthly and the heavenly realms. This requires an end to self-seeking, unchaste love and a turning instead to that which will most benefit the communal good. For Christ, this meant suffering pain and death for the redemption of humans; for Bassanes, it means not looking to ease his pain or grief, not looking for death or escape. He is the only character whose use of the breached body trope reflects the suffering of Christ: 'Rip up my bosom', he cries when Penthea is taken away from him(3.3.188). 'Sweats, hot as sulphur, / Boil through my pores. Affliction hath in store / No torture like to this' (4.2.96–8). Ithocles, however, never really articulates his suffering as anything distinct from his yearning for Calantha. And his suffering for his crime against his sister is quick to depart when he finds Calantha returns his love. When Ithocles is sure the Princess loves him, he announces in over-blown joy to Orgilus: 'the sweetness / Of so imparadised a comfort, Orgilus! / It is to banquet with the gods' (4.3.127–9). The heights of Ithocles' pride are evidenced in his belief that Calantha's love is a divine feast. He is on precisely the road that leads Orgilus and Penthea to their

'Excellent misery!': the chastity of Christ's broken heart 79

destruction: rejecting the sustenance of communion because of an erroneous belief that their earthy passion for each other is the only sustenance on which they can survive.

From the very beginning of *The Broken Heart*, Orgilus mistakes his passion for Penthea as divine. Orgilus' teacher, Tecnicus, who like the Friar in *'Tis Pity* is the only consistent voice of religious wisdom, senses the wildness and pride of Orgilus' passion and counsels him to 'tempt not the stars' with whom 'thou canst not play'. 'In thy aspect' he warns, 'I note / A consequence of danger' (1.3.1–7). But despite Tecnicus' warning not to elevate earthly love above divine love, Orgilus departs from his teacher, musing:

> Love, thou art full of mystery! The deities
> Themselves are not secure. In searching out
> The secrets of those flames which hidden waste
> A breast made tributary to the laws
> Of beauty, physic yet hath never found
> A remedy to cure a lover's wound.
>
> (1.3.36–41)

Orgilus attributes to love the mysteries which, in seventeenth-century theology, properly belong to God.[39] He does this to such a degree that he perceives the gods themselves as vulnerable to earthly passions and the envious 'flames which hidden waste a breast'. The human art of physic may not, as he observes, have found a cure for lovers' wounds but the heavenly arts which Tecnicus teaches do provide the cure: penance. He chides Orgilus for his 'extremities' which 'care not / For harms to others' but 'contemn their own' misfortunes. Bassanes, however, does understand the importance of his penance for the health of the whole community, both heavenly and earthly. When preparing to avenge Penthea, Orgilus promises Bassanes: 'I will acquaint'ee with an unmatched secret, / Whose knowledge to your griefs shall set a period.' Bassanes answers: 'Thou canst not, Orgilus.'Tis in the power / Of the gods only' (5.1.37–40).

For the brief time that it lasts, Ithocles' requited love for the princess offers him the prospect of being elevated to a status far above his own. But Ithocles remains like the other lovers who allow human passion to function in their lives as though it were divine providence or punishment, and like them, he dies for love. He is not raised above his station.

---

[39] Romantic love was for many writers a means of evoking and describing divine love. See Elizabeth Clarke, *Politics, Religion and the Song of Songs* (Basingstoke: Palgrave Macmillan, 2011). However, Ford's focus on pride makes a clear moral distinction between the two forms of love.

Bassanes, however, is so raised. His deserving comes from his true repentance and his unique understanding that extreme passion can only properly exist, can only be properly chaste, when it does not undermine the passion from which all human action and affection must take its compass: Christ's passion. In his own grief, Bassanes consoles others who grieve. On the death of Ithocles, he counsels Armostes to 'rent not / Thine arteries ... Thou'st lost a nephew, / A niece; and I a wife. Continue a man still' (5.2.54–7). 'Make me', he continues:

> a pattern of digesting evils,
> Who can outlive my mighty ones, not shrinking
> At such a pressure as would sink a soul
> Into what's most of death, the worst of horrors.
> But I have sealed a covenant with sadness,
> And entered into bonds without condition
> To stand these tempests calmly. Mark me, nobles,
> I do not shed a tear, not for Penthea.
> Excellent misery!
>
> (5.2.58–66)

These lines justify readings of Bassanes' reform in terms of stoic restraint. However, he uses specifically religious language (covenant, evils, a sinking soul), and although he tries not to cry for Penthea, his 'excellent misery!' betrays the sadness to which he is now bound. These are not Bassanes' last words. On the death of Calantha, and her bestowal of leadership on him, Bassanes weeps and mourns and abandons any stoic or reasoned resolve: 'Alas, great mistress, reason is so clouded / With the thick darkness of my infinite woes' (5.3.22–23). Here, Bassanes uses words which recall the penitent in *Christes Bloodie Sweate*, who looks on Christ's wounds and is so sorrowful that 'remorce confounds / Reason and sence' (1438–9).

It is Bassanes who survives and points the way forward for Sparta. Of all the plays' passionate lovers, he alone learns that human passion is only chaste when it does not occlude the chastity of Christ's own passion for his bride, the people who incorporate his body. Human passion which damages the body of Christ cannot survive in a world which is, from the Christian perspective, always being compelled towards the just realignment of unchaste and misdirected relationships. In this way, the narrative thrust of *The Broken Heart* is in good measure tragicomic. The play may not conclude with the wondrous reuniting of lovers, families, and friends but it does provide a profound consolation. Through his willingness to see how his actions have injured all of Sparta and to make appropriate amends, Bassanes represents a future Sparta properly orientated towards the one passion which chastens all others through its redemptive grace. Bassanes proves the play's hero because only he learns to overcome the heartbreak suffered from the loss of the one he loved improperly and comes to share instead in what Ford in *Christes Bloody Sweate* describes as the 'contrite and broken' heart of Christ (471).

Ford's vision of chastity was subtle but deeply engaged with the various discourses of chastity emerging in early Stuart medical and theological thought. His understanding of the virtue not only informed the extreme degrees of romantic and sexual unchastity to which his characters succumb but also the broader vision that shaped the communities on which his plays focus. Like Leontes before them, pride is the error into which Ford's unchaste characters descend; their unchastity is itself a form of pride. But it is a pride for which healing is always available. Whether they fail spectacularly to realise the penitence, healing, and community integrity of tragicomic reform (or, in the case of Bassanes, quietly achieve it), Ford's characters are built from the same vision that was being articulated by the Caroline cult of chastity through masques, tragicomedies, and the doctrinal innovations championed by Charles himself and churchmen such as Andrewes and Laud. With their hope for the healing of religious schism, their trust in the moral and spiritual benefit of penitential purging, and their celebration of those skills so exemplified by Hermione and Paulina (reform, fertility, healing, wonder), the cult of chastity and the early Stuart theatre were informed by the same vision of chastity. Against this vision, court-critics wielded arguments, in sermon and pamphlet form, that instead interpreted communal chastity as the purging of diseased members. Their accusations of pride were conversely directed to those who espoused a view of inclusiveness, healing, and forgiveness. Focussing instead on images of unchastity that drew on the anti-feminist tradition embodied by Leontes, court-critics represented those proud 'tyrants' at court as the moral contagions against which the truly chaste Church/nation/person needed protection. The clear gendering of the two opposing views of chastity that I am tracing is something I will develop further in subsequent chapters; in my next chapter, however, I want to look more closely at how arguments for pride as a form of unchastity began to centre closely on the Throne of State, and therefore took on a more pointed political agenda.

CHAPTER 3

Chastity, William Harvey's demonstrations and court ceremony

One of the arguments this book suggests is that early seventeenth-century disagreements over the nature of chastity helped pave the way for the revolutionary struggles that resulted in the Civil Wars. A virtue so bound up in discussions of the body politic and its relative integrity, and in those forms of pride that so damage community cohesion and political stability, chastity was an important touchstone for controversialists seeking to sway popular opinion. In this sense, I am tracing the subtle influence chastity had on the revolutionary thinking and writing that would emerge after the period on which this book concentrates; the arguments I will be analysing in this chapter are not part of the core of texts which we consider revolutionary in the proper sense – those pamphlets surfacing in the 1640s and 1650s as motivations for and defences of military action. Instead, I intend to show how chastity underpinned the cultural and intellectual changes from which revolutionary writing sprung and provided a powerful rhetorical tool through which polemicists and dramatists alike could engage in the political ferment of the early seventeenth century. Crucially, polemicists and dramatists were working in forms that were each uniquely suited to the definition of chastity they espoused: the early Stuart theatre and masque celebrated that definition of chastity also embraced by the court's cult: feminine, inclusive, gestural, adorned, pietised, refined, Marian and grounded in the celebration of female procreative capacities and a spirituality of wonder. In their attempts to wrest chastity away from its close identification with the court, prose controversialists instead deployed the chastity figures I have detailed in such a way that could be said to constitute an opposing vision of the virtue: one more masculine, intellectualised, Protestant, internalised, isolationist (in its arguments against inclusivity and the healing of corporate bodies), and its persuasiveness located less in gesture, beauty and wonder and more in prose language, argumentation and disputation.

In the 1630s, chastity was becoming increasingly popular: as a virtue, an idea and a set of images that could legitimate revolutionary arguments, be they the polemical arguments of pamphlet writers and printed sermons or the gestural and spatial arguments of court ceremony and performance. This chapter extends my argument about tyranny and pride as forms of unchastity by addressing Caroline disagreements over the relative chastity of thrones (particularly the Throne of State). It is from within these disagreements that chastity emerges most precisely as a point of political conflict between pro-Parliamentarian writers and the court: two increasingly opposing sets of voices that were each attempting to claim chastity for their own cause. In my last chapter, I began to map out the ways in which unchastity-as-pride situated the division between tragicomedy (and those anti-Calvinist theological and liturgical preferences which shared the tragicomic vision) and the radical-Puritan pamphlet writing of the same period. This division is revealed most especially by focussing on arguments about thrones because a throne is at once a word that signals authority (either chaste or unchaste) and an object on which and in which political authority was contested, claimed and embodied.

The chaste throne at court

The numerous descriptions of earthly government emerging in the early modern period sought to describe the proper, stable functioning of power and authority and to warn against its dissolution, and many did so by concentrating on the Throne of State as that emblem of centralised order which, when debased, would unravel all the threads that held society together. The image of an 'unchaste' Throne as a sign of tyranny (a spoiled, bloodied, or contaminated seat of lust) had a strong Elizabethan precedent. John Knox concentrated his horror at the prospect of a woman monarch into his depiction of a monstrous Throne of State which overwhelms all who are subject to it, transforming them from upright citizens to 'foolish', 'fond' and 'coward[ly] ... women'.[1] He argued that 'the erecting of a woman to [the Throne] is not onely to invert the ordre, which God hath established: but also it is to defile, pollute and prophane ... the throne and seat of God, which he hath sanctified and appointed for man onely' (34). The woman monarch would, Knox argues, infect the Throne with her own 'imperfections', 'naturall weaknes, and inordinate appetites'. For history reveals that women 'have burned with such inordinate lust, that for the

---

[1] John Knox, *The First Blast of the Trumpet against the Monstruous Regiment of Women* (1558), p. 11.

quenching of the same, they have betrayed to strangers their countrie and citie: and some to have bene so desirous of dominion, that for the obteining of the same, they have murthered the children of their owne sonnes. Yea and some have killed with crueltie their owne husbandes and children' (13).

In the seventeenth century, the possibility that tyrannical monarchs could infect ('defile, pollute and profane') the Throne itself with their own lust and pride bolstered arguments that the Throne and its props be separated and protected from unstable humanity. Yet, these arguments generated a series of figures in which thrones became metonymic extensions of monarchs' virtue or vice. The writers of *Novembris Monstrum* (1641) depict its various unchaste characters as co-terminous with their thrones: Bacchus' throne is a cask of wine, Pan's a rock, and Phocas' the couch in which occurs the titular miscarriage of the child which the whore of Babylon begot by the corrupt emperor (28, 73). Depicting the vulnerability of the Throne of State to the unchastity of tyrannical monarchs spoke efficiently and effectively to commonplace fears that the vice of rulers spread quickly to the instruments and machinery of government and to the more abstract ideals of purity, peace, and stability which they signified. As Knox made clear, a century earlier, in his caustic description of a woman in State, the props of power were signs of justice and authority – 'the royall crowne upon her head, the sworde and sceptre borne before her, in signe that the administration of justice was in her power' – and to sully the objects through misuse was to throw proper order into chaos. One of the most terrifying practices attributed to seventeenth-century witches was their use of swords, scepters, and orbs for demonic purposes.

When we pay attention to the prevalence of throne imagery in a number of early seventeenth-century fields, we see that in varying contexts, the figure of the sovereign Throne was shorthand for any nucleus of power and virtue. Further, any chair or seat could under most conditions signify authority. As Laud himself admitted, even while defending the importance of a centralised earthly authority: 'Thrones, or Chairs, or Seats, (call them what you will, the thing is the same)'.[2] Early modern thrones or seats figured authority in such general terms because from antiquity, the main purpose of a chair was to contain and display only the most powerful figures in a room. More specifically, however, chairs signified central

---

[2] William, Laud, *A sermon preached on Monday, the sixth of February, at Westminster at the opening of the Parliament* (1625), p. 35.

authority because the early modern conception of systematic organisation usually assumed a ruling and central force of power and governance. For Ford, the heart is the seat of man's virtue: God 'gently yet again attempt's to winne / The Monarchy of hearts usurp't by sinne', and for William Gilbert, the pole of a magnet is the 'the seat, the throne'.[3] Yet, it was this very moment in history in which the figure of the throne was also used to question not only the legitimacy of those enthroned in state but the very concept of centralised government. This is not only true within the period's political debates; William Harvey scandalised the medical world by shifting his attention from the central control of the heart as 'seat' and 'monarch' of the body to the more dispersed governance of the blood.[4]

At Charles I's court, however, the Throne was very much a singular object of reverence, given a degree of prominence and ritualised significance far greater than it possessed under James. This was not only the case in Caroline court masques, in which the Throne of State enjoyed an unprecedented position both dramatically and morally, but throughout Caroline court ceremony. Shortly after Charles' accession, it was noted that he had reinstated the 'antient form' of ceremony when in state, practices that emphasised the authority, majesty and mystery of his kingly body.[5] Of particular interest is the degree to which the Throne of State was separated as a sacred space to which all present must show reverence. The King, 'of all European princes, was served on bended knee, and when the French ambassador complained because neither chair nor stool was set for his wife – as was done for the English ambassador's wife in France – he was told that on official occasions no lady of the English Court except the Queen herself, not even the Princess Royal' was allowed to sit.[6]

At the initial assembly of Charles' first Parliament in London in 1625, it was noted that the King wore his crown for the entire duration, even though his Coronation had not yet taken place. The crown remained veiled except when Charles delivered his speech. By revealing the crown only when he spoke and, obscuring and mystifying it when silent, Charles marked with high ceremony the divinity of his words and his throned body

---

[3] John Ford, *Christes Bloodie Sweate*, pp. 5–6 and Gilbert, *On the Magnet* (1600), p. 17. See Elizabeth Spiller, *Science, Reading and Renaissance Literature* (Cambridge: Cambridge University Press, 2004).
[4] William Harvey, *De Motu Cordis*, in Geoffrey Keynes (ed.), *The Anatomical Exercises of Dr. William Harvey* (London: The Nonesuch Press, 1928), pp. vii–viii.
[5] In a letter from John Chamberlain to Sir Dudley Carleton, April 9, 1625. *Court and Times of Charles I*, I: 7–8.
[6] Wedgewood, *The King's Peace*, p. 55.

in state (I:33–4). Perhaps this performance failed to instil in Parliament the awe it was calculated to inspire, or perhaps it did little to camouflage the King's lack of natural majesty. Charles did not share Elizabeth's and James's gift for oratory and, unable to produce in his address to Parliament the gravity with which he wished to imbue his throned person, he decided that during his subsequent appearance he would not speak at all. When next seated before the House at the Oxford session of his first Parliament, Charles issued decrees through 'the king's mouth to the house', the Lord Keeper (I:81). Charles' new ceremonialism was as much an expression of his love for beauty and formality as it was a cure for, and at times a symptom of, his awkwardness. However, his attention to the ceremonious presentation of his throned body in official appearances was far from consistent and provided a number of opportunities for his detractors to resent those in his favour who were excused from observing ritual decorum. It was this resentment that fuelled scandal when it was reported that Buckingham had been carried in the King's box to St. James' while the King walked beside him. Parliamentarians also noted bitterly the report that when Charles was seated in state during a Christmas performance at court and Buckingham arrived at the end of the first act, the players were made to start again from the beginning (I:191).

While these breaches of Caroline ceremonial decorum were not committed on occasions whose explicit aim was to assert the monarchs' chastity (as in some court masques), the King's critics often attacked him on such grounds, reinterpreting the Caroline chastity of state as its opposite. Charles left himself open to such attacks. Throughout his reign, the Crown continued to bear the figure of the Virgin Mary. Married to a Catholic Queen who shared the name of the mother of God, Charles had to work hard to diminish the effect of this conspicuous object. When painted in state, he was always depicted from behind. But this was not enough to allay the concerns of those who, in *The Great Eclipse of the Sun, or Charles His Waine Over-clouded* (1644), argued that the crown had been sullied by the King's love of Popish ceremony and the inordinate power he granted Archbishop Laud. Drawing an easy parallel between unchastity, Catholicism, and tyranny, the writers argued that the King's love of his Parliament and the true Church had been so darkened by the seductions of the Queen and the popish Bishops that the Throne and the props of State had all been contaminated. They asserted that Charles' true subjects needed 'to pray that [the King] may recover the light of his scepter and the love of his subjects' and that war against him was justified because 'desperate diseases must have desperate cures'. The King's unchaste disease of pride and idolatry was thought to be so desperate that he would even 'pawne his Crown (if he could get it from *Westminster*) to maintaine the Miter'.[7]

A more sustained criticism of the chastity of the Throne of State under Charles occurs early in *Novembris Monstrum* (1641). The authors describe two thrones, one chaste and just, the other unchaste and tyrannical. In the chaste throne, Eliza sits with Peace asleep contentedly on her lap: an image reminiscent of the Pietà, still popular in early seventeenth-century prints. In the other throne, the Pope fornicates with Phocas. A narrative account of the Gunpowder Plot printed in 1641, the tract looks askance at Charles' ties with Catholicism. Through its depiction of a tyrannical and unchaste throne, *Novembris Monstrum* articulates the growing Caroline interest in distinguishing the objects of state from the monarch, and the conceptual innovation of resisting royal authority while asserting loyalty to the Crown. The writers insist that the Throne of State is itself incorruptible and only sullied by those who inhabit it: 'Peace flyes not Scepters, but dread Tyranny'. Eliza, however, was not a tyrant and Peace was at home in her England:

> When blest Eliza swai'd proud England's rod
> And ballanc't in her hands the golden ball:
> Peace sat by hir, laid downe her head to nod
> Within her Princely lap, and there did fall.
> Into a slumbring sweet-security.
>
> (62)

Although Peace lives contentedly in Eliza's throne, her slumber is interrupted when the Queen leaves to fight her Catholic enemies. The women's mutual comfort is also disturbed when Peace has a gruesome and prescient dream of the Gunpowder Plot. Where Eliza's throne sits in radiance and glory overlooking and defending English shores, Rome's throne is in Peace's dream buried deep in a close cellar 'full as darke as jett' and surrounded by its evil advisors (71). The Synod is made up of the familiar stock of unchaste Catholic female personifications, including the 'incestuous' Devotion (72). Drawing on all the watery and fleshly imagery of unchastity as a broken or sluiced body, the tract depicts the 'purple whore' as an over-gorged body which cannot fit into its Throne: the Pope, 'that man of sinne', is 'quite surfetted with goare, / Gorg'd with the flesh of Saints at Plutos feast, / Bathed in Nectar blood, pancht with mans

---

[7] Anon., *The Great Eclipse of the Sun, or Charles His Waine Over-clouded* (1644), p. 5.

flesh, / As if it were high Ioves Ambrosia dish' (2). In the same way, the throne Pope Gregory creates for the corrupt Phocas will not contain him. Mounted on his 'high imperiall seate', Phocas is 'brim-full of Honour'. Such an excess of 'honour must runne o're' and from the breach, 'shall flee / Supremacy to swell the Bishops See' (90). Over-gorged with ill-gained honour, Phocas' uncontainable, liquid corruption is the unchaste seed by which the tyrannical emperor impregnates the Holy See. Where under the chaste Eliza, the throne is shared only with Peace, and certainly with no consort or overseas Catholic power, the Throne of Phocas (and Charles) is the very place where the earthly ruler fornicates with Rome. The period's figure for unchaste broken bodies as, to use Leontes' phrase, 'knee deep' in blood and fluids is evoked throughout the tract when describing the thrones of Phocas or Rome, both of whom struggle to remain in state for all the blood in which their thrones are drowned.

In 1631, the court's assertion of the Throne of State's chastity under Charles, and anti-court depictions of the Throne as watery, fleshly, prideful, and unchaste, were in direct and very public conflict throughout the trial of the Earl of Castlehaven. The trial was an unprecedented spectacle in which the Crown sought to punish the transgressions of a peer accused of gross unchastity and tyranny in his own home. The trial of a peer was historically an extremely rare event but by 1631, Charles had already punished a number of noblemen for crimes against chastity. However, none had committed acts as cruel as those of which Castlehaven was accused and none were peers. Castlehaven's son had appealed to the King on the grounds that his father had performed sexual and fiscal acts that represented a diabolical inversion of every category in the natural hierarchies. The Earl reportedly lavished his money and attention on his servants, while denying them to his heir. He was said to prefer the company of his male inferiors, valuing them emotionally and sexually while humiliating his wife and children. He sought to have his man penetrate his wife before him. The Countess of Castlehaven, older and very much her husband's social better, claimed that her marriage was a constant battle over her honour. Her husband, she asserted, repeatedly humiliated her sexually and verbally, forced her on his favourites, and threatened her with rape if she did not consent willingly. The Earl's son and daughter-in-law appeared to loathe each other and had separated after three years of marriage. It was alleged that Castlehaven subsequently encouraged a sexual relationship between his son's estranged wife and his favourite, Henry Skipwith, a man of no social or financial standing. Castlehaven was said to have expressed a desire to claim Skipwith's offspring as his heir, rather than that of his son. Even before this affair began, Castlehaven had rewarded Skipwith with money and property, and had him sitting at table with the family and referred to as 'mister' (18).

In a legal trial of such high profile, the moral and disciplinary power of the Throne as a guarantor of sexual chastity and a check to its subject's pride was key to its success, but Charles' personal desire to chastise his wayward subject was given particular voice. Before the trial commenced, Charles announced that he was disappointed to discover that 'some great ladies intended to be spectatrices' of the 'obscene tragedy'. He instructed all woman, regardless of their status, that they attended the trial 'upon pain of ever after being reputed to have forfeited their modesty'.[8] The narrative of the prosecution made it perfectly clear that the Crown expected a guilty verdict, emphasising that it fell to Charles to maintain and protect chastity just as God had done when he annihilated the tribe of Benjamin for refusing to surrender a brutal rapist, and had destroyed Sodom and Gomorrah for their sins. Attorney-General Sir Robert Heath declared that 'if these offenses be not punished … certainly a heavy judgement must fall upon the land' (50, 83). To this end, the Throne of State was given a prominent position in the performance of the trial.

The trial's extensive ceremonials were aimed at the glorification of the Throne and the assertion of its authority to chastise Castlehaven. Scaffolding was built into the courts of the King's Bench and Chancery in Westminster, converting these spaces into theatres which could accommodate the crowds that attended. At the opening of the trial, the twenty-seven peers acting as judge and jury ascended twelve steps to the gallery and sat themselves in order of precedence at a long table, at the head of which stood the Chair of State. Seven judges and legal advisers followed, then the four prosecuting lawyers and all the clerical officers of the court. An hour after this procession began, seven sergeants-at-arms bearing seven maces entered. Behind them, in 'greater state' than had been witnessed before, came Thomas Coventry, Keeper of the Great Seal and (for this occasion) Lord High Steward of England. A considerable series of salutes, greetings, and announcements were then observed (58). Coventry sat in the Throne of State before the Usher of the Black Rod knelt and presented him with the white rod of State. This was held upright throughout the proceedings, and, at the end of the trial, the white rod was broken over the Steward's knee. The staff, its white symbolising the purity of the monarch and of English justice (a theme on which Coventry spent considerable time

---

[8] Herrup, *A House in Gross Disorder*, p. 50.

in his accusation of Castlehaven), marked the King's presence in the person of the Lord High Steward and its breaking marked his departure and the conclusive delivery of the monarch's punishment.

The breaking of the white rod of State at the end of Castlehaven's trial was officially a mark of the Crown's triumph over unchastity. However, for some commentators, the action did not so definitively signal the purification of error, which continued to fester in the pride of the Lord High Stewart. One pamphleteer noted that Coventry was seated in 'greater state than ever I saw before'. A second commentator agreed. To him, 'my Lord High Steward his grace / with many a rich mace' came 'into the palace', guarded and with much pomp. The theme of the verse, as is to be expected, is sexual unchastity. But unlike other bawdy commentaries on the trial, this one lampoons the high ceremony of the proceedings, suggesting thereby that there is something ridiculous about the chastising of criminal excess through a process marked precisely by such unchaste and proud effeminacy and pomp. The author details Coventry's horror that 'so vile a thing' has damaged 'the happiness of the King' who has lived so long without one of his peers going astray. Of Coventry, the anonymous author notes:

> He used much scripture text
> which many there perplexed
> who did not think it possible
> That a man of his trade
> who so much profit had made
> Should be so well read in the bible.[9]

Seated in state, Coventry so 'liked the canopy ... and the chair he sat in' that it was thought he would have been contented to be 'The Red Flap of the Law'. The bawdy connotations of 'red flap' are numerous. The term referred as much to a loose woman as to loose lips (a flap-mouth). It also referred to flap-like valves both on tunnels and ducts (like a sluice) but especially to the epiglottis. Given that the verse jeers at Coventry's overzealous speech, this meaning is surely one to which the term refers. Another possible meaning is the proverbial 'to be flapped with a fox tail': to dismiss contemptuously, a womanish action. For our purposes, it is important that the author overturns the trial's claims to chastise the grossly erroneous Castlehaven by depicting instead Coventry's unchaste pride, his lust for high ceremony, verbose and hypocritical speech, avarice, pomp,

---

[9] Cited in Appendix of Herrup, *House in Gross Disorder*.

and effeminacy (162). The author expresses this unchastity through the image of the Throne of State as the red flap from which, in the image of unchastity as a broken (female) vessel, chastity drains away. The jibe is aimed directly at the Lord High Steward's claim that the peers who tried Castlehaven were men 'whose heads and hearts are as full of integrity as their veins are full of blood' (66). In his statement at the trial, Coventry specifically chose this image to contrast the fullness and integrity of the monarchs' veins with Castlehaven's lack of integrity, in body and spirit. But in the satirical verses, Castlehaven's willingness to ravage his family and sluice his own veins, is shown to be only as unchaste as Coventry's pride and verbosity. Seated in the Throne of State and enthralled by the power it granted him in such a sensational event, Coventry's vainglory in fact drains the chaste blood of the sovereign out of the Throne through his canting 'red flap'.

Throughout the 1630s, Charles and Henrietta Maria developed their cult of chastity in order to promote the monarchs' virtue. Castehaven's trial was in many ways a function of this: the peer, in failing to maintain properly orientated relationships, the legitimacy of his family's unions and issue, or the integrity of any of the family's bodies, became an example within a trial almost as spectacular as a royal masque. Crucially, however, Castlehaven's trial was designed to assert the integrity of the nation – that body which the monarchs' bodily integrity was, within the Caroline cult of chastity, supposed to figure. Disorder and unchastity were by no means singular to Castlehaven's household. Unlike other men, however, he had failed to keep such problems within the sphere of his control, and, by placing his heir in a position in which he felt it necessary to involve the Crown, the Earl had also implicated the King himself. To restore the chastity of the Throne of State, Castlehaven was required to repent of his crimes and submit to the King's punishment. Instead, Castlehaven resisted the role prescribed to him by the trial. He was never contrite, never ashamed, but rather asserted consistently that he had done nothing wrong and that his family, whom he described as greedy and murderous, were conspiring against him. His resistance made explicit not only his failure to maintain his sovereignty over the house, but made public the abuses, the jealousy and rivalry, lust, and resentment that must have at times been present in most households, including that of the King. Where Charles I worked to present himself as a stalwart leader, whose virtue influenced the behaviour of his subjects, Castlehaven openly blamed those over whom he was expected to exercise control and refused to take responsibility for the unruliness of his house. In doing so, he demonstrated that he too was a subordinate that the King could not control, thereby undermining the royal image of moral and bodily perfection.

Through the language of his prosecution and the physical presence of the Throne of State, Heath was re-articulating and consolidating the vision of chastity upheld by the Caroline court. While Castlehaven's resistance to the King's authority confirmed in the minds of spectators how crucial chastity was to the nation's moral well-being, it also argued powerfully against the Crown's assertion that the monarchs could, by embodying the virtue themselves, will it of their subjects. The Crown's intention for the trial was that Castlehaven would acknowledge his crimes and, implicitly, his treason. Had he been contrite, Castlehaven would have confirmed the power of the Crown by enacting the reabsorption of transgressive forces into the chaste community that royal masques argued were flourishing under the monarchs' influence. However, by maintaining his resistance to the Crown's decree and insisting upon his own innocence, Castlehaven asserted an individualism that initially made Heath's task of presenting him as perverse easier, but ultimately created uncertainty about the validity of the verdict and the operations of power from which it proceeded. Instead of claiming responsibility for his crimes and showing contrition, Castlehaven threw the accusation of unchastity squarely back upon the women in his family, accusing them of sexual voraciousness. His wife was a 'common whore' who had borne a bastard shortly after their marriage. He argued that it was his inability to fulfill his wife's gluttonous desires that had motivated her to bring about his ruin and murder. Broadway, Castlehaven's servant on trial for his part in the crimes, said that the Countess lay commonly with other inferior men of the household and had 'made away' with her own bastard (76, 80, 96). One pamphleteer took a similar angle in his commentary on the trial:

> I need no trophies to adorn my hearse
> My wife exalts my horns in every verse
> And placed them so full upon my tomb
> That for my arms there is no vacant room
> Who will take such a Countess to his bed
> That first gives horns and then cuts off the head?[10]

Popular default to commonplaces of female sexual unchastity was itself one reason why Attorney-General Heath had to work so hard to depict the extreme unchastity of Castlehaven himself, while arguing that his wife and

---

[10] Quoted in Herrup, p. 160.

daughter-in-law were chaste and innocent victims. To this end, Heath built his argument against Castlehaven upon the claim that even the most wicked man would still wish his partner and family chaste, whereas Castlehaven forced unchastity on others. This claim was delivered after a long narration of the history of rape and sodomy and the lament that until Castlehaven, Charles I's reign had been free from aristocratic scandal.

Crucially, the accused's breach of chastity was explicitly linked to his damaging of the royal doctrine of chastity, which was being promoted in court masques as a force strong enough to reform not only England but the heavens, and which was throughout the trial represented in the throne erected high upon the stage. Heath's speech invoked war and suggested that Castlehaven had created a war of sorts in his own house and in the nation's house (60). Linking nationhood with chastity, an argument integral to Caroline masque rhetoric, Heath also repeatedly linked Castlehaven's sodomy with treason (62). We have seen from those writings which present England's very soil, streets, and buildings as vulnerable to the infectious spread of unchastity how powerful Heath's strategy must have been. Connecting the image of a penetrated, broken, and unchaste body with that of a soiled life or ravaged England inspired a degree of psychological and spiritual fear in early modern men and women that was perhaps unique to this moment in English intellectual history.

Chastity and the throne in the theatres of John Ford and William Harvey

In the late 1620s, Ford made particular use of the Throne of State in *The Broken Heart*, a play in which Orgilus murders Ithocles by trapping him in a throne and accusing him of both tyranny and unchastity (4.4.29). Ithocles bitterly articulates the convergence between ambition, unchastity, and tyranny: 'Ambition!' is 'of viper's breed, it gnaws / A passage through the womb that gave it motion'. 'Like a seelèd dove' it 'mounts upward, / Higher and higher still, to perch on clouds, / But tumbles headlong down with heavier ruin' (2.2.1–5). Although he can diagnose his own unchastity and ambition, Ithocles is not freed from it: a truth which Ford explores through his use of chairs. The text stipulates clearly that Ithocles and Penthea are sitting together on the same chair when he begs her to put him to 'any penance' for his 'tyranny' (3.2.63). Outside, Penthea's jealous husband waits, convinced that the siblings are committing incest. Throughout the play, Ford used chairs and thrones to stage his most fraught scenes. After Penthea's death, her body is brought onstage, seated in a chair and veiled. The song accompanying her entrance is an ode to her 'chaste' life and her 'endless' death as a martyr to love (4.3.142–53). We discover that she in fact died in the same posture in which she is presented, seated and veiled: a ceremonial flourish so recently reintroduced at court by the King, but one also reminiscent of the churching ritual: an event for which Penthea, who would never be mother to 'pretty prattling babes', both longed and mourned (4.2.88). Penthea's body is set onstage between two other chairs, that on her right being the engine which Orgilus has planted in order to trap Ithocles. In fact, we find the whole scene has been orchestrated by Orgilus, who, with characteristic self-aggrandizement, attempts to become the play's dramaturge. He dismisses Penthea's ladies (her 'prompters'[4.4.11]), who have so far been the narrators of Penthea's end, in order that he might stage his elaborate revenge. Having arranged the three chairs just as he wants them, Orgilus commands Ithocles to 'Take that chair'. 'I'll seat me here in this. Betweene us sits / The object of our sorrows' (4.4.16). There may be no canopy marking Penthea's death-chair specifically as the Throne of State, but, veiled and flanked by two princes, she is presented by her lover as majestic, queenly. As soon as he is seated, Ithocles is trapped in the engine. 'Caught, you are caught / Young master; 'tis thy throne of coronation' (4.4.22–3). Wishing to punish Ithocles for the pride that drove him to force Penthea into an unchaste union, Orgilus stages a murder that mocks the princely ceremonies his enemy once sought. The glory for which Ithocles had laboured is delivered instead as a fatal rebuke for his assault on female chastity, that 'monarch[y]' which Bassanes earlier came to see was the 'Soul, and elixir of the earth's abundance' (4.2.25–30).

By demonstrating how easily chaste love can be distorted by ambition and the human desire for self-gratification, *The Broken Heart* could be said to mock Charles' and Henrietta Maria's claims to a virtuous authority based on chastity in love and religion. Orgilus certainly mocks Ithocles for his error on this point by arguing that Ithocles' blissful and penitential discovery of chaste love is merely another form of that ambition for which he condemned his sister to an unchaste union: 'Thou fool of greatness. See, I take this veil off; / Survey a beauty withered by the flames / Of an insulting Phaeton her brother' (4.4.24–6). But Ogilus is himself the prime example of the error he so longs to punish. His overblown sense of the heroic value of his revenge, and his desire to prove at all costs that the only throne worth a coronation is that of chaste and mutual love, misses the point being made by the play. The same point which was made, however simply, by the Queen's masques: to truly value chaste love leads not only to the object of one's love (in Ford: a lover, at court: the monarchs) but ultimately away from the self, the self's desires, and toward heaven.

In his loss and penitence, Bassanes does come to realise this truth. He laments that he 'who was made a monarch / Of what a heart could wish for, a chaste wife' loved her too possessively. Chaste love, he realises is a 'Temple built for adoration only' and to have ruined such a heavenly gift was 'a sacrilege so impious' (4.2.29–34). Ford's exploration of the throned body reveals just how tragic his erroneous lovers are: in their devotion to chaste love, they come very close to realising that through it one can attain salvation, yet they fall just short of redemption by continuing to worship their lost lover and ultimately seeking martyrdom on the throne of chaste love rather than reconciliation with God and community. Ford's incestuous lovers in *'Tis Pity* demonstrate this alleged error most explicitly. Giovanni recalls his enjoyment of his sister's body, claiming there was 'wonder in every portion of that throne' (2.5.54). Their love was a bliss that raised him to majesty: 'nine months I lived/ A happy monarch of her heart and her' (5.6.42–5). When in *The Broken Heart*, Ithocles and Orgilus martyr themselves on either side of Penthea's throned body, they continue to locate her as the object of their self-sacrifice. Striving for a glorious death, they look to 'Penthea's sacred eyes' to 'lend new courage' (4.4.57). The scene's tragedy extends from the error of its three players, but visually, it speaks to a truth which the play shares with Caroline court masques: that the throne is the site of chaste married love, whose passion is the devotion by which believers can see the face of God.

With Orgilus's suicide by phlebotomy (5.2.99–159), Ford made inventive use of the unchaste throne's capacity to figure vainglory. In a manner that recalls the richly emblematic suicide of Shakespeare's Cleopatra, Orgilus stages his own death as a purifying and heroic act of majestic proportions. Ford's audience, however, witness in his final act a near-treasonous, and certainly a blasphemous, claim to exit the world a martyr to love, throned in State. Seated for his suicide, Orgilus takes a staff in his hand, exposes a vein, and, opening it, narrates the heroism of his final surrender. The barber's pole – an object familiar to most in Ford's audience who would have had blood let regularly by their barber, surgeon or physician – only differs from a royal scepter in its symbolic function and its lack of finery. Where one has at its tip, a shining finial, the other has attached to its base, a bowl for catching blood. This difference aside, the two objects are held in the same manner by a person seated, his arm extended and his hand clenched around the centre of the pole. When Orgilus calls for his 'staff', he is clearly asking for an instrument that will, like a barber's pole, assist in bringing a vein closer to the surface of his skin. But the only staffs present on stage at the play's final scenes are those carried by the nobility. Therefore, both the chair on which Orgilus sits and the staff he grasps in his hand would have borne a greater likeness to those of a throned and scepter-bearing monarch than of a man being bled by his barber. His tragic mockery of the Throne of State is a gruesome warning to Ford's audience against the unchastity of pride. Like the blood-drenched thrones of the fornicating tyrants in *Novembris Monstrum*, Orgilus sits in State covered in his own blood, with the blood of his victim (if only figuratively) on his hands, and all the while pridefully believing he is sacrificing himself at the altar of his chaste love.

Ford's message is clear: Orgilus dies condemned of the greatest pride since he, unlike everyone observing him, does not realise how closely his bloody and enthroned death approximates the purifying and medicinal image, which Ford himself depicted in *Christes Bloodie Sweate*, of the throned Christ, bleeding from his heart. Ford's use of the throne also draws on other early modern acts of purification, each one contributing to his aim of extracting as much tragic irony as possible from the convergence of two such opposing experiences, salvation and damnation, within the one emblematic image. For instance, the similarity between Orgilus's kingly posture and the more pedestrian scene of a barber's bloodletting would have brought to the minds of his audience a cluster of associated ideas about chastity. Even at the physical level, the King's body in state was as relevant to an individual's awareness of their physical purity and impurity as was the common experience of bloodletting. Not simply a source of heavenly virtue, the purity of the chaste Caroline throne could bring soundness of body to those who came to be touched for the King's Evil – one of the many ceremonial practices whose regularity marked the new ceremonialism of Charles' reign. Further, when early moderns sat to have their blood let, they in fact took on the posture, if not the grandeur, of their King in State, in order to be cleansed of impurities. Impurities, which, as Orgilus and the tradition of lovesickness confirms, were thought to be caused as much by unchastity in body, mind, and passions as any other vice or disorder. In its aping of a barber's bloodletting, Orgilus's death is a medically accurate picture of cleansing. As a picture of a criminal seated in state, his death is in one sense accurate since he is cleansing the state of his crime. But Orgilus claims to die a martyr to chaste love in the very Throne of State which at Whitehall was being promoted as the site of heavenly chastity: in this, he demonstrates that he has failed to learn the lessons being taught by the King and Queen. The play's tragic loss argued for the true virtue of the chastity its characters failed to realise, but it did so by staging a treasonous and erroneous possession of the Throne in the name of earthly love.

While assessing in Chapter 2 the place of Ford's plays in disputes about new medical technologies, I pointed to the similarities between Ford's staging and the staging by which Harvey demonstrated his thinking on the circulation of the blood. I want now to look more closely at the chair in the performance of Harvey's lectures and demonstrations because it is another field in which the correlation between unchastity and pride was engaged, and because Harvey himself would eventually play a role, however unwittingly, in the decline of Charles' authority and the eclipse of the Caroline cult of chastity. Although we have no first hand account of Harvey's lectures or demonstrations, we know from his notes that the staging of his anatomies were much like those he himself attended in Padua, with the cadaver lying flat on a raised table at the centre of a conical gallery. Under Fabricius, Harvey learned to deliver lectures and demonstrations that were as much a theatre of the virtues as any royal masque or popular drama. How much more theatrical must have been those spectacles in which he unveiled his controversial discovery. When it came to demonstrating his thinking on the circulation of the blood, Harvey needed to use a living subject. Most often these were animals, but he must surely have at times demonstrated on a human. The engraved plates illustrating the movement of the blood in *De Motu Cordis* show a man's arm outstretched, clutching a barber's pole and tied with a tourniquet as though the arm were being prepared for phlebotomy. The plates were copies of the well-known images in Fabricius' *De Venarum Ostiolis* (1603, 1624) (See Figure 3).

Although the images could be said to illustrate a man lying flat like a cadaver in an anatomy hall, his arm stretched out beside him, it is more likely that when demonstrating his ideas on circulation, Harvey used the posture so routine and conducive to the letting of blood. As such, the staging of Harvey's demonstrations would have recalled the Throne of State with all its props, as did Ford's *The Broken Heart*. Harvey's explorations of the human body and the divine truths it reflected were, in an important sense, performances in which the throned body – the body of the King, of Christ, of all men – was revealed, its mysteries peeled away. However, as much as his demonstrations exposed divine and human truths, Harvey was also adding to the wonder of the body enthroned: revealing its unseen movements, he uncovered further questions. He may have demystified Galenic views

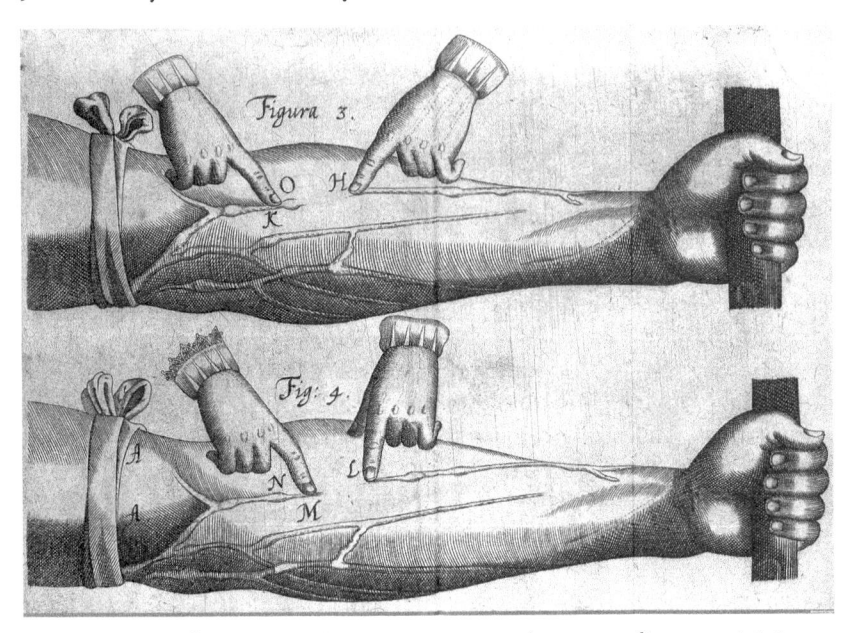

Figure 3: William Harvey, Exercitatio anatomica de motu cordis et sanguinis in animalibus (G. FitzerFrankfurt, 1628). Wellcome Library, London. https://creativecommons.org/licenses/by/4.0/

of the blood's behaviour, but at the same time he demonstrated that the body mimicked the mysterious circulation of the heavens even more closely than Galen had ever thought.

I have detailed the conflict between those who, suspicious of the new medical technologies, presented the new and greater knowledge of the interior of the body as a form of unchaste pride epitomised by 'Adam and Eve' books (See Figures 1 and 2).[11] Harvey himself attracted accusations of pride not only from proponents of this view but from his fellow medical men because his methods rejected so much institutional knowledge. Further, by demonstrating his discovery on a throned body, astute observers might have noted that Harvey's investigation was an assault on the very chastity with which the monarchs infused the state. Cowley's ode to Harvey, 'Coy Nature', draws on the classical literary tradition of chastity in order to praise the great anatomist as a plunderer of nature's secrets and a methodological trail-blazer:

---

[11] See pp. 65–6

> Coy Nature (which remain'd, though aged grown,
> A beauteous Virgin, injoy'd by none,
> Nor seen unveil'd by any one)
> When *Harvey*'s violent passion she did see,
> Began to tremble and to flee,
> Took Sanctuary, like *Daphne* in a Tree:
> There *Daphne*'s Lover stopt, and thought it much
> The very Leaves of her to touch:
> But *Harvey* our *Apollo*, stopt not so,
> Into the Bark and Root he after her did go.[12]

In an attempt to escape Harvey, Daphne/Nature leaps into the human bloodstream and hides in the heart. But Harvey pursues her. His investigation of the heart is as much a triumphant rape of chaste nature as it is a dethroning of the sovereignty which Galen ('*Daphne*'s Lover') had enjoyed before the empirical Harvey pushed beyond him into nature's 'Bark and Root'. Harvey, unlike his peers, can truly know her, given he alone 'sought for Truth in Truth's great book' and investigated 'the creatures' who were 'writ' by 'God himself'. Unlike his fellow medics, Harvey 'wisely' thought it fit 'not to read comments only but 'on th' original itself to look'. His fame is secured by his empirical methods, his bold scrutiny of God's original, while his peers are held back by their insistence on medicine's intellectual fidelity to its philosophical tradition.[13] Cowley's Harvey may have performed an act of unchastity upon coy nature but ultimately, his investigation revealed those truths written on the body by God himself.[14] In an inversion not unlike Donne's 'Batter my heart three-person'd God' or the 'inviolate' blood of the violated Christ in Ford's *Christes Bloodie Sweate*, the sanctifying revelation which Cowley's Harvey enables undercuts the violence of the doctor's search, turning ravishment into the revelation of God's truth.

In the early modern medical world, the sovereignty of the heart was a commonplace, deriving ultimately from Aristotle. John Halle referred to it in 1565: 'Let us call the heart of man a king, the brain and the liver the chief governors under him.'[15] However, by the time William Harvey's career was at its peak and the popularity of the King was waning, the belief that the

---

[12] Abraham Cowley, *Verses, written upon several occasions* (1663), p. 18.
[13] See also Patricia Parker on Harvey's 'ocular'opening in relation to the presentation of dark, foreign, feminine, and unchaste truths in 'Fantasies of "race" and "gender": Africa, Othello and Bringing to Light' in Susan Zimmerman (ed.), *Shakespeare's Tragedies* (Palgrave MacMillan, 1998), pp. 167–211, 171.
[14] See Jonathan Sawday, *Body Emblazoned*, pp. 241–42.
[15] J. Halle, *An Historicall Expostulation* (Percy Soc., London, 1844), p. xxii.

heart was the throne of the body had become one of the most notoriously disputed claims in the medical world.[16] Harvey was overturning long-held medical beliefs that the heart was the Throne of the human person by suggesting instead that the multitudinous blood was sovereign. In 1628, Harvey claimed that on earth it is from the King, as in the body it is the heart, from which 'all power arises and all grace stems'. However, in 1649, the year in which Charles was executed, Harvey renounced his earlier opinion: he 'dethroned the heart'.[17] He no longer believed the source of life and vitality stemmed from 'the sovereignty of the heart' but from the 'the prerogative ... of the blood'.[18] While in 1628 Harvey invited the King to 'contemplate the Principle of Mans Body, and the image of your Kingly power', twenty years later, Harvey's view of the body was, however unwittingly, in sympathy with Parliament's view of how English society ought to be governed.

One of the events which influenced Harvey's unwitting dethroning of the heart involved Charles himself and has been read as marking the end of the royal cult of chastity and the King's authority. In approximately 1640, Harvey brought the young aristocrat, Montgomery, to the King's attention. Montgomery had suffered a wound to his chest which, though healed, remained an open cavity. It was kept clean and covered throughout the young man's life, but the curious were able to place their fingers into the hole and feel his heart beating. The fact that Montgomery could not feel the hand that touched his heart was of great interest to Harvey since it suggested, contrary to traditional medical belief, that the heart had no sensation, and thus, little vital spirit of its own. How, therefore, could the heart be deemed the monarch of the body? It is reported that when Harvey brought Montgomery before the King in order that he might touch his heart and verify its senselessness, Charles' responded: 'Sir, I wish I could perceive the thought of some of my nobilities' hearts as I have seen your heart'.[19] This event was crucial to the shift in Harvey's thinking from the centrality of the heart to the importance of the blood. It is for this reason, and the fact that the event took place in the year in

---

[16] For an analysis of this shift in thinking, not only to the relationship between King, people, and Parliament, but to the mixed-plot of tragicomedy and emerging commercial economies, see Richard Kroll, *Restoration Drama and 'the Circle of Commerce'* (Cambridge: Cambridge University Press, 2007), pp. 32–56.
[17] Christopher Hill, 'William Harvey and the Idea of Monarchy', *Past and Present* 27 (1964), pp. 54–72. See also Richard Sennett, *Flesh and Stone: the Body and the City* and John Rogers, *The Matter of Revolution* (Ithaca: Cornell University Press, 1996), p. 16.
[18] Hill, 'William Harvey and the Idea of Monarchy', p. 55.
[19] Quoted in Whitteridge, *William Harvey*, p. 235.

which Parliamentary power reached its height, that John Rogers has attributed an elegiac quality to the scene in which Charles is asked to participate in his own dethronement by acknowledging the heart's senselessness. Harvey, in Rogers' interpretation, asks Charles to agree that the body's 'most principal member' in fact cannot 'function as a governing center or sentient locus of reason and organisation'.[20]

However, we must also acknowledge the deeply theological resonances of the scene: the similarity between the King's investigative touch and that of Thomas when he placed his fingers into Christ's side might not have been lost on those present, nor on those who related the story to each other. Thomas' narrative only enhances the scene's evocation of a King facing his own dethronement. Before he placed his hand in Christ's side, Thomas was unable to accept the truth that Christ had been transformed and did not yet understand that he would soon ascend to his heavenly Throne from where he would institute the true Church. It could be said that in the same way, Charles, when he met Montgomery, had not yet accepted that the Church was changing in ways contrary to his hopes and would soon dethrone him as its head. At the beginning of a decade that would end in his trial and beheading, the King unwittingly played the tragic part in an emblematic scene narrating the fall of monarchy. Enthroned in state, the King was invited to accept the truth that God had inscribed in the bodies of his creatures a divine plan whose central governance was in fact not as total as Harvey had once assured Charles it was.

Throughout Charles's reign, the Throne of State emerged as a particularly potent site on which to stage debates about the relative chastity of the King, and of centralised royal government generally. In these debates, the correlation between unchastity and pride was crucial. During Castlehaven's trial, Coventry's and Heath's attempts to claim for the Throne of State the same chastity and authority within the theatre of the law that it asserted in court masques meant presenting the Throne's influence on the real and figurative bodies it protected as unifying and sanctifying. Critics of the trial instead presented the Throne as an unchaste seat of pride, stained and fleshly, and thus as damaging to England's unity and sanctity. Castlehaven's unrepentant stance was a denial of the court's charge of unchastity. Yet, his refusal to submit to penitential humility would have conversely suggested to many onlookers his insistent clinging to the kind of unchaste pride embodied by one of Ford's unrepentant and

---

[20] Rogers, *The Matter of Revolution*, p. 33.

unchaste lovers. Castlehaven's death scene might in this way be read as a version of Ford's death scenes. From the perspective of those who identified with the Caroline cult of chastity, this scene could be read as depicting a proud individual who resisted contrition, defended his own passions, and refused to be drawn back into the chaste body of the community. To court critics, however, the scene could be interpreted along the same lines as both Castlehaven and Orgilus interpret their own death scenes: a valiant individual refusing to relinquish his sense of his own moral right and his chastity. Where Castlehaven refused to bend to the unchaste will of a tyrant, Orgilus refused to see his passion as anything but good and heroic: he may not have denied the earthly authority that determined his punishment but he denied the heavenly decree that called him back from his sin. Both men were adamant that they remained chaste, and thereby, denied claims on the part of their community that true chastity existed in their penitent reabsorption into the body politic.

Charles's own figurative dethronement in the theatre of William Harvey's career potentially placed the King in precisely the compromised moral position from which the court's presentation of the Throne sought to protect him. If indeed we can read the Montgomery scene as a legitimate philosophical and medical challenge to crucial early modern justifications of divine right monarchy, then the scene becomes another 'death' scene, like those of Castlehaven and Orgilus, in which an individual is forced to accept his own decline and either be penitently absorbed back into the body politic or else cling to his own moral right and risk the accusation of pride. Certainly, Charles was, in 1640, regularly being accused of pride and tyranny. The King's persistent defence of his own position for the remainder of the 1640s might, however, suggest that to onlookers he had himself chosen the role of the unrepentant, unchaste tyrant. Crucially, the strength of the Caroline cult of chastity did not centre on Charles alone. As my next chapter argues, the cult's popularity (at least in the 1630s) needs to be attributed to Henrietta Maria herself, and to her own presentation of the Throne of State as an object whose supreme chastity was upheld by its association with that courtly chair in which the Queen routinely triumphed: the royal birthing chair.

CHAPTER 4

Marian chastity: Caroline masques and Henrietta Maria's chaste births

My reading of early modern thinking on chastity identifies those two distinct modes – prose sermons or pamphlets and tragicomic or masque performances – that were each developing visions of chastity in direct opposition with each other. Under the influence of Charles I and Henrietta Maria, the court of the 1630s developed a cult of chastity, the values of which drew on those aspects of Catholic and Laudian theology and liturgy that intersected with the formal and stylistic devices of tragicomedy and masque: communal participation, gestural worship and celebration, piety, visual beauty, female fertility, wonder, and spectacle. The cult invested deeply in the mysticism of the Throne of State but its popularity in the 1630s was also indebted to another royal chair: the Queen's birthing stool. Through Henrietta Maria's celebration of female fertility and female monastic communities, the culture of chastity she espoused grew to such prominence that court critics had to work hard to discredit it. The anti-court response to this cult evidenced a crucial rhetorical awareness that chastity was a virtue of such importance to early modern thought that it needed to be reclaimed from the court and re-inscribed as a virtue which signified those values of importance to Parliamentarian plain-religionists: a masculine and individuated moral struggle, verbal and internalised worship, intellectualised and highly rhetoric disputation, and a suspicion of centralised authority. The most astute pro-parliamentarian voice was John Milton's, but before Milton can take his place in this story, I want to establish the means by which the Caroline cult of chastity claimed its version of the virtue, and in doing so drew on the devices of tragicomedy.

The Winter's Tale continues to be my point of reference; it is the play that most clearly realises those themes and formal elements in which all tragicomedies are invested – especially the Shakespearean romances. These plays espoused a confidence in God's providentialism that was fundamentally bound up in familial unity and strength, and the unity of royal families in particular. While this most fortuitous and confident of visions was socially conservative, it was also feminist. *The Winter's Tale* makes clear that redemption depended on women's procreative capacity. While Leontes seeks to undermine the procreative capacities of the women in his household, Paulina, Perdita, and Hermione work to protect the legitimacy of their sexuality and the truth of the divine (Delphic) decree that supports their claims to chastity. Their efforts are rewarded in the statue scene when the words of the oracle are fulfilled and everyone, both onstage and in the audience, experiences the wonder of being granted that for which they most hoped but least expected: the return of the family's lost members.

Before his remorse began, Leontes was deeply threatened by Hermione's fertility, forcing her to give birth in scandalously debased conditions and then ordering the murder of her child. He violently attacks her reproductive capacities while 'publish[ing]' her 'on every post' 'a strumpet' (2.1.98/3.2.99–100). In the play's final scenes, however, the frequent anti-feminist slurs against women's sexuality and midwives become instead figures for birth as chaste and wondrous. In reporting the court's joy at finding Florizel and Perdita, Paulina's steward is described as able to 'deliver' more news, the truth of which is 'pregnant by circumstance' (5.2.23–8). Mimi Still Dixon notes that in the providential final scenes of Shakespearean tragicomedy 'metaphors of rebirth ... collect naturally'.[1] With the restoration and recreation of the court's 'unity', integrity, and chastity, reproductive imagery suddenly departs from the misogynist language of feminine deceit. Instead, it draws closer to the paradoxical language of divine grace associated with the Virgin Birth. In *Pericles*, 'Thou beget'st him that did thee beget' (5.1.195), and in *The Winter's Tale*, truth becomes pregnant with more truth, goodness breeds goodness and wonder 'beget[s] wonder' (5.1.132).

Over the sixteen years of Leontes' penance, Paulina cares for both the King and the Queen, overseeing the physical, moral, and spiritual health of both. The symbol for this deeply maternal and creative act is the statue, which everyone at court believes Paulina has been whittling away at over the sixteen years she has lived in retirement in her chapel. Through the 'issue' of Paulina's creation, the violence with which Leontes destroyed his family in the trial scene is finally redeemed. Crucially, Paulina's fruitfulness emerges from a cloistered female community. In the sixteen years of her apparent death, Hermione has lived in solitude with Paulina. She effectively retreats into a holy life of silence while she waits in hope for the return of her daughter. 'For a woman to opt out of a marriage that has

---

[1] Dixon, *Tragicomic Recognitions*, p. 57.

humiliated her is not necessarily implausible, and many medieval as well as Renaissance women made such choices.'² Hermione and Paulina contrive the statue scene so that Leontes might evidence how he has changed: 'O, thus she stood, / Even with such life of majesty—warm life / As now it coldly stands—when first I wooed her. / I am ashamed' (5.3.34–7). However, in an important sense, the statue scene is not about Leontes at all. Hermione has primarily been waiting for the return of her heir: 'knowing by Paulina that the oracle / Gave hope thou wast in being, have preserved / Myself to see the issue' (5.3.126).

The significance of the statue scene as an affirmation of the redemptive capacity of women's procreative ability becomes clear when we recognise that Leontes initially sought to align Hermione with Eve. *The Winter's Tale* makes thoughtful and very specific use of the doctrines of the Fall and the Virgin Birth; understanding this offers a vital background for reading Henrietta Maria's own use of Marian imagery to underpin her queenship. On suspecting Hermione of adultery in 1.2, Leontes imagines that her 'issue / Will hiss me to my grave' (1.2.187). As though confirming his suspicion, Hermione, like Eve, then leads Polixenes into the garden. Even before this moment, the two men's nostalgia for the shared childhood they interpret as pre-lapsarian immediately registers Hermione and all women as sexually dangerous. The play makes it clear, however, that the real threat to Leontes' and Polixenes' souls is not their wives but their desire to imagine themselves as fellows in a vision of innocence built on a dangerously prideful denial of original sin. Eden was not a purely male world containing 'two lads that thought there was no more behind / But such a day tomorrow as today / And to be boy eternal' (1.2.62–5), and error cannot be avoided by imagining a world in which the Fall never occurred. Convinced by this misconception, Leontes can only interpret Hermione's and Polixenes' exit into the garden as confirmation of the human fallenness he has attempted to elide. However, watching his wife and friend going into the garden, he also experiences his absence from it. Not only is he not there with his wife (as, in keeping with Christian ontology, he should be), but he is not there with Polixenes, whom he had imagined was his pre-lapsarian partner. Leontes thus experiences isolation from both his imagined relationship with Polixenes and his real relationship with his wife: the former because it is by nature unstable and the latter because he has always been afraid of fully participating in it. Leontes' fear and his fantasy walk together into the garden without him and he feels precisely

---

² Vanita, 'Mariological Memory in *The Winter's Tale* and *Henry VIII*', p. 314.

that rejection from Paradise from which both were designed to protect him. When detailing what he perceives as evidence of Hermione's and Polixenes' adultery, Leontes registers the feeling of loss as expulsion: 'O, I am out!' (2.1.72). When on trial, Hermione later refuses Leontes' charge of treason and his interpretation of her as Eve, arguing that the only 'disobedience' she might have committed would have been her negligence of duty had she not shown Polixenes the affection due him as her husband's friend (3.2.68). Denying the action through which Eve first erred, Hermione refutes the charge of 'conspiracy', claiming 'I know not how it tastes, though it be dished / For me to try how' (3.2.70–71).

If for Leontes Hermione is like Eve, the play is instead at pains to depict her as Mary. Heavily pregnant for the first two acts of the play, Hermione then, on the loss of her child, becomes the mother of sorrows in Antigonus' dream:

> To me comes a creature,
> Sometimes her head on one side, some another;
> I never saw a vessel of like sorrow
> So filled and so becoming. In pure white robes
> Like very sanctity, she did approach
> My cabin where I lay; thrice bowed before me,
> And, gasping to begin some speech, her eyes
> Became two spouts.
>
> (3.3.20–5)

Hermione's transformation into one of the leaky figures to whom generations of early modern Englishwomen and men had dedicated their devotions, shocks Antigonus into ignoring the King's instructions and preserving her second child's life.[3] Finally, in the tableau, Hermione takes on the statuesque quality of the many Marian icons which had been systematically defaced by 1611.

Despite the zealous degree of anti-Marian sentiment in English acts of iconoclasm, theologians and divines, who wrote profusely about the Fall, remained relatively silent on the doctrine of the Virgin Birth – most likely because its scriptural documentation was clear and difficult to refute. Despite commentators' relative silence on the issue, the doctrinal and scriptural truth remained that Mary conceived a child by God. Leontes exemplifies a common early modern masculine desire to fix Eve as the biblical figure for women and deny them the potency of Mary. Certainly,

---

[3] See Jocelyn Wogan-Browne, 'Chaste Bodies: Frames and Experiences,' in Sarah Kay and Miri Rubens (eds.), *Framing Medieval Bodies* (Manchester: Manchester University Press, 1994), pp. 24–42.

the structure of *The Winter's Tale* requires that Leontes relinquish his view of his wife as Eve and acknowledge her status as a chaste exemplar worthy of precisely the veneration granted her by Paulina in the statue scene, and by Antigonus, whose dream of Hermione's leaky ghost accords her Marian status. The play ultimately requires Leontes to stand and admire Paulina's creation, a work of art so good it appears life-like. It also demands that he be transfixed by wonder when the statue does come to life. While his wonder stems largely from his joy that Hermione is in fact alive, he is also, together with the audience, invited to respond with awe to a creative act which exemplifies and celebrates the female capacity to beget life as much from stone as from flesh.

When it is first read aloud in Act Three, the record of the oracle's decree does not impress Leontes, who is convinced that his own reading of events is the most true. This is despite Dion's and Cleomenes' certainty prior to the trial scene that the moment they read aloud the words of the oracle, something as 'rare' as the experience they themselves had at Delphi will 'rush' to the knowledge of the King. However, at the conclusion of the play, when events most suddenly conform to the words of the oracle, the universal experience of wonder is such a 'rush' of knowledge that no textual reproduction (by ballad-makers) could be equal to the experience of the event itself. When the divine will ultimately reveals itself in the fullness of providence, bringing into being the very outcome most wished for by all in the theatre, it can only be experienced as miraculous. This typically tragicomic pattern offers a paradoxical and simultaneous cultivation of the inevitability and impossibility of that grace which brings enlightenment to those who did not have faith in it and reward to all those who did. *The Winter's Tale*'s providential vision locates the divine will in acts of female creation: both Hermione's procreative capacities and Paulina's artistic virtuosity, which, even if it did not make a statue, conceived of and executed the deceit of the statue, thus ensuring the family is reunited. The play's providential vision, as much as its depiction of redemption, are crucially located in spaces of female community: both the cloistered space into which Paulina and Hermione retreat, and the extended contrition into which Leontes enters under Paulina's guidance.

By enacting *The Winter's Tale*'s great mystery among themselves, the play's women bring about the wonder of both a resurrection and a Marian act of chaste begetting. Paulina instructs her work of art, Hermione, to 'Strike all that look upon with marvel—come, / I'll fill your grave up' (5.3.100–1). She is not only calling Hermione back from the dead – filling up her grave and the graves of those who look upon the miracle – she is also 'beget[ting]' her from stone by calling life into her. In so doing, Paulina and Hermione embody the divine source of the play's providential love, drawing into the theatre space an experience of providence as female creation and recreation. The statue 'moves', 'transport[s]', 'stirs', 'amaz[es]', 'breathes', and 'awake[ns]' the 'faith' of onlookers (5.3.88;68;73;87;78). When all the play's lost characters are reunited with each other, the response from everyone on the stage is a 'passion of wonder'. 'There was speech in their dumbness, language in their very gesture'. In their transfixed state, the reunited household 'seemed almost with staring on one another to tear the cases of their eyes'. This statue-like state is caused by such a mingling of paradoxical emotion that the emotion itself cannot be named: 'the wisest beholder that knew no more than seeing could not say if th'importance were joy or sorrow' (5.2.14–5). Such a wondrous tableau, an experience of somatic awe and speechlessness, is akin to the spectacle created by court masques, which draws participants into the communal experience of wonder and celebration at the masque's conclusion, and which invite participants to believe that the truths they are embodying are touched by the divine. *The Winter's Tale*'s vision of chaste familial unity as that which is both divinely inspired and brought about by women's creative capacity is distinctly Marian and the kind of social and spiritual experience that, some decades later, Henrietta Maria also sought to realise in her cult of chastity.

As the most popular and prominent 'leader' of the Catholic Church in England, an exemplar of married chastity, and the fertile mother of numerous Stuart heirs, Henrietta Maria was the perfect embodiment of the emerging Caroline cult. That her public life was built from an appreciation of, and participation in, Marian devotions and the genre of performance most associated, since Shakespeare's late plays, with the divinity of female chastity only consolidated the Queen's status as fertile, chaste, and a holy Marian leader. What I am calling Henrietta Maria's 'Marian fertility' (her chaste and divine maternity) was promoted at court by her masques and performances, by her devotional practices, birthing rituals, and by her religious supporters. It was a form of queenship that recalled that wondrous vision of the chaste and feminised divine will expressed most succinctly at the conclusion of *The Winter's Tale*. Crucial to Henrietta Maria's cult of chastity was the celebration not only of female procreative capacities but of female monastic devotions: two modes of female experience that would be contradictory for enclosed religious but which suited elite laywomen in Counter-Reformation Europe and were supported by the immensely popular writings of St Francois de Sales.

The new tone of chastity and refinement at the Caroline court was indebted to Henrietta Maria's introduction of a culture familiar to her and to Charles' attempt to chasten the crudeness of his father's court. It stemmed from their own personalities as much as it did from their shared love of piety, refinement, performance, innovations in Continental art and architecture, and ceremonial worship and governance. Early in Charles' reign, John Chamberlain noted that the King was observed by many as devout, cheerful and amiable, and intolerant of the drunkenness that had been acceptable under his father. Under Charles, the court was 'more straight and private'. Optimistically, Chamberlain believed that this change was 'a sign that the world will every way amend'.[4] Malcolm Smuts has also noted that Charles was known to preach decorum to the younger men at court, to blush at obscenities and fine courtiers for swearing. The Countess of Carlisle bemoaned the new sombre tone at court and the steady decline of gallantry.[5] The portraiture commissioned by Henrietta Maria and Charles depicted a court that valued both moral and artistic refinement as much as domestic and familial integrity. At the centre of this new domestic monarchy was the Queen, whose chastity was celebrated by Van Dyke's portraits, which depicted the Queen taming unruly forces of nature with the touch of her hands and surrounded by objects – roses, pearls, glass vases – traditionally associated with chastity.[6]

Henrietta Maria's cloistered chastity

Henrietta Maria's interest in chastity was not only moral but firmly religious. Her devotional life was marked by close association with enclosed female religious orders and, both in England and in France, she maintained a position of leadership within the religious communities she established and protected. In Henrietta Maria's vision of queenship, secular leadership was as important as leading a community of prayer. From the little evidence we have of Henrietta Maria's early education, we know that she was formed in the renewed Post-Tridentine spirituality by her Carmelite instructors. She was also tutored in riding, singing, and dancing, and regularly participated in court theatricals. She lived largely at St Germain until 1622 when, at thirteen, she was more often in Paris,

---

[4] *Court and Times of Charles I*, vol. I, pp. 7, 8, 12.
[5] Malcolm Smuts, *Court Culture and the Origins of a Royalist Tradition in Early Stuart England*, p. 193.
[6] Gudrun Raatsen, 'Merely Ornamental? Van Dyke's Portraits of Henrietta Maria' in *Henrietta Maria: Piety, Politics and Patronage*, pp. 159, 161–63. See also Erin Griffey, 'Devotional Jewellery in Portraits of Henrietta Maria' in *Henrietta Maria: Piety, Politics and Patronage*, pp. 165–94.

where she had a household of 200, many of whom accompanied her in 1625 to the English court and were still with her in her final years back in Paris. Caroline Hibbard notes that Henrietta Maria arrived in England not only with her considerable entourage but with a vast trousseau of furniture, jewellery, clothes, pictures, books, plate and vestments for her chapel, and, after three years of living as the sole remaining daughter in her mother's household, 'Henrietta Maria brought from France to England firm ideas about how a court should function and be housed'.[7]

Just as the court in which she was raised contained a religious community, so did the one she established in England. The Queen reproduced in her palace what she referred to as 'un couvent de l'Incarnation', the Carmelite retreat she had enjoyed in her youth at the Convent of the Incarnation in Paris.[8] Salvetti, whom Caroline Hibbard notes is a detached observer, reported that at Easter in 1626, Henrietta Maria and her ladies retired to Somerset House where cells, a refectory, and an oratory had been set up 'in the manner of a monastery' and there they 'sang the hours of the Virgin and lived together like nuns.' A few months later he again reports that the young Queen retired for a week so as to 'with greater devotion attend the religious observances of the most holy jubilee'.[9] Henrietta Maria heard Mass every day, communicated monthly, and was regularly hearing sermons and chanting the hours.[10] Once her chapel opened, she established two confraternities, dedicating herself to both the Virgin Mary and St Francis of Assisi. In the spiritual observances of each, chastity is of great importance, not only in the avoidance of sensuality but in the mortification of the body through fasting, almsgiving, and the offering of personal sufferings.[11]

The Queen's love of monastic devotion and her belief in its centrality to public office continued throughout her life. Once exiled in France, she spent considerable time with the Carmelites and eventually established a house for the Visitation order in Chaillot, in which she had her own quarters: a house that became her 'beloved and most delicious retiring place'.[12] Cyprian notes that, following her wishes, the Queen's body was

---

[7] Caroline Hibbard, 'The Queen's Patronage of Artists and Artisans', in Erin Griffey (ed.), *Henrietta Maria: Piety, Politics and Patronage* (Aldershot: Ashgate, 2008), p. 117.
[8] M. Houssaye, *Le Cardinal de Bérulle et le Cardinal de Richelieu, 1625–1628* (Paris, 1875), pp. 8–9, 33–34.
[9] Hibbard, 'Henrietta Maria', *Court Historian*, p. 20.
[10] Hibbard, 'Henrietta Maria', *Court Historian*, p. 21   [11] *Court and Times of Charles I*, vol. 2, p. 317.
[12] Alison Plowden, *Henrietta Maria: Charles I's Indomitable Queen* (Stroud: Sutton Publishing, 2001), p. 224.

opened after her death and her heart taken to the sisters at Chaillot.[13] In a short space of time, the Queen was able to establish in France a court in which enclosed, monastic life was fundamental architecturally, spiritually, and culturally. This was the living arrangement in which she had been raised and the one she had worked to introduce in England: that it was her vision for a Christian court for the entire span of her life attests to her abiding belief that royal authority ought to be rooted in all the rigour of enclosed monastic life.

Although Charles would come to share and endorse his wife's plan for the organisation of court life, he was initially resistant. In the first year of Charles and Henrietta Maria's marriage, the King was greatly offended by the ease and frequency with which the Queen's friars accessed her private chambers.[14] A Protestant king, he believed he had sovereign rights to the Queen's most intimate space and person. But for a woman of Henrietta Maria's devotional temperament, the company of her spiritual advisors was of very great importance, especially in the early years when she did not yet enjoy a close relationship with Charles. As Caroline Hibbard notes, when the King complained that 'the French were 'attempting to steal away' his wife, one of his grievances was no doubt the frequency of those seasons in the Catholic calendar during which sexual abstinence was observed. The Venetian ambassador noted that the Queen 'severely observes all the vigils','[15] and Sir Dudley Carleton complained that 'today is such a saint, tomorrow is the feast of such a saint, your majesty has the rope, girdle or pacienza of such a blessed one, you must not let the king approach; she believed it all, and conversation with her husband was made difficult'.[16] Yet, even after the royal marriage grew warmer, Henrietta Maria continued to practice her religion with great strictness and piety.

It has been widely noted by critics that the marriage – both the private relationship between the monarchs and the marital iconography through which their shared rule flourished – did not settle into its full stride until after Buckingham's assassination in 1628 and Charles' initial dismissal of Henrietta Maria's French entourage. Only then did the monarchs begin to turn their energy towards developing a shared culture built around their now more exclusive relationship. The Carlomaria tradition, through which the monarchs' shared rule was grounded in images of chaste, loving marriage, represents a level of unified leadership that was never part of the iconography of James I's and Anne of Denmark's reign, and it recalls the

---

[13] *Court and Times of Charles I*, vol. 2, p. 470.   [14] *Court and Times* I, vol. 1, p. 40.
[15] Quoted in Hibbard, 'Henrietta Maria', p. 24.   [16] Quoted in Hibbard, 'Henrietta Maria', 24.

images of shared rule prominent in the French court in which Henrietta Maria was raised. The Carlomaria tradition can also be seen as extending from the spiritual vision of married love espoused by St Francois de Sales. De Sales was, of course, another of Henrietta Maria's imports, and the popularity of his teachings in Counter-Reformation France has been widely noted by critics. Exemplary of the renewal of lay piety which followed the Council of Trent, de Sales' *Introduction to a Devout Life* (1609) and *Treatise on the Love of God* (1616) are spiritual guides directed in the first instance to women, particularly those in public life. In them, he exhorts his readers to think in new ways about the interior struggle, the daily life of devotion and prayer, and the cardinal virtues, thereby assisting the laity to enrich their lives with the degree of sanctity usually expected only of religious. De Sales made the pursuit of sanctity more available to those in public life by encouraging a greater understanding of the virtues conventionally thought so at risk in positions of power, most especially chastity. By seeking perfection in chastity, his followers did not simply resist courtly impurity but became themselves forces for good, sanctifying courtly life through their participation in it and bringing souls to God through their ability to purify and beautify what had traditionally been thought occasions for sin: conversation between men and women, theatrical performance, sensuality, and power.

The Counter-Reformation interest in chastity did not only clear a way for women to take more prominent places of authority, it put women's experience at the very heart of a piety which all believers, both men and women, were encouraged to pursue. Under the influence of de Sales especially, renewed Counter-Reformation piety took the virtue of chastity and a devotional language grounded in women's experience and made it the means by which nations as a whole could reach God. In his preface to *Treatise on the Love of God*, de Sales chastises those male readers who dismissed his *Introduction to a Devout Life*, written some years previous, on the basis that it was addressed to women. He explicitly intended all his work to be read by both men and women, though his spirituality was everywhere marked by devotion to feminine figures. Among these figures were the many religious and lay women with whom he developed his spirituality, the mother of God, and the Church as divine lover: de Sales was especially fond of the depiction of the Church as the chaste but passionate lover of Christ in the *Song of Songs*.

The spirituality of the Queen's Capuchin friars was also grounded in feminine devotions and female figures, especially Henrietta Maria herself. They were very aware that their mission was enabled and guided by the

Queen and they, like her, were particularly attuned to the power of chastity as a means of evangelisation in England. When the friars first arrived in London, they perceived the English as particularly unchastened: to men used to the devotional practice of self-denial, poverty, and chastity, the English appeared great lovers of pleasure. The people of London also struck Father Cyprian of Ganache as significantly wealthier than their French counterparts, which he attributed to the fact that they had not paid taxes since Charles dissolved Parliament. To the Catholic outsider, the English appeared all the more unchaste for spending their greater bounty on themselves: they evidently did not spend any of it adorning their churches. Cyprian narrates the reintroduction of splendid liturgy and priestly poverty in London, noting that the English Catholics who flocked to see him and his fellow Capuchins on their arrival were fixated by the monks' cassocks. They 'could not turn their eyes from that dress, in which they contemplated the poverty of Jesus Christ, in the humility of the Gospel and the contempt of wealth. They compared this simplicity with the luxury of the ministers, and thanked God for having kept them in that religion ... which they had received from their ancestors, and had ... always boldly maintained, at the expense of their fortunes, their honour and their blood.'[17]

With the arrival of the new Queen came two new religious perspectives on chastity: self-mortification and self-denial of the body to curb concupiscence, and the need to maintain the decorum of God's house through material glorification: both practices which to most Protestants would have conversely appeared unchaste and erroneous. The anonymous *Novembris Monstrum*'s damning 1641 depiction of Catholicism as a grotesque stage-play was an attack on the Queen and her court's devotional temperament. The tract depicts Catholic spirituality in a series of grotesque feminine personifications. Ignorance is 'a wizled Dame'. The Church walks on the 'crutches of the whore [of babylon]'. Error is a drunkard and fornicator, her naked feet 'all scurfy growen / With dirty pennance'. Superstition is dressed gaudily, in 'chang of costly cloaths still varying'. Her maid is 'counterfit Devotion, / Who carrys after her some holy shrine / Stole from the Virgin Ladies sacred brows, / To which with supple knees she humbly bows'. The women are all 'old' and 'meager' and, presented as players in an anti-masque, are further corrupted by their love of performing.[18]

This view of the Queen's devotions was shared by William Prynne. Much critical attention has been given to Prynne's reference to Henrietta

---

[17] *Court and Times of Charles I*, vol. 2, p. 302.   [18] *Novembris Monstrum* (1641), p. 119.

Maria's stage performances in *Histriomastrix*, where he condemns woman actors as 'notorious whores'.[19] But Prynne is liberal with his abuse of anyone who enjoys performances on the grounds that altering the body in any way from its God-given form is unchaste. His criticism of cross-dressing players is extended to religious sisters, who cut their hair. Such 'polled' nuns are 'lewd Adultersses and notorious Whores', 'unnatural', and 'shameless', not only because they remove their hair but because they live unmarried, 'espoused unto Christ', and 'freed from all subjection to men, or to their husbands'. For Prynne, this is 'An unnaturall unchristian shamefull practise'.[20] Prynne goes on to depict the devil's religious house as a female order, led by a prioress whom he equates to every English woman that 'singeth in the dance'. By rejecting as unchaste both Catholic, all-female devotions and female performance, Prynne implies that his vision of a chaste Protestant woman is one in which her beauty and pleasure are fostered strictly for the enjoyment of her husband. She does not alter her body and remain celibate for love of God, nor does she live in female community, nor perform publicly. For Prynne, nuns are just as unchaste for shutting themselves away as female performers are for showing their talents to the world. Prynne goes on to argue that both groups of women are no better than animals: 'for as when Hogs are strayed, if the Hog heard one call, all assemble themselves together'.[21] It was assemblies of women that worried Prynne and many of his fellow critics of the court. His promotion of heterosexual, Protestant marriage sought to place individual women under the sovereignty of their husbands and divided those women who, whether professed nuns or courtly ladies, gathered together to pursue their own shared interests and beliefs. Embedded in Prynne's vision of chaste womanhood is his more submerged but perhaps even more scandalous libel: he condemns as unchaste the two forms of womanhood which were central to Henrietta Maria's idea of queenship. She and her ladies not only regularly participated in performances but, in their observance of a strict devotional life, were said to sometimes live 'together like nuns'.[22] Indeed, the Queen's pastoral performance, to which Prynne directed his criticism, staged a world in which women could escape the perils of the court and take a vow of chastity in an enclosed community governed by the Queen.

---

[19] *Histriomastix: The players scourge, or, actors tragaedie, divided into two parts* ... (1633), pp. 203, 184.
[20] *Histriomastix*, pp. 201–02.   [21] *Histriomastix*, p. 230.
[22] Hibbard, 'Henrietta Maria', *Court Historian*, p. 20.

Prynne's criticisms of the 'unholy orders' are not dissimilar to those which the King himself directed at the young Queen's devotional life. H. Haynes records that the official explanation for the 1626 expulsion of Henrietta Maria's French retinue was because the priests had 'wrought the Queen's person, as it were to a kind of rule of monastic obedience, so far as to make her do things base and servile'.[23] The French ambassador was requested by the King 'to wean the queen from certain degrading ceremonies ... and especially from betaking herself on solemn festivals to some small rooms built like a monastery at the top of her palace, where she remains without decorum, as she did lately on All Saints' Day'.[24] The Ambassador does not elaborate on the base and servile acts, but John Pory reports in 1626, that the Queen's penitential acts of self-mortification included going barefoot, waiting on her own servants at table and being careful of how much she kissed the King. In Pory's report, these acts are forced on her by her priests and he hopes that after they have been dismissed, 'the queen will by degrees find the sweetness of liberty, in being exempted from those beggarly rudiments of popish penance'.[25] But Henrietta Maria was not compelled to observe strict devotions by anyone but herself. Reportedly, even François de Bassompierre, whose task it was to ensure the Queen kept her Catholic retinue in England, expressed his own disapproval of Henrietta Maria's devotional practices, but she was 'obstinate and very determined'.[26]

In France, the early seventeenth-century movement for spiritual renewal both within enclosed orders and among the laity drew on the interconnections between dynastic and religious houses. It did so by developing the spiritual integrity of the enclosed while at the same time making available to adjunct lay communities a greater share in the rigorous devotional observations taking place within religious houses.[27] Some of the challenges

---

[23] Haynes, *Henrietta Maria* (London, 1912), pp. 321–22.   [24] Hibbard, 'Henrietta Maria', p. 24.
[25] *Court and Times of Charles I*, vol. I, p. 122.   [26] Hibbard, 'Henrietta Maria', n. 68
[27] A full survey of recent work on changes to post-Trent court and monastic life in France is beyond the scope of this study. Monastic houses, and those of women especially, were in Henrietta Maria's childhood enmeshed more deeply in the architectural and bureaucratic life of the court than they had ever been. And throughout Henrietta Maria's childhood, these changes took place in a court increasingly saturated with images of chaste deities. Sheila Ffolliot, 'The Italian "Training" of Catherine de Medici: Portraits as Dynastic Narrative', *The Court Historian* 10 (2005), pp. 36–54: 44–45; Susan Broomhall, *Women and Religion in Sixteenth-Century France* (Palgrave, 2005), p. 18; Joanne Baker, 'Female Monasticism and Family Strategy: The Guises and Saint Pierre de Reims', *Sixteenth Century Journal* 28 (1977), pp. 1091–108; Joan Davies, 'The Montmorencys and the Abbey of Sainte Trinité, Caen: Politics, Profit and Reform', *Journal of Ecclesiastical History* 53 (2002), pp. 665–85; Barbara Whitehead (ed.) *Women's Education in Early Modern Europe* (London: Garland, 1999); Harline, *The Burdens of Sister Margaret* (NY: Doubleday, 1994), p. xii; E.A Lehfeldt,

of this new approach can be seen in Henrietta Maria's later life when, having established a house for the Order of the Visitation in which she could have her own quarters, the sisters refused to live among the costly furnishings Henrietta Maria provided and on occasion had to ask that the Queen limit the number of visitors she received. The spirituality of figures like Francois de Sales was aimed especially at the growing interdependence between enclosed houses and the houses of elite and courtly families. It did this by offering a form of devotional piety coexistent with feminine elegance and worldliness. It recognised the important place of women in public life, and systematised the sophisticated culture of early modern European courts within a life of sanctity and holiness. Henrietta Maria was not the only queen to establish or live within a Salesian house of the Visitation: Anne of Austria, Catherine of Braganza and Marie of Modena all dedicated themselves to the order.

Henrietta Maria's influence on English culture and writing was significant.[28] John Cosin's controversial *Collection of Private Devotions* (1627) was written after the Queen's French ladies chided their English counterparts for having no private devotions. Francis White of the Durham House group advised the King to commission Cosin to produce the book. It took the 1560 Elizabethan primer as its model, reintroducing to his readers the calendar of feast days, instructing them on the lives of the saints, and the hourly cycle of prayers and observance, and teaching them how to calculate moveable feasts. It gave guidance on the Lord's Prayer, the Creed, the Ten Commandments, the Beatitudes, virtues and vices, and included meditations and prayers for every occasion from dressing in the morning to childbirth and death. It even contained an unacknowledged poem by St Ignatius Loyola and a frontispiece whose Jesuit overtones did not go unnoticed by controversialists. Notably, the book remained free of any Marian devotions. In his preface, Cosin emphasised that the book was a guide to private prayer and was not an intervention in the common prayers of public services.[29]

For Cosin's critics, the book, however private, was dangerous. John Mead, a moderate with Puritan leanings, notes that only 150 copies of the

---

'Discipline, Vocation, and Patronage: Spanish Religious Women in the Tridentine Microclimate', *Sixteenth Century Journal* 30 (1999), pp. 1009–30. See also Robin Briggs, *Early Modern France 1560–1715* (Oxford: Oxford University Press, 1977), p. 169. And for the French courtly investment in chaste deities, see Philippa Berry, *Of Chastity and Power* and Sheila Ffolliott, 'Catherine de Medici as Artemisia: Figuring the Powerful Widow' in *Rewriting the Renaissance*, pp. 227–41.

[28] In evidencing the Queen's influence on court writers and thinkers, Erica Veevers points to the work of Cosin, Stafford, and Hawkins in Chapter 3 of *Images of Love and Religion*.

[29] *A collection of private devotions: in the practice of the ancient church* (1627).

book were initially printed, intended only for private use but that by subsequently going into public print, it was made 'offensive'.[30] With a subtlety characteristic of his letters, Mead points to the shift in court policy evidenced by the simultaneous authorisation of Cosin's book and the recalling of Burton's unlicensed *Baiting of the Pope's Bull*. Cosin's *Private Devotions* was immensely popular: it went through three editions in 1627 alone, and five more before Cosin's death. Some passages were later adopted in the Scottish prayer book of 1637.[31] Three generations after the religious houses had been closed in England and in the absence of any structured guide to daily devotions (the collection published early in Elizabeth's reign was no longer in print), the style of piety that came to court with Henrietta Maria soon spread across the country. The Little Gidding community in Cambridgeshire is one example of an initiative among the laity to establish a semi-monastic life, structured by regular worship, shared property, a taking of vows (of which chastity was the most important, given that the community was made up of both sexes), and a preference for high worship.[32] Before establishing the community, Nicholas Ferrars had been in Italy where the spirituality of de Sales had impressed on him the style of lay piety so popular at Henrietta Maria's court. The King, who was himself regularly in attendance at the Queen's chapel in the 1630s, was a great advocate of Little Gidding and a sponsor of their gospel concordances, which was full of the Catholic devotional images Ferrar brought back with him from the Continent. Another devotional group sprung up in London in the 1620s and 1630s under the direction of William Austin. There is less evidence of how the group of friends, or *consanguineorum*, was organised than there is for the Little Gidding community, but Graham Parry believes they met in private houses for spiritual exercises.[33] Their spirituality was markedly Laudian and Parry has suggested that the group may have been directly associated with Laud, as Austin lived close to Laud's London base, Winchester House.[34] In 1635, Austin produced his own book of meditations, *Devotions Augustinianae Flamma*, which went into a second edition in 1637.

In 1635, the first Protestant devotional text with a Marian focus was published by Anthony Stafford. *The Female Glory* not only recalled the life

---

[30] *Court and Times of Charles I*, vol. 1, p. 227.
[31] Anthony Milton, 'Cosin, John (1595–1672)', *Oxford Dictionary of National Biography* (Oxford University Press, 2004).
[32] Adam Smyth, '"Shreds of holinesse": George Herbert, Little Gidding, and Cutting Up Texts in Early Modern England', *ELR* 42, pp. 452–81.
[33] *Glory, Laud and Honour*, p. 122.   [34] *Glory, Laud and Honour*, p. 121.

of Mary, but meditated upon it before advancing the good of enclosed female orders whose lives of chastity and prayer Stafford offers as the model for all pious souls:

> You who have lived spirituall Amourists, whose spirits have triumphed over the flesh, on whose cheeks solitude, prayer, fasts and austerity have left an amiable pale; you who ply your sacred Arithmaticke, and have thoughts cold and cleare as the Christall Beads you pray by; you have voud Virginitie mentall and corporall; you shall not only have ingresse here, but welcome.[35]

Stafford's book is so Marian and so marked by his adoration of female chastity and piety that Parry does not believe that *The Female Glory* could have been considered Protestant at all. It certainly met with resistance. His earlier work even discomforted the woman to whom it was dedicated. His 1611 *Stafford's Niobe*, which laments the degeneracy of his age, was dedicated to Anne, Countess of Dorset, a very pious woman whose soul, Parry notes, Stafford found most beautiful. However, she rejected the dedication. Two decades later, *The Female Glory* was dedicated to another pious and learned woman, Lady Theophila Coke. When defending the Protestantism of his piety, Stafford used the language of chastity to argue that he had not transgressed the limits of decorum nor sullied the Virgin Mary by crossing into popery. In his address to his female readers, Stafford makes the point that he is a great admirer of the Virgin Mary, though he is not her idolater. 'I no way allow of their profane custome, who do robbe God of his Honour, and bestow it on her.' Yet, 'truly I believe that the undervaluing of one so great, and deare in Christ's esteeme, cannot but be displeasing to him, and that the more we ascribe to her (setting Invocation apart) the more gratious we appear in his sight.'[36] Despite Stafford's attempts to defend his advocacy of Marian devotions, the book was immediately attacked for its indebtedness to the piety popular in Henrietta Maria's chapel. Henry Burton condemned Stafford's praise of Mary's ability to convert men to God, a teaching which Burton perceived working well at court, where Catholic women were drawing men back to the old faith.[37]

In 1638, an English translation of Jacques du Bosque's *The Secretary of Ladies*, was entered into the Stationer's Register. It is a collection of letters between courtly women, which Diana Barnes has argued was influenced

[35] Quoted by Prynne in *Canterburies Doome*, p. 215.
[36] Quoted in Parry, *Glory, Laud and Honour*, p. 127.
[37] *Glory, Laud and Honour*, p. 128. See Prynne, *Canturburies Doome* and Veevers, pp. 99–109. See also Helen Wilcox, 'Entering The Temple: Women, Reading, and Devotion in Seventeenth-Century England', in Donna Hamilton and Richard Strier (eds.), *Religion, Literature and Politics in Post-Reformation England 1540–1688* (Cambridge: Cambridge University Press, 1996), pp. 187–207.

by de Sales and may also have shared values with the culture that existed in and around Henrietta Maria's court circle. The letters are exchanged between a community of women who value refined manners, an educated appreciation of the arts, modesty and rationality, and a passionate pursuit of moral and religious truth. Husbands and children are markedly absent from the letters and are only mentioned when they are being persuaded by their mother or wife to enter a seminary or nunnery. For the letter writers, 'civility and integrity' are the grounds for intelligent and warm female community and 'devout life is a manifestation of ... dialogue, dialectical reasoning, friendship and community'.[38] Importantly, the letter-writers value their epistolary community for the fact that it exists outside the court and thus limits their temptation towards worldly pleasures. English women reading the letters in the late 1630s, when Henrietta Maria's influence was at its peak, were encountering a devout, chaste, all-female society which existed both in the world (the letters contained news and commentary on current affairs) but also outside of it. The group's sense of independence of the world was created by the letters themselves: through their exchange, they established a refined, devout, and enclosed community which enabled them to draw closer to God.[39] In this, the community of letter-writers developed a culture like that at Henrietta Maria's court by allocating themselves an all-female devotional space that depended on the learning, moral culture, and social etiquette of the court but was also importantly separated from the courtly perils of pride and disorderliness.

The book that appeared most marked by the influence of Henrietta Maria's Marian court piety is Henry Hawkins' *Partheneia Sacra* (1633). Hawkins was actually a Jesuit, but as Parry has observed, his book would most probably have been acceptable to Laudian Protestants: its tone is more courtly than Austin's or Stafford's but its emblematic devotions are explicitly Marian. It was published in Rouen and is addressed to 'The Parthenian Solidaritie', a group of exiled English Catholics who printed the book in order that it might reach their English counterparts and so ease their suffering. Erica Veevers and Graham Parry have both noted how proximate the tone of *Partheneia Sacra* is to the devotions practiced at Henrietta Maria's court.[40]

---

[38] Diana Barnes, '*The Secretary of Ladies and Feminine Friendship* at the Court of Henrietta Maria', in Erin Griffey (ed.) *Henrietta Maria, Piety, Politics and Patronage* (Aldershot: Ashgate, 2008), pp. 39–56, 55–56.
[39] Diana Barnes, '*The Secretary of Ladies and Feminine Friendship* at the Court of Henrietta Maria', pp. 45–46, 55–56.
[40] Graham Parry, *Glory, Laud and Honour*, pp. 128–29.

Cyprian reports that Laud met secretly with the Papal envoys in London, because he wished to 'bring the Protestant religion so near to the Roman Church, that a union should ensue almost imperceptibly'.[41] However, following Gordon Albion, Karen Britland argues that the relationship between Laud and Rome, certainly between Laud and Henrietta Maria, was a hostile one, in which the Queen and the Archbishop were both 'determined to protect and promote their own faith'.[42] Yet, it is impossible to imagine the Laudian movement progressing so swiftly without the presence of the Queen and her Catholic party, not least because the King himself, who favoured Laud, was a supporter of that reverent worship which he had first encountered on his trip abroad with Buckingham to woo the Infanta and of which he remained a firm advocate all his life. We cannot know exactly how Laud felt about the growing presence of monastic communities in London during the 1630s, but in *Canturburies Doome*, Prynne notes with venom the number of monastic and lay devotional texts in Laud's library, including those of Francois de Sales. Laud may have refused to sanction the English translation of de Sales, but he knew his work well and no doubt found much in de Sales' spirituality which suited his own style of prayer.

The Protestant devotional manuals I have described and the style of faith they fostered in individuals and communities in and around the court during the 1630s are steeped in a piety that welcomes monastic devotions, longs for the chastening of vows, and covets the cloistered and female world of passionate, strict, and beautified worship, a world that de Sales had helped to make popular on the Continent and which Henrietta Maria introduced into the heart of London. Through the Queen, the virtue of chastity became a crucial aspect of female authority, not only that popularised in France by the romances of Honoré D'Urfé but, more directly, the spiritual chastity of female monasticism. It is only when we recognise the impact of the Queen's piety on her leadership that we can understand the extent to which she influenced England's changing religious landscape in the 1630s. Henrietta Maria's reintroduction of monastic devotion to the London court was celebrated in *The Shepherds' Paradise* (1632). In Montagu's pastoral, the King of Castile sanctions and protects from afar an enclosed society in which members take a strict vow of chastity and over

---

[41] *Court and Times of Charles I*, vol. pp. 2, 317.
[42] Britland, *Drama at the Courts of Queen Henrietta Maria*, p. 148; Gordon Albion, *Charles I and the Court of Rome* (London, 1935). See also Rebecca Baily, *Staging the Old Faith*, pp. 149–66; Anthony Milton, *Catholic and Reformed* (Cambridge: Cambridge University Press, 1995), p. 228.

which a woman reigns. More critics are now recognising how the society in *The Shepherds' Paradise* reflected the culture over which Henrietta Maria presided at court, but they have looked to the values espoused by the pastoral's society – chastity, honour, beauty, justice, love, female authority – as indications of Henrietta Maria's influence on local political negotiations and court intrigue.[43] Little sustained attention has been paid to the monastic quality of the play's pastoral world beyond the disagreement over whether it does, indeed, advocate or denigrate monastic life.

Veevers notes that the pastoral world of *The Shepherds' Paradise* is 'not unlike ... a religious order ... with its vows, ceremonies, priests, altar, temple, and prayers'.[44] Sarah Poynting disagrees on the grounds that the community welcomes both male and female inhabitants and is thus in keeping with hostile Protestant stereotypes of secluded Catholic communities as unchaste. For Poynting, the world of *The Shepherds' Paradise* is a largely secular one. Britland has countered Poynting's claims in her detailed study of the degree to which Henrietta Maria oversaw the pastoral's production and the fact that the community's structure in every way besides its mixed-sex inhabitants matches those of the religious communities in which Henrietta Maria was raised and to which she would return in her later life.[45] The community offers its inhabitants regular prayer, the strictness of vows, and a radically communal life in which all personal property is relinquished. Its leader is always a woman who is selected democratically by the community's female inhabitants only. Yet, even Britland stipulates that the pastoral's 'allusions to faith provides a spiritual framework within which women's conversation with men can be enacted' and that this 'certainly makes the Shepherds' Paradise more like a Parisian *salon* than a Catholic convent'. She concludes that the pastoral ultimately asserts the 'importance of faith as a way of conserving chastity within the secular sphere'.[46] I propose instead that the devotional culture Henrietta Maria introduced into her adopted court was promoted by the Queen through the performance she sponsored, not to ensure her active role at court but because she believed its moral and spiritual tenets to be true.

---

[43] Tomlinson, *Women on Stage in Stuart Drama*, Chapter 2. And Britland, *Drama and the Courts of Queen Henrietta Maria*, p. 125.
[44] Veevers, *Images of Love and Religion*, pp. 43–44.
[45] Britland, *Drama and the Courts of Queen Henrietta Maria*, pp. 125–30 and Sarah Poynting, *The Shepherds' Paradise* (Oxford: Oxford University Press, 1997), pp. 156–57. See also Bailey, *Staging the Old Faith*, p. 110 and John Peacock, 'The French Element in Inigo Jones's Masque Designs', in David Lindley (ed.), *The Court Masque* (Manchester: Manchester University Press, 1984), pp. 149–68, 156.
[46] Britland, *Drama and the Courts of Queen Henrietta Maria*, p. 128.

A woman formed within one of Europe's most formidable dynasties, Henrietta Maria did not need to exploit religious teachings on chastity to justify her full participation in court life. Even her predecessor, Anne of Denmark, who was not a Medici, was nonetheless a powerful and prominent leader of her own court, especially during the long periods when James was away from London, and she did not need to advertise her own chastity in order to maintain this role. It can certainly be argued that assertions of female chastity within court performances worked to justify women's enhanced role onstage, most notably the unprecedented speaking part performed by the Queen herself. However, while performances by royal women onstage may have been a new phenomenon, the prominent place of queens within early modern European courts was well established.[47]

More importantly, to claim that Henrietta Maria's faith was a means by which the Queen and her entourage ensured a reputable place in the public and secular sphere is an inversion of the hierarchy of truths held by a woman of her piety. If the numerous reports of the Queen's passionate devotional life are to be accepted as true, then it follows that her faith demanded chastity as a means to salvation, not because it enabled her to enjoy courtly conversation. *The Shepherds' Paradise* is indeed a world in which men and women meet to discuss love in a philosophical manner and in this it does resemble a *salon*. But such conversations take place within the context of curing moral and spiritual injuries suffered at court. The community offers healing to courtiers disappointed in love, seclusion to those wishing never to love, and a moral education for those who have loved erroneously. In its vision of civilised and chaste heterosexual relationships at court, the pastoral is instructive. It is itself a chastening of the very courtiers it entertains. Britland notes that the secluded and enclosed space amid the court, which the community in *The Shepherds' Paradise* enjoys, resembles the 'youthful idyll' established by the King of Navarre in Shakespeare's *Love's Labours Lost*: a place where vows of chastity extend the initial possibilities for heterosocial conversation that ultimately lead to love.[48] But the Shepherds' Paradise also resembles those spaces, enclosed within and protected by the court, to which Henrietta Maria and her women routinely retreated in order to live 'like nuns'.[49]

---

[47] See especially *The Court Historian*, p. 10.
[48] Britland, *Drama and the Courts of Queen Henrietta Maria*, p. 128.
[49] Caroline Hibbard, 'The Queen's Patronage of Artists and Artisans' p. 20.

The Shepherds' Paradise depicts a court that sanctions and protects an enclosed, chaste, devotional community, ruled by a queen: a space that is separate and contained, while remaining geographically proximate and morally and culturally central to the court. As such, the pastoral's chaste community very accurately reflects the Queen's achievements in London during the 1630s, where she re-established monastic orders and maintained leadership within them, not simply as their patron but as their leader and guide. The only legal Catholic monastic communities in London at the time depended for their existence on her sovereignty. In this, she was the most prominent and powerful figure in the Catholic Church in England, a role for which her upbringing had prepared her. Even more than a 'symbolic figurehead for Catholicism's generativity', Henrietta Maria was, as her confessor acknowledged, the 'foundation' of the 'Catholic religion ... in England'. 'As the life of the Queen kept [the Caroline Catholic mission] alive, so her decease was death to it.'[50]

The 1636 court masque, *The Temple of Love,* also advocates monastic devotions and the maintenance of a secluded place of Catholic prayer at the centre of the court. In the masque, Henrietta Maria is Queen Indamora, the Queen of chaste love. She and 'the beauties of her train' are celebrated for 'rais[ing] strange doctrines' at court. Their fellow courtiers are 'Carthusian Poets', 'cloistered ... in an Hermitage', while the anti-masquers are wild magicians who love and worship erroneously.[51] Scholars since Veevers have interpreted the 'true temple' in Davenant's masque, which is hidden in mists until the Queen reveals its location, as a figure for the Queen's religion if not more specifically for the Queen's chapel at Somerset House, which was officially opened not long before the masque was performed.[52] *The Temple of Love*'s final image of Charles and Henrietta Maria seated in state, beholding the revelation of the temple, has prompted Bailey to observe that the 'regal image of chaste love projects the potentially explosive symbol of religious union'.[53] Britland has noted more specifically that *The Temple of Love*'s anti-masque 'clearly associates Calvinist Protestantism with Chaos and disruption': its erroneous magicians call upon 'a sect of modern devils ... that claim / Chambers and tenements in heaven as

---

[50] Frances Dolan, *Whores of Babylon, Catholicism, Gender and Seventeenth-Century Print Culture* (Notre-Dame: University of Notre-Dame Press, 2005), p. 136; See also Cyprian in *Court and Times of Charles I*, vol. 2, p. 464.
[51] *The Dramatic Works of Sir William D'avenant*, vol. 1 (New York: Russell and Russell, 1964), pp. 292–94. All subsequent quotations will be cited in text.
[52] Veevers, Britland and see especially Bailey, *Staging the Old Faith*, Chapter 3 and 4.
[53] Bailey, *Staging the Old Faith*, p. 148.

they / had purchased there'. She suggests that the masque may have worked to consolidate the relationship between Catholicism and Arminianism by locating Calvinism as the source of chaos, thereby 'rendering English Catholics less threatening by showcasing their virtues' and the doctrinal similarities between them and Laudian Reformists.[54]

In the years between *The Shepherds' Paradise* (which tentatively marked the opening of the temporary Capuchin chapel) and *The Temple of Love*, the popularity of Henrietta Maria's style of devotion had grown considerably. Not only does the masque celebrate a monastic space within the court, which in *The Shepherds' Paradise* was the secret retreat of a few, it also heralds the glorious revelation of the hidden space and the conversion of all who behold it. I propose further that in *The Temple of Love*, Henrietta Maria is not merely celebrated as the head of a monastic community, as she was in the earlier pastoral, but as the embodiment of the Church itself: as the chaste and mystical bride of Christ. In *The Temple of Love*, Charles and Henrietta Maria offer their chaste union as an emblem of virtuous conduct on which the nation can model its own behaviour. Fate is so beloved of Charles that she has placed him – 'the monarch of men's hearts' – on the throne specifically to reveal to his people 'love's blessing' (290). But it is Henrietta Maria who reveals to him and his subjects the true temple: a temple which is distinguished from its false counterpart by its chastity. The masque argues that the Queen will reveal the true temple when those who have been worshipping and loving erroneously are reformed by her chaste example. As critics have noted, this claim is a playful promotion of Henrietta Maria's court culture of Platonic love, but in an important sense, the masque's claim was also exactly the same as that being made repeatedly in prose pamphlets about the visible Church. *The Temple of Love*, like the tracts of so many divines writing outside the court, posited that the true Church was both chaste and obscured and that it could only be revealed, and schism overcome, through the pursuit of particular virtues and doctrines. Not surprisingly, *The Temple of Love* argues that the virtues and doctrines which will bring about the revelation of the true Church are those popularised by the Queen: chastity, beauty, piety and the arts. What is remarkable is that the masque argues that the Church will be revealed by the Queen once her influence has cleansed art of its profanity and made it sacred again. Only when the masque's poets have been 'purifi'd', can they herald 'what Indamora comes to show': the location of the true Church (289).

---

[54] Britland, *Drama at the Courts of Queen Henrietta Maria*, p. 148.

Henrietta Maria's queenship was built on a celebration of her reform of court spaces and the arts, a fact most extravagantly attested to by Gentileschi's ceiling paintings for the Queen's House. Charles shared his wife's love of Continental arts, most controversially in his liturgical taste. By celebrating the Queen's ability to chasten the arts and thus to restore them to their sacred agenda, to guide the King, and to reveal the true Church, the masque comes very close to admitting the truth of anti-court accusations that the King's taste for beautified ceremony and ornament, especially in worship, owed much to his wife's Catholicism. However, the masque's argument for the chastening of love poetry had its own tradition. From Sidney's 'Leave me, O Love', Robert Southwell's *Marie Magdalene's Funeral Teares* to Ford's *Christes Bloody Sweate* and the devotional poetry of Richard Crashaw, the call to bring love poetry back from its earthly dimension and return it to the heavenly one was one more early modern use of chastity.[55] Where this tradition advocates the redirection of carnal desire toward God as a chastening influence on both poet and poetry, *The Temple of Love* presents the Queen herself as the mechanism by which profane desires and erroneous worship are redirected to the truth and chastity of the true temple. In the true Church, earthly love poetry will be supplanted by the 'grave frosty Homilies, / And Anticke lawes of Chastitie' already being enjoyed by certain 'Carthusian Poets' in 'an Hermitage' (294). That is, the arts and worship currently enjoyed by the King's subjects will be replaced by the style of monastic worship which the Queen and her Capuchin friars had already introduced into the centre of London. But the new teaching will be made attractive because the Queen will embody it herself. When Henrietta Maria, as Queen Indamora, descends from the heavens and onto the masquing stage, she is saluted as both the object of adoration and the authority by which adoration is chastened and spiritualised. 'She' and 'each Princesse in her traine' are

[55] In his preface to *Christes Bloody Sweate*, Ford announces that he is attempting to chasten the poetry of his time: 'Poetrie is so every way made the herald of wantonnesse, as there is not now any thing too uncleane for the lascivious rime; which among some (in whose hearts God hath wrought better things) hath bin the cause, why so generall an imputation is laid upon this ancient and industrious Arte. And I, to cleere (as I might) verse, from the soyle of this unworthinesse, have herein (at least) proved that it may deliver good matter'. In this intention, he follows Robert Southwell, who, in his dedication of *Marie Magdalene's Funeral Teares*, bolsters his arguments for the chastening of poetry with chastity's watery imagery: 'For as passion, and especially this of love, is in these daies the chief commaunder of moste mens actions, and the Idol to which both tongues and pennes do sacrifice their ill bestowed labours: so is there nothing nowe more needfull to bee intreated, then how to direct these humors unto their due courses, and to draw this floud of affections into the right channel. Passions I allow, and love I approue, only I would wishe that men would alter their obiect and better their intent'.

praised by the 'wise enamor'd Poets' as most beautiful (300–301), but they are also kind and instructive. Where in the realm of earthly love poetry, chastity is cruel, in the new divine poetry advocated by the Queen, it becomes the source of true passion: that passion which she and her ladies expressed when cloistered within their court 'like nuns'. The Queen's chastity is not cold and pitiless, but a loving and spiritual instruction. While she and her ladies 'subdue' the hearts of those who behold them, they are also 'kind' and 'take a care / To free, and counsell, whom their eyes ensnare' (301). It is through the person of the Queen that love is chastened and redirected to God as sacred, passionate devotion.

For all the non-conformist-Calvinist and pro-Parliamentary efforts to recast the marital image of the Church in terms that secured the King from Popish influences, little had been done to displace the still-widespread figure of the Church as the chaste, mystical bride of Christ. Amid the growing popularity of Henrietta Maria's style of worship, *The Temple of Love* suggests that the true and chaste temple is not only the Queen's Capuchin chapel but the Church, the bride of Christ, which the Queen herself embodies. The Queen searches 'ev'ry Heart' to heal the wounded, clean the tainted, and teach all how they 'should love'(289). She is the Church in the *Song of Songs*, the mystical bride on whose passionate chastity de Sales regularly meditated in the works that so informed the Queen's spirituality. In *The Temple of Love*, the monarchs' two crowning virtues are personified by Sunesis (Understanding) and Thelema (Will). Understanding says to Will: 'Come, melt thy soule in mine, that when unite, / We may become one virtuous appetite'. Will responds: 'First breathe thine into me, thine is the part / More heavenly, and doth more adorne the heart'. Both together conclude that 'Thus mix'd, our love will ever be discreet, / And all our thoughts and actions pure, / When perfect Will, and strengthened Reason meet, / Then Love's created to endure'(303). We can assume that Will is the King's virtue in particular since he wields the sceptre. Henrietta Maria therefore embodies Understanding, a claim in keeping with the masque's vision: she is both beautiful and wise and directs her husband and all his subjects to God. To conform the will to God by first deepening one's understanding of his divine plan is standard and timeless Christian ontology, but William Davenant and Henrietta Maria did something unique by arguing that such a process constitutes chastity, since chastity was also the virtue by which commentators of all confessions were describing the true visible Church.

The masque argues that the true temple will be revealed when the King unites his will to the Queen's understanding, when Queen Indamora breathes into the King's heart her 'more heavenly' soul (303). By presenting the Queen's body as the mystical bride itself, which is welcomed into the heart of the King and of his subjects, the masque offers a direct reversal of those images frequent in anti-Catholic court commentary that cast the Queen as an unruly body in need of containment by the King. Where Dr Meddus and his correspondents had urged the possession of the Queen's foreign Catholic body by the King as the means of securing the health and stability of the country and its safe deliverance from plague and war, the masque argues instead that the King and all his subjects will be truly healed when they have allowed themselves to be chastened by the Queen and welcomed into her temple. When the temple is revealed, Will and Understanding enter its gilt archway, united. Henrietta Maria remains seated at the foot of state richly dressed, like all her ladies with her, in blue, yellow, white and gold, their dresses and head-dresses embroidered in silver and plumed with feathers, their bodies everywhere reflecting 'beaut[iful] light' (291): a final tableau whose radiance matched exactly that of the true, chaste Church in de Sales' much-read interpretation of Psalm 68:13:

> Propose unto yourselves a fine dove amidst the sun's rays; you shall see her change into so many divers colours, as you behold her diversely; because her feathers are so apt to receive the light that the sun spreading his splendour amongst them there is caused a number of transparencies, which bring forth a great variety ... of colours so agreeable to the eye, yea the enamel of richest jewels; colours that are glittering and so quaintly gilt that the gold gives them more life. In consideration hereof the Royal Prophet said unto the Israelites: *Although affliction rudely [...] your face/ Yet shall your hew henceforth to men appear/ As pigeon's plumes, when silvers trembling grace,/ And burnished gold do make them shine the more.* The Church is indeed [so] adorned'.[56]

These are the same 'painted feathers' which Milton in *Eikonoklastes* accused Charles of wearing to 'set him off so gay among the people'. Milton denounced *Eikon Basilike*, the King's 'Idoliz'd Book', as little more than 'rosarie prayers' and 'sweet rapsodies of Heathenism and Knight-errantry' by which he drew the 'ignorant and wretched people' to 'go a whoring after him'.[57]

From Charles' perspective, the masque may have simply claimed that the Church of England was, under him and his Queen, discovering its true catholicity while remaining firmly within his rule. But Henrietta Maria and her supporters could only have read one way the masque's claim that

---

[56] *A treatise of the Love of God* (1630), preface. [57] *Eikonoklastes*, CPW, 3: 364–7.

the King must conform his will to her chaste and heavenly soul. The masque did not refute the claims of anti-court commentators that the Queen had seduced the King to popery; it merely argued that his marriage to the Catholic Church was chaste.

Henrietta Maria's Marian fertility

The many royal births of the 1630s, each coincident with a lavish court masque, were especially interested in celebrating the Queen's chaste fertility. One key reason for this must surely have been the fact that commentators immediately after the Queen's arrival in 1625 perceived Charles' and Henrietta Maria's inter-religious marriage as a suspiciously unchaste source of royal issue (a view which some thought vindicated by the first, and still-born, Charles II). The Queen's birthing rituals were events in which her Marian fertility – her status as the chaste 'door' between heaven and earth – was promoted through the birthing rituals' use of all the decorative arts deployed in the more public ceremonies of court masques. Under the Tudors, the royal palace chosen for most births was Greenwich and Henrietta Maria also chose this location for the birth of her first child on 13 May 1629. However, the son, baptised Charles, was either still-born or died within a few hours of delivery and Henrietta Maria chose not to return to Greenwich for her subsequent labours, the first five of which took place at St. James's Palace (Charles, Prince of Wales, 29 May 1630; Mary, 4 Nov 1631; James, Duke of York, 14 Oct 1633; Elizabeth, 28 Dec 1635; Anne, 17 March 1637). Her sixth, seventh, and eighth children were: Katherine (died), born at Whitehall, 9 Jan 1639; Henry, Duke of Gloucester, born at Oatlands, 8 July 1640; and Henriette Anne, born at Exeter, 16 June 1643. Despite Henrietta Maria's apparent decision that the Greenwich Palace was a space blackened in some way by her misfortune, she did subsequently build on Greenwich's Tudor reputation as the site of royal fertility by embedding into the fabric of the more recent Greenwich building (Inigo Jones' Queen's House) iconography which clearly marked it as a space in which Stuart fertility was to be celebrated. The grotesque ceiling of the bedchamber at the Queen's House contains four emblems which describe the space in terms that appear to be designed specifically as a celebration not only of the fertile and chaste union between Charles and Henrietta Maria but of the space itself as pure and purifying: emblems which constitute a direct rebuttal of her detractors' accusations that her religion and sexuality had an unchaste effect on the architectural spaces of the court.

The four emblems draw on French and English courtly imagery – including two conjoined palms for married fertility and three lilies for purity – and bear the titles *Mutua Fecunditas, Spes Reipublicae, Ardet Aeternum, Cum Odore Candor*. The strength of the commonwealth is secured by the eternal love and fertility of Charles and Henrietta Maria, whose marriage is the source of that pure essence, the goodly perfume, which dispels disease.[58] By drawing the image of healing perfume into its celebration of the Queen's fertility, the painting makes a contentious claim for the space as the site of a birthing ritual that is concerned at once with the physiological and spiritual health of humans. While the burning of herbs to purify the air of houses appears to have continued uncontroversially throughout the century as a form of health care, the burning of herbs for devotional purposes was, like candles, silver, music, and gesture, an adornment under intense scrutiny by religious disputants in the years of Henrietta Maria's reign.[59] Acceptable as a form of physiological purity, burning incense before an idol was seen as erroneous by advocates of plain religion who, with Thomas Adams, believed that Christian prayers 'are onely perfumed by the Incense of Christs prayers and righteousnes'.[60] By asserting that the agent by which the monarchs' fertile union sustained the health of the commonwealth was incense, the bedchamber's grotesque ceiling made both the benign claim that the physiological purity and health of the Queen's fertility secured England's future and the more controversial claim that the heirs to the throne, future heads of the English Church, were begotten by a Queen whose birthing rituals were built from the unchaste Popish adornments of elaborate religious worship.

The evolution of incense into increasingly contradictory functions capable of chastening a space (by healing its air of disease) and unchastening it (by turning it into a darkened 'grove' of idolatrous worship) is on its own reason enough to recognise how embroiled were the Queen's birthing rituals (and the bedchambers in which they either occurred or were promoted through architectural and decorative fabrics) within Caroline disagreements over the chastity of space. Yet, Henrietta Maria's birthing rituals were also built from adornments which to advocates of plain

---

[58] My thanks to Sophie Carney for permission to consult her 'The Queen's House at Greenwich: the Material Cultures of the Courts of Queen Anna of Denmark and Queen Henrietta Maria, 1603–1642' (Unpublished Doctoral Thesis, Roehampton University).

[59] See Holly Crawford Pickett, 'The Idolatrous Nose: Incense on the Early Modern Stage'in Williamson and Degenhardt (eds.), *Religion and Drama in Early Modern England* (Farnham: Ashgate, 2011), pp. 19–38.

[60] Thomas Adams, *The Happiness of the Church* ... (1619), p. 375.

religion were explicitly unchaste: she filled the spaces of her bedchamber with paintings of the Virgin and Child. Erin Griffey and Sophie Carney have both analysed the material acquisitions of the court during times of birth and their findings reveal the vast purchase of herbs for burning and strewing around the bedchamber, of paintings to adorn it, and of linens with which to adorn the Queen and the baby.[61] Regardless of which palace Henrietta Maria chose to give birth in, we can speculate that she spent her labour in a birthing chair under a great cloth canopy, not unlike those which sat above the Throne in State, and she surrounded herself with paintings of the Virgin and Child, which were brought especially from other palaces to be hung in the bedchamber for the occasion. She also, Griffey has found, pinned canvases of the Virgin and Child to the inside of the canopy that surrounded her. The floors were strewn with fresh flowers and the air was full of the smoke of incense and perfume. Her ladies, spiritual guides, doctors, and midwives, would have attended her in the hierarchised formations befitting a court solemnity, and music was perhaps played without. Regardless of their finer details, these rituals were some of the court's most elaborate and important ceremonies. They were not open to as many observers as other court ceremonies, yet they were occasions of the greatest solemnity and ritualised splendour in which the material and spiritual health of mother and child coincided with that of the nation and in which God's grace might enter the world in the form of a divine leader through the body of a chaste Queen. Or, as in the case of Henrietta Maria's first birth, it would not.

The implications of the Queen's still-birth ought not to be underestimated and its relevance to my analysis of early modern chastity is considerable. To the Queen's detractors, the still-born Prince would have been a sign of precisely the unchastity with which her erroneous religion marked the monarchs' marriage. As Julie Crawford has argued, monstrous births (which included still-born and sickly babies), were a morbid sign of more than the mother's unchastity: they were also 'outcasts from God and irrefutable testament to their parents' own spiritual reprobation'.[62] The association between the sexual act, the relative chastity of the partners, and the issue of birth itself is attested to most vividly by the widespread belief that a marked or damaged child was a direct result of unchastity at

---

[61] Sophie Carney, 'The Queen's House at Greenwich: The Material Cultures of the Courts of Queen Anna of Denmark and Queen Henrietta Maria, 1603–1642'; Erin Griffey, 'In the Bedroom: Ritual, Display and Personal Identity in the Stuart Bedchamber', paper given at the University of Nottingham on 7 March 2012.
[62] Julie Crawford, *Marvelous Protestantism*, p. 20.

conception. James Reuff's *The Expert Midwife* (1637) has a special section on monstrous births. Such afflictions could be 'attributed and ascribed to the Judgement of God'. Yet, 'the corruption and fault of the seed is to be acknowledged'. Rueff recounts the instance of a monstrous birth, attributing it to the sins of the parents. 'We allege the immoderate desire of lust to be a cause, whereby it commeth to passe, that the seedes of men and women are caused to be very feeble and imperfect, whereby of necessity a feeble and imperfect Feature must ensue'. Keith Thomas notes that Tudor and Stuart 'moralists had always taught that incest, adultery and other forms of sexual immorality were punished by ill health and monstrous births'. It was with 'relish' that Puritan commentators ascribed monstrous births to the evil of the times.[63] An anonymous tract printed in 1645 rejoices that the King has resolved to return and be reconciled to his Parliament, to which 'there is no good Subject (unlesse he be a desperate Malignant or some arch Papist) but will say Amen'. The happy moment is described as especially timely since, in the months when Charles and the Parliamentarians were at war, many monstrous wonders had visited the country. Of greatest note is the baby born in Shoe Lane with no legs or arms and instead of a head, a hollow of flesh from which another limbless body proceeded.[64]

For non-elite women as much as royals, chastity dominated the discussion of all stages of pregnancy, labour, and childbirth because it was a time when the vulnerable infant was at the mercy of the vagaries of the (female) flesh and the checkered world of female medicine. The close early modern association between 'bawdery', midwifery, and witchcraft is well known.[65] *The Expert Midwife* warns against unchaste medics: 'doe not use ... the counsell of unskilled Physicians' or the 'wicked Arts and policies of old Witches and Harlots'. Rueff argues that such women ought to be 'remov[ed]' and 'punish[ed]' by 'Magistrates' because only these 'fathers of the people' can protect the innocent 'virgins' and 'widows' who have been 'insnared and intangled with the Arts and divellish practices' that threaten not only the 'tender Babes and Infants' but the world of legitimate and sanctified medical practices. Reuff's ambivalence over the chastity of midwives is also evident in the fact that throughout his treatise, he does not use the term midwife at all, but rather the synonymous title

---

[63] *Religion and the Decline of Magic*, pp. 109–10, 124, 125.
[64] *The Most Strange and Wonderful Apparition* (1645), pp. 7–8.
[65] James Reuff, *The Expert Midwife* (1637), p. 58. See also Leah Donnison, *Midwives and Medical Men* (New Barnet: Historian Publishers, 1988).

'grave and modest matron'. For Reuff, a good female midwife is a chaste woman and a bad one, a 'witch' or 'harlot'. When he goes on to provide instructions on nursing children, the chastity of the nursemaid is also given particular emphasis. Sexual abstinence in nursemaids is crucial, he insists, as is a chaste demeanor, since, following Galen, sex and sensuality 'troubleth the blood' and so by consequence the breast milk.[66]

From a spiritual and Galenic perspective, the new mother's body was especially vulnerable to corrupting influences. In the month between her labour and her churching, the new mother was in receipt of elaborate treatments: her body was covered in ointments and wrapped in fresh animal skins. Ideally, her diet was scrupulously designed with a view to purity. The process sought to deliver her safely and untainted from the long trial of her pregnancy and birth and to secure her from further illness. However, often its ultimate and ideal goal was the restoration of the virginal state. Reuff notes that this ought to be the aim of postpartum care, since Vestputius Florentius had spoken of 'those perpetual virgins that dwell beyond the antarctic pole'.[67] When we turn to royal births, it is easy to see how the relative chastity of the Queen's body and of the spaces in which she gave birth were interpreted as influencing the fortunes of the royal line and the health and stability of England's connection to God. More than any other body, the Queen's body was the vessel in which royal life, touched by an especial divine favour and decree, entered the world.

We have seen how wondrous and divine are the moments in tragicomedy and masque when the lost child, loved-one, or state of grace is finally returned to those who most long for it. In the same way, we can be certain that one year after the death of the first Charles II, the majority of Caroline subjects were attentive to the Queen's second labour, both its result and its conditions. The fact that this second labour produced a healthy boy who, again named Charles II, would go on to become King makes this second birthing ritual at St James's Palace a crucial moment in the Caroline reign: one which produced the very wonder and celebration conjured by similar scenes in tragicomedy. This birthing ritual would have brought real conviction to the masque's image of Henrietta Maria as holy, fertile, and chaste Queen. The conditions of the ritual are therefore of crucial importance to understanding the 1630s – they can tell us much about the country's increased loyalty to the Queen after 1630, and its greater investment in her devotional, moral, and aesthetic cult of chastity.

[66] Jacques Guillemeau, *The Nursing of Children* (1612), p. 4.
[67] Jacques Guillemeau, *The Happy Delivery of Women* (1612), p. 195.

From the few traces of evidence we have, we can 'read' the conditions of Henrietta Maria's successful labour at St James' and, where there exists no evidence, we can speculate on the perceptions of observers. This is especially so for the birth of Charles II because the extant evidence suggests that even those living in London at the time were not sure which of two possible 'scenes' were taking place. The first possible scene, in which a Huguenot doctor of dubious reputation attended the birth, was caught up in and determined by the greatest levels of bravado and controversy which the masculine professional medical world could produce. The other was steeped in the figures and rituals of a Catholic world that had not been seen in England for generations. From the perspective of those observing the court, the second scene was most likely to have taken place. The ritual's Catholic conditions can thus be viewed as one crucial reason that Henrietta Maria's cult of chastity proliferated throughout the succeeding decade. That is, in this single birthing ritual, the Queen's interpretation of chastity as feminine, pietised, Marian, Catholic, and spectacular was galvanised. Where her opponents could draw only on rhetoric to further their own claims to chastity, the Queen's first successful labour confirmed the chastity of the monarchs' union and issue; it returned to the nation the lost Charles II; attested to God's divine favour, drawing his blessing onto the earth; and consolidated the strength of the nation, uniting it into one body.

We know that Henrietta Maria's first birth, the still-born Charles, was attended by Peter Chamberlen the elder. The attendant at the second birth, that of the healthy Charles II, is less clear. Radcliffe very reasonably assumes that because Dr Peter Chamberlen, the son of Peter Chamberlen the younger, succeeded to his aged uncle's Royal appointment after the Queen's first pregnancy, he therefore attended the birth of Charles II in 1630.[68] Charles II himself appears to have believed he was delivered by Dr Peter Chamberlen.[69] However, we also know that around the time of Charles II's birth, the French midwife, Mme Peronne, arrived at court and was given a handsome allowance for this and all her subsequent services to the Queen throughout the decade.[70] That Marie de Medici would have sent over one of the French court's most competent midwives is in no way surprising: France had at the time an excellent reputation for professional

---

[68] Radcliffe, *Milestone in Midwifery*, p. 30.
[69] W. R. LeFanu, 'Huguenot Refugee Doctors in England', *Proceedings of the Huguenot Society of Great Britain and Ireland* 19 (1955), pp. 113–127, 118.
[70] Caroline Hibbard, 'The Queen's Patronage of Artists and Artisans' in *Piety, Politics and Patronage*, p. 135.

midwifery. Louise Bourgeois Boursier, who had attended all of Marie de Medici's births, including that of Henrietta Maria, was an educationalist and scholar and had produced some of the best seventeenth-century manuals on midwifery. Boursier had retired by the time Henrietta Maria began to have children, but one of her pupils and successors, Mme Peronne, shared her teacher's reputation, and the reputation of the Hôtel-Dieu de Paris.[71]

Chamberlen had a more complicated reputation. Throughout the seventeenth century, the Chamberlen men were performers in the grand style of any anatomist, building up the brand of their family name and their mysterious instruments by promoting their peculiar abilities and challenging the power of the College of Physicians who chastised them for routinely stepping outside their official area of practice. However, the family's unorthodoxy did not bar them from court where they played a crucial role in the Caroline theatre of birth. The theatrical spectacle of a Chamberlen birth was enhanced by the family's demands for enclosure. How they ensured secrecy during labours remains a subject of speculation. We do know that they arrived in a flourish at the house of their patient with the carved and ornamental wooden chest in which they kept the forceps and other tools.[72] These were carried inside and the room was cleared. Did they then cover the seated patient with a large white sheet tied around her neck and stretching down to the floor? This was common practice in Holland, where male midwives attempted to maintain decorum for their patient by sitting on a stool outside the sheet and, their arms tucked beneath it, delivered the baby without ever observing the mother below her neck.[73] For the Chamberlens, the purpose of the sheet would not have been to conceal the mother's sex from their own view but rather to conceal their instruments from the view of the mother and her attendants. Peter Dunn argues that this method would have been impossible as the instruments, especially in their initially large and clumsy form, could

---

[71] On the basis of gender alone, Louise Bourgeois Boursier would not have approved of Chamberlen's attendance upon the Queen: she once denounced French gentlewomen who preferred male physicians over female midwives as '*coquettes*'. Louise Bourgeois, *Observations diverses sur la stérilité, perte de fruict, foecundité, accouchements, maladies des femmes et des enfants nouveaux niz* (Paris, 1617), II: 215.

[72] Walter Radcliffe, *The Secret Instrument* (London: Heinemann, 1947); *Milestone in Midwifery* (Bristol: John Wright & Sons, 1967); Adrian Wilson, *The Making of Man-Wifery* (London: UCL Press, 1995).

[73] Walter Radcliffe, *Milestone in Midwifery*, pp. 31–2; Leah Donnison, *Midwives and Medical Men*, pp. 23–4.

not have been applied successfully in dim light.[74] Did the Chamberlens take candles with them beneath the sheet? Or, as William Prioleau has speculated, did they blindfold the patient instead?[75] Either of these scenes presents a grimly emblematic inversion of state: the mother's body, enthroned beneath a canopy and surrounded by a huge white shroud, blood-smeared, and she either blind-folded or lit from beneath her skirts by the glow of candle light projecting onto the inside of the white sheet the looming shadows of the iron forceps, their long blades clattering loudly against each other.

The French court can only have felt that their own care would be superior to that of Peter Chamberlen, a Huguenot and a naturalised Englishman with a reputation for dubious theatrics. But they clearly also felt that their own care would be more chaste: a quality essential in birth as in all aspects of a woman's life. Boursier's condemnation of mothers who request male midwives as *coquettes* reveals how scathingly she disapproved of men in the birthing room and the French may have felt that the English court's provision of a male midwife for Henrietta Maria was a grossly inadequate defence against a second tragic birthing scene. However, England also responded with concern over the care given by their court to the Queen and the dead Prince. In one correspondence, it was noted that there 'may be cause to add fears to our sorrows, that Chamberlen's help was used in her majesty's labour' (2:14). Both Peter Chamberlens, the elder present at the Queen's first pregnancy and his successor, shared equally in their family's complicated reputation, so it is no surprise that the replacement of the one by the other did not inspire confidence in all. For English observers, however, the new Chamberlen appointment was preferable to that of the French, which was noted with suspicion. 'The queen's majesty, having no fancy, it seems, to our English midwives and nurses, had sent into France for both'. Crucially, the French midwives and nurses did not come alone but 'together with a dwarf, and, as some say, twelve nuns' (2:70). Their ship followed shortly after the ship which contained not only the Queen's Capuchin friars but a French Bishop and a Catholic physician 'to be near [the Queen] in any occasion of her sickness' (2:47).

The new decade began with the Queen's second pregnancy and with it, two quite different royal birthing scenes began to be anticipated by court

---

[74] P.M. Dunn, 'The Chamberlen Family (1560–1728) and Obstetric Forceps,' *Archives of Disease in Childhood: The Journal of the British Paediatric Association: Fetal and Neonatal Edition* 81.3 (1999).

[75] William H Prioleau, 'The Chamberlen Family and Introduction of Obstetrical Instruments', *Proceedings of the Huguenot Society of Great Britain and Ireland* 27.5 (2002), pp. 705–714, 707.

observers. Each scene was highly emblematic, with its own distinctive characters, whose props and (in the case of the Catholics) costumes were novel, foreign and threatening. In the first scene, the country's future was in the hands of Chamberlen, who, despite the frightening theatrics he brought to the birthing chair, his dubious instruments, and his French extraction, was nonetheless a naturalised Englishman, a Protestant, and a servant to the King. This scene was, to the English, perhaps preferable and the one thought best able to secure a happy outcome. The other scene contained a series of figures lifted directly from the stock of those unchaste characters least welcome at such an important occasion: nuns, Capuchins, a Bishop, a Catholic physician, French nurses and midwifes, and a dwarf. We are unlikely to ever know for sure which scene actually took place. Yet, even if Mme Peronne, her French nurses, the Capuchins, the 'Catholic physician' (and the dwarf) did not attend the birth, they were certainly present after it to care for the Queen and the new Prince, taking up residence at court and enjoying a degree of welcome they would not have enjoyed had their arrival coincided with a second unhappy outcome.

It is crucial for our understanding of the rise in the 1630s of the Caroline cult of chastity that the new cast of 'unchaste' French figures arrived on English shores to attend what proved to be a successful birth and that, even if they were not actually in attendance, they continued to be associated with the fortuitous occasion. The Queen's first tragic birthing scene, however, was associated with Peter Chamberlen. We can therefore read Henrietta Maria's birthing rituals as events which occupied a pivotal place in the history of English monarchy. The success of the Queen's second birth – its issue both healthy and male – contributed to the consolidation of the Queen's status as Marian exemplar, not least because her fertility was ultimately fostered by those attendants most associated with her Marian devotional spaces. A birthing ritual whose potentially idolatrous staging (incense, paintings of the Virgin and Child) and Catholic attendants might have proved to confirm English suspicions of the unchaste influences which Henrietta Maria had introduced into the royal Palaces and bloodline, in fact turned out to be the catalyst of a softening of attitude towards the French faction at court. It also proved an opportunity for Henrietta Maria to celebrate and promote the chastity of the royal marriage, and the chastity of her own newly-arrived 'temple', in the masques of the 1630s.

The monarchs' chaste marital union was celebrated on the royal masquing stage in almost exactly as many performances as the issue it produced. In the minds of onlookers, the Queen was perhaps understood to have sat in the masque's Throne of State as often as she sat in her canopied birthing chair. Both performances claimed to chastise the spaces in which they occurred and to radiate blessing from the monarchs' chaste bodies to all subjects. Henrietta Maria's birthing rituals were, as the ceiling paintings at the Queen's House asserts, the means by which purity and love were made available first in the space of the bedchamber and then throughout all of the commonwealth. In the same way that *The Shepherds' Paradise* made it clear that the chaste and sequestered space of its community healed all the court and the many nations beyond its walls, the grace and purity of Caroline royal birthing spaces radiated chastity and sanctity outwards. Henrietta Maria's fertility ensured that the bedchambers' paintings of the Virgin and Child, its incense, and Catholic attendants, did not transform them into those dark and sequestered 'groves' of idolatry described by Burgess, but rather into the blessed spaces which, like the Queen's chapels and masque stages, made available to all a wondrous experience of the divine will as both chastening and feminine.

CHAPTER 5

Protestant chastity: the language of resistance in Milton's 'A Maske' and A Maske

Amid the success of Charles' and Henrietta Maria's cult of chastity in the 1630s, the young John Milton began to assert his own version of the virtue. Although he articulated it most completely as early as his 1634 masque, Milton's vision of chastity can be seen as paving the way for the cultural and political events of the late 1640s, through which the court's spectacular, feminised, and pietised cult of chastity was eventually eclipsed by the more masculine and prosaic pro-Parliamentary vision of the virtue. Indeed, we could say that it was Milton's vision of chastity which led to the definitive separation of the virtue from its association with tragicomedy and, with the closure of the theatres, brought an end to chastity's and tragicomedy's pervasive hold on early seventeenth-century language and culture. In Milton's corpus we see how important chastity was to the emergence of those early seventeenth-century intellectual processes through which royal authority was resisted and from which would emerge, preeminently in Milton himself, a powerfully articulated voice for political and religious reform. What makes Milton so interesting as a figure through which to assess early modern perceptions of chastity is that he, like Charles I and Henrietta Maria, displayed not only a canny sense of the polemical force and the moral and conceptual relevance of chastity to his cultural moment but also a deeply personal investment in the virtue. This is, perhaps, to be expected: the central ideas by which identity is structured and by which the rhetoric of major controversies are made convincing and relevant in any given moment in history are usually powerful for the very fact that individuals believe in their importance.

In its subtle criticism of the court, Milton's *A Maske Presented at Ludlow Castle,* makes brilliant use of the Throne of State as the emblematic focus for Milton's re-coding of chastity and, as such, evidences the extent of his thinking about Caroline masques and the cult of chastity's efforts to associate its own vision of the virtue with the Throne of State. In this,

Milton demonstrates why he was so eligible to become the chief promoter of the commonwealth project. He knew as well as Cromwell, and perhaps even better than the King, Queen, and those who created their masques, how to use the props of power to assert the integrity and ascendency of his view of true chastity over the inordinate number of competing views being offered by his contemporaries. Milton's sense that the Throne of State was a powerful means by which to explore chastity suggests he was also aware of the numerous prominent instances, both on and off the stage, in which thrones and the virtue were associated.

In the previous chapter, I argued for an interpretation of royal birthing scenes as a form of public performance crucial to the theatre of monarchy. At the centre of these performances was the royal birthing chair, an object at once medical, ecclesial, and royal: a prop of power and divinity which marked the gates between heaven and earth and through which the continuance of the royal line was either secured (a grand testimony to royal chastity) or damaged. The royal birthing chair and the performance that surrounded it were seen by few but were nonetheless evoked in the Throne of State which, in the masques of the 1630s, proclaimed the monarchs' fertility, chastity and sanctity. In the Caroline court's cult of chastity, the Throne was a sign of the monarchs' own chastity: of their legitimate union with each other and their many legitimate issue; of their power to bring back to virtue those who, embodied by the anti-masque, had strayed from the Crown's chaste influence; and of the bodily integrity of the monarchs themselves and, figuratively, of the nation. The court masques, ceremonies, and birthing rituals offered a bold and emblematic claim for the chastity of the Throne of State under Charles and Henrietta Maria's rule – a claim that was a difficult symbolic feat for dissenters to unravel. They did so by re-coding the Throne as a site of moral struggle in which the tyranny and pride of princes who had lost all just sense of their proper place in relation to the divine allowed not only their own bodies to be broken and unchastened but, figuratively, the body of the nation also. While Milton's masque made the expected generic use of chastity – the return of the lost children to their parents, the celebration of the Bridgewater family's union, the threat to the Lady's bodily integrity – it was fundamentally a sustained exploration of the moral struggle against pride and towards a proper relationship with God. Wrestling chastity away from the Throne meant re-coding the Throne as a seat of trial, in which virtuous leaders could become tyrants, spoiling the Throne itself, themselves, and the nation with the blood that flowed from their breached and unchaste bodies.

To reveal this more fully requires turning to Milton himself and his very personal engagement with chastity. Milton's sonnet 'How Soon Hath Time' and his University exercise, the 'Sixth Prolusion', reveal how closely bound Milton's early thinking on chastity was to his developing ideas on pride, subjection, authority, and upright Christian citizenship. By the 1630s, Milton's own developing understanding of what constituted a chaste subject, a chaste throne, and the genre through which chastity was best realised, became a central concern of his masque. Through a reading of both the printed and performed versions of Milton's masque of chastity, with which this chapter concludes, I will assess how Milton's re-inscription of chastity within the printed word and away from the spectacular world of court performance constituted a powerful attack on the cult of chastity and paved the way for those who, writing in the following decade, began to win popular support for their criticism of the King and court.

Chastity and the young Milton

Milton's *A Maske Presented at Ludlow Castle* was commissioned by the Earl of Bridgewater and performed on 29 September 1634 at the new family home, Ludlow Castle, in Herefordshire. The Earl had recently been appointed Lord Lieutenant of Wales and President of the Council. The masque is thought to have marked his investiture, though it was performed months afterwards. Three of the Earl's children played the principal roles: Lady Alice Egerton, aged 15, played the Lady, and her brothers John Viscount Brackley, aged 11, and Thomas Egerton, aged 9, played the two brothers. The Bridgewater children had all performed in royal masques. In 1632, they appeared in *Tempe Restored*, which, like Milton's masque, included Circe and the transformation of men into beasts. The two boys were also torch-bearers in the 1634 *Coelum Britannicum*. The children's music teacher, Henry Lawes, played the Attendant Spirit in the Bridgewater masque, composed the music, and is said to have engaged Milton for the task, as he was acquainted with the young poet's father. Lawes had recently enlisted Milton for verses to be included in *Arcades*, commissioned by the Earl of Bridgewater's mother-in-law, Alice Spencer, Dowager Countess of Derby. Both the Countess of Derby and her son-in-law's family had recently been at the centre of the scandal surrounding the Earl of Castlehaven, who was another of the Countess' sons-in-law. While the relevance of the scandal to Milton's masque has long been disputed by scholars,[1] my treatment of Castlehaven's trial will remain limited to its more general role in the Throne of State's capacity to signal chastity and unchastity, which I have already explored.

Milton's replacement of the theological virtue of charity with chastity in his masque speaks to his interest in chastity as a preservation of the self. Where charity is a giving of the self, chastity, in Milton's view, is a restraint and protection of the self. This is, of course, the anxious and rather limited interpretation of the virtue which *The Winter's Tale* forces Leontes to reject in preference for a more expansive, generous, relational, and mature interpretation. In *Milton and the Culture of Violence*, Michael Lieb describes Milton's deep anxiety over the threat of physical assault and his attendant interest in images of the body safe and intact. Whatever positions Milton held on Christian doctrine and ecclesiology in the years leading up to 1634, it is clear from the masque as elsewhere in Milton's corpus, that he believed in the necessity of chastity to an upright and virtuous life, realised through a sound and disciplined body, and that the opposite of chastity was effeminacy: a tendency to vice – ambition, pride, sensuality, lust – to which those in authority were particularly prone. Milton's early writing on chastity evidences a particular interest in avoiding the pride produced by the unchastity of an erroneously-oriented relationship with God. He expresses this interest through a resistance to the cult of chastity's interpretation of the virtue.

St Paul writes that 'man ... is the image and glory of God: but the woman is the glory of the man'.[2] While recounting his own strict practice of chastity in *Apology Against a Pamphlet*, Milton argues that Paul's words can be taken to mean that 'if unchastity in the woman ... be such a scandal and dishonour, then certainly in a man who is both the image and

---

[1] Barbara Breasted, 'Comus and the Castlehaven Scandal', *Milton Studies* 3 (1971), pp. 201–24; John Creaser, 'Milton's Comus: The Irrelevance of the Castlehaven Scandal', *Milton Quarterly* 4 (1987), pp. 25–34; Leah Marcus, 'The Milieu of Milton's Comus: Judicial Reform at Ludlow and the Problem of Sexual Assault', *Criticism* 25 (1983), pp. 293–327; Nancy Weitz, 'Chastity, Rape, and Ideology in the Castlehaven Testimonies and Milton's Ludlow Mask', *Milton Studies* 32 (1995), pp. 153–68; Catherine Thomas, 'Chaste Bodies and Poisonous Desires in Milton's Mask', *SEL* 46 (2006), pp. 435–59. Castlehaven was a close relative of the Egerton family. However, I am inclined to agree with Cedric Brown that Milton's masque could not have been referring directly to the scandal. Not only was it an occasion demanding a degree of decorum prohibiting such aspersion but Milton himself was a young man too scrupulous to breach the requisite polity. More importantly, chastity and its staged interrogation through the stately props of authority was widespread enough in the early-seventeenth century that Milton's trial of chastity was surely understood by observers as participating in a broad tradition rather than referencing directly any single incident. Brown, *John Milton's Aristocratic Entertainments*, p. 14.

[2] I Corinthians 11:7.

glory of God, it must, though commonly not so thought, be much more deflowering and dishonourable'.[3] While not denying the crucial importance of chastity to women, Milton claims the virtue as also importantly masculine and crucial to the Christian search for perfection. He recognises that schooling in the virtue of chastity is a complex, life-long process, essential to salvation. But Milton's earlier work evidences that for him the struggle for chastity is a distinctly Protestant battle: intellectualised, masculine, and individual. He does not, for instance, learn the depth of the virtue from women as Leontes does from Hermione and Paulina. Nor does he arrive at it through a deeply affective encounter with God and his own limitations, as do Leontes, Bassanes, and the speaker of Ford's *Christes Bloodie Sweate*. Most of all, he does not arrive at it through the celebration of the divine will as feminine, through the Queen's cult of pietised fertility, or through the spectacle and ornament of a masque or Laudian communion service. Milton may have brought to the English language a feminine and Baroque ornament[4] and his thinking on gender was, in an important sense, revolutionary regarding women's emancipation in certain contexts,[5] but Milton's morality viewed the affective and the feminine as too proximate to the vice of effeminacy, and contrary to truly masculine and rigorous chastity.

Referring to Milton's prose, Gina Hausknecht observes: 'where Milton's most closely held principles are at stake' gender emerges. 'He describes the world through a discourse of manliness in which privilege accrues to male gender, not male sex: men can be insufficiently masculine, and women are not unequivocally subordinate'.[6] The same can be said for much of Milton's poetry, in which both men and women are defined morally as either manly or effeminate, but the pursuit of perfection through chastity is a manly struggle out of effeminacy. For Milton, the struggle is deeply existential, as it was for Leontes and Bassanes. But unlike Leontes and Bassanes, it is not the fear of contamination and loss caused by a beloved woman's unchastity that initiates an exploration of the virtue. Instead, we see in Milton's early work that a fundamental aspect of his pursuit of virtue was an awareness that the risk of infection from unchastity or effeminacy

---

[3] *Complete Prose Works* (New Haven: Yale University Press, 1953–82), 1: 892. All subsequent references will be cited in text.
[4] Gordon Campbell and Thomas Corns, *John Milton: Life, Work, and Thought* (Oxford: Oxford University Press, 2008), pp. 83–84.
[5] Catherine Gimelli-Martin (ed.), *Milton and Gender* (Cambridge: Cambridge University Press, 2004).
[6] Gina Hausknecht, "The Gender of Civic Virtue", in *Milton and Gender*, pp. 19–33, 32.

Chastity and the young Milton

lurks in the prideful desires that plague man from the earliest moments of adulthood. His descriptions of chastity as spiritual combat and moral perfection are always attended by the search for maturity and an instinctive resistance to authority. To this end, Milton's interest in chastity as a means of battling pride and fostering virtue concentrated on the practice of refinement, both of the body and of language.

In the sonnet, 'How Soon Hath Time', which Milton wrote to mark his twenty-third birthday, he observed:

> Perhaps my semblance might deceave the truth,
> That I to manhood am arriv'd so neer,
> And inward ripeness doth much less appear,
> That som more timely-happy spirits indu'th.[7]

His physical youthfulness and femininity misrepresent his true (inner) manliness, his moral and vocational maturity. The fruit of that manliness (poetic repute) has not yet arrived: 'But my late spring no bud or blossom shew'th' (119). Indeed, with nothing worldly to show for his inner ripeness, how can he say that he is a man at all? Untimely youthfulness at his age, a failure to take his place in the world of responsibilities and reputation, could easily constitute effeminacy. But does he want his blossoms to show in order that he might appear a man or be a man? Acknowledging the potential presumption in his resentment of how time has treated him, Milton moves towards a position of acceptance and then submission to God:

> Yet be it less or more, or soon or slow,
> It shall be still in strictest measure even,
> To that same lot, however mean or high,
> Toward which time leads me, and the will of heav'n;
> All is, if I have grace to use it so,
> As ever in my great task-maister's eye.
>
> (119)

The sonnet narrates Milton's early vision of maturation, in which the desire for worldly manliness must be overcome and true manliness, which is something for God's eyes first and foremost, must develop in its place. Although Milton claims that his 'inner ripeness' has not bloomed in any evidence of poetic greatness, the sonnet itself constitutes exactly such evidence. It is the work of a promising young poet and therefore the

---

[7] All references to Milton's poetry, except his masque, are to Shawcross' edition. *The Complete Poetry of John Milton* (New York: Anchor Books, 1971), p. 119. All subsequent references will be cited in text.

bloom of worldly maturation and achievement. But for Milton, the truly mature man and poet is one who explicitly disavows any significance in the work except the dedication of it to God.

The sonnet describes an act of self-dedication that is also an act of self-definition, one which depends on the initial questioning comparison between the poet and others and the ultimate denial of the world as a measure of greatness in favour of a singular, manly fidelity to God. This is the *felix culpa* operating at the level of individual consciousness: subjectivity – for the manly, chaste self – is constituted in the simultaneous and triumphant moments of worldly self-assertion and chaste self-dedication, in the oscillation between pride and humility, unchastity and chastity. One cannot be chaste without first asserting the self as great in the world's eyes, for there would otherwise be nothing worthy to offer God, nor can one be chaste without dedicating the self to God, as to do so signals self-interestedness and moral immaturity, qualities that precisely constitute the effeminacy of pride. A knowledge of unchastity is therefore essential if the chaste adventurer is to realise their goal, just as the Lady in her trial must encounter Comus, debate with him, and even be partially physically altered by his unchaste throne before emerging triumphant.

'How Soon Hath Time' appears to be mostly interested in chastity as the perfection of language and of the poet's proper relationship with his work and with God. But it is also in some measure concerned with the body, and I do not refer here solely to Milton's concern for his lack of physical maturation. The humility of the sonnet's speaker has been described by Michael Lieb and Richard Halpern as the self-emptying or self-offering of Christ, his *kenosis*.[8] Halpern argues that it is Christ's chastity, expressed in the 'Nativity Ode' through the unifying totality of his infant body that chastises the 'foul deformities' of nature and the pastoral world of sexuality. Where sexuality 'decompose[s] the body', 'Christ's mastery over nature is figured by his ability to repel these sexual threats and thus retain the chaste integrity of his bodily form'.[9] In *A Maske Presented at Ludlow Castle*, Milton would again figure the effeminacy of unchastity as a contagion that liquifies and deforms the body.

---

[8] Michael Lieb, 'Milton and Kenotic Christology: its Literary Bearing', *ELH* 37 (1970), pp. 342–360, 352; Richard Halpern, 'The Great Instauration: Imaginary Narratives in Milton's "Nativity Ode,"' in Mary Nyquist & Margaret W. Ferguson (eds.), *Re-membering Milton: Essays in the Texts and Traditions* (New York: Methuen, 1987), pp. 3–24, 7. See also Stephen M. Fallon, *Milton's Peculiar Grace* (Ithaca and London: Cornell University Press, 2007), p. 60.

[9] Halpern, 'The Great Instauration', pp. 12–13; and 'On the Morning of Christ's Nativity' (Shawcross, *CP*), p. 65, line 44.

While debating their sister's safety and the nature of chastity, the Elder Brother tells the younger that:

> when lust,
> By unchaste looks, loose gestures, and foul talk,
> But most by lewd and lavish act of sin,
> Lets in defilement to the inward parts,
> The soul grows clotted by contagion.[10]

This clottedness is an excess of the flesh which 'imbodies and imbrutes' until 'the divine property' of the person is, like the Church in Burton's vision, so swamped by unchastity that it comes to resemble the 'thick and gloomy shadows damp / Oft seen in charnel-vaults and sepulchres' (485–91). The Elder Brother's depiction of a damp grave to which the brutish, 'degenerate', and 'degraded' soul is attached by its 'carnal sensuality' is a prefiguring of the stately palace in which Comus later entraps the Lady (495). There, her refined, chaste soul or 'mind' is forced to linger in the fleshly world where her own flesh is momentarily 'clotted' by the release of its 'gums of gluttenous heat' (957). As the visions of fleshly thrones discussed in Chapter 3 evidence, the unchastity of leaders was caused by more than sensuality. Like Shakespeare and Ford before him, Milton interprets pride, the desire for the fleshly and worldly over the divine, as most characterising unchastity. But Milton retains that part of Leontes' anxious thinking which seeks to chasten the body and protect it from assault through 'rigour', armour, and self-enclosure. Where the healing vision of chastity in *The Winter's Tale* and *Christes Bloodie Sweate* depicted the virtue as the breaking of Christ's body, Milton perceives chastity instead as a Protestant armour against unchaste influences, a virtue that is fought for through the refinement of the mind and the preservation of the body, but primarily through the dedication of the self to God. For Milton, with his difficult relationship to authority, chaste self-dedication was a complex ontological process played out most vividly in his early poetry.

For Milton, resisting the version of chastity articulated by the Caroline cult of chastity meant re-gendering it. However, while he masculinised the struggle for chastity, he did not limit its benefits to men alone. The self-conquest involved in the sonnet's final act of submission is an act of manly chastity that in fact anticipates Eve's decision to desist from questioning.

---

[10] Line 483–7. All references to both the 1637 printed and 1634 performed versions of the masque are to Sprott's edition. S. E. Sprott (ed.) *A Maske: The Earlier Versions* (Toronto: University of Toronto Press, 1973).

This is the most significant decision of its kind in Milton's corpus. Waking from her divine dream, Eve prepares to enter the post-lapsarian world, 'all her spirits composed / To meek submission' (12:516): submission to her 'task-master'. Crucially, Eve moves away from the effeminacy that marked her self-involvement, her susceptibility to temptation, and her fall. Her arrival at the muscular moral practice of self-conquest and the dual process of self-betterment and the dedication of that best self to God is a move away from effeminacy and towards masculine chastity.

The movement from effeminacy to chaste manliness described by the sonnet is the arc that Milton's Adam and Eve follow, but it is also the arc of Milton's own arrival from a youth characterised by his peers as effeminate to a manliness elevated enough that he can use it to denounce his critics as themselves effeminate. Milton's University oration, the 'Sixth Prolusion', illustrates Milton's development of manly chastity as a virtue constituted in and through the transformation from adherence to worldly opinion to an alliance of the chaste individual with God – an alliance that is superior to the world's demands on the self. The 'Sixth Prolusion' narrates this process as one that takes place amid distress. In it, Milton's initial effeminacy is a charge his peers level at him in an expression of 'hostility and dislike'.[11] The effeminacy of which they accuse him suggests physical weakness, moral scrupulousness, and high ideals. Milton articulates his doctrine of manly chastity by re-defining manliness as a virtue predicated on high ideals and moral scrupulousness and a moral muscularity that refuses physical strength any significance. Indeed, in Milton's redefinition, the physical prowess of his attackers becomes a sign of their effeminacy. Through their sporting antics and sexual adventures, they fail to step up to the truly manly battle with the self: a battle in which such low exhibitionism and venal pleasures must be overcome. As Michael Lieb has argued, Milton's rhetoric in this exercise reveals a personal investment more vexed than any of his other work.[12] He responds to his new popularity among the group of young men, by whom he has clearly felt persecuted for the majority of his undergraduate terms, with a mixture of resentment and outright abuse, masking disdain with condescension and disgust with vulgar humour. In this, Milton's thinking about the tension between chastity and pride can be seen in its very nascent, and

---

[11] *Private Correspondence and Academic Exercises*, translated by Phyllis B. Tillyard (Cambridge: Cambridge University Press, 1932), p. 86. All subsequent references will be cited in text.
[12] Michael Lieb, *Milton and the Culture of Violence* (London: Cornell University Press, 1994), pp. 83–113.

very personal, form. His defensive and self-protecting assertions of chastity risk falling into that unchastity of pride which Milton would later interrogate in his sonnet and, more fully, in his masque.

Milton opens the oration by describing the way he was dragged from his study to perform for his peers. In doing so, he acknowledges the view, held by his audience, of himself as studious and exacting. He has been 'commanded to transfer that zeal, which I had intended to devote to the acquisition of knowledge, to foolery and the invention of new jests'. But he will deign to such a lowly task since he is not the first great champion of chastity to do so. 'If Junius Brutus, that second founder of Rome and great avenger of the lusts of kings, could bring himself to disguise his almost godlike mind and wonderful natural talents under the semblance of idiocy, there is assuredly no reason why I should be ashamed to play the wise fool for a while' (85–6). Milton's actual project is to avenge his own past belittlement by those whom he no doubt both actually and defensively considers foolish by re-inscribing as greatness the capacities that mark his difference from them. In marking his difference by aligning himself with Brutus, Milton is again both playfully and actually claiming for himself a degree of greatness and virtue that far outstrips that of his audience. Milton says something very specific when he aligns himself with Brutus: the man who had to hide his true greatness was also the man whose valiant response to the rape of Lucrece was the founding of a new nation on the claims of chastity against the 'lust of kings'. Milton then goes on to remind his audience that they recently contradicted their usual conduct towards him by offering a 'new-found friendliness' when he last gave an academic oration. It is rhetorical skill that distinguishes Milton from his persecutors, just as it was between Brutus and his peers at the moment of Lucrece's suicide. Milton's use of language marks his ascendency over his audience at the same time that it wins the approval he no doubt both desires and feels compelled to scorn.

The claim Milton must defend in his oration is that 'Sportive Exercises on occasion are not inconsistent with philosophical Studies'. The task is quite complex for Milton, who must defend the very act he is performing whilst rebuking those to whom it is designed to give pleasure. He has also clearly been ridiculed himself as a figure not unlike the studious boors he is expected to attack:

> ... if a man does not desire to be considered cultured and witty, he must not be annoyed if he is called a clown and a boor. There is a certain mean kind of fellow, often enough met with, who, being themselves incapable of wit or gaiety and conscious of their own dullness and stupidity, always

> conclude that any witty remark they may hear is made at their expense. It would indeed serve them right if their unreasonable suspicions were to be realised, and if they should find themselves the butt of everyone's witticisms, till they were almost driven to suicide. But such dregs of mankind as these cannot stand in the way of the pleasantry of polite society. (90)

Milton distinguishes himself here from an extreme example of the personality he has himself been forced to occupy by the ridicule of his peers. Where another tormented man is driven to annihilate himself, Milton is immune. Unlike his hypothetical man, Milton himself is cultured and witty but is not – he is anxious to assert – concerned with the opinions of others. However, prior to his first most public opportunity to defend himself, Milton had in fact been taunted by his listeners, if not as a clown and a boor, then certainly as a Lady.

Milton then moves to the section of his exercise which has proved most embarrassing to his nineteenth- and twentieth-century readers. His grotesque and gastronomic humour appears to be an expected element of the performance and Milton throws himself into the task with energy. However, he is careful to equate the vulgarity of his language in this section with the vulgarity of his audience and to distance himself from both. Wherever he may lower himself to 'barbarity and meanness', it is because that is what his audience both wants and deserves; he is merely descending to the task. Yet, in proving consummate at such a task, Milton wins approval precisely at the moment that he defines his difference from and supremacy over his listeners.

> In a moment we shall shake off the fetters of rhetoric and throw ourselves into comic license. If in the course of this I outgo by a finger's breadth, as they say, my usual habits and the strict rules of modesty, I beg you, gentlemen, to accept this explanation: it is to give you pleasure that I have put off and for the moment laid aside my usual habit, and if anything I may say is loose or licentious, put it down to the suggestion, not of my real mind or character, but of the needs of the moment and the genius of the place. (93)

Milton proves that he can, if he chooses, put off his usual habit of chastity, modesty and refinement in order to be as vulgar as the next man. He then changes direction by announcing that 'I will now turn to what concerns me more closely' (98):

> Some of late called me "the Lady." But why do I seem to them too little of a man? Have they no regard for Priscian? Do these bungling grammarians attribute to the feminine gender what is proper to the masculine ...It is, I suppose, because I have never brought myself to toss off great bumpers

like a prize-fighter, or because my hand has never grown horny with driving the plough, or because I was never a farm hand at seven or laid myself down full length in the midday sun; or last perhaps because I never showed my virility in the way these brothellers do. But I wish they could leave playing the ass as readily as I the woman. (98–9)

Milton's behaviour, which his peers have deemed unmanly, is, in fact, 'proper to the masculine'. Those who overlook this are themselves effeminate, not only because they are morally inept (requiring a brothel to prove their virility) but because they are 'bungling grammarians'. While through his oration Milton has proved himself a consummate rhetoretician, Milton's peers reveal in their inability to correctly gender a pronoun their lack of basic grammar. As we will see, this vision of chastity, as a battle against pride as much as a refinement of the body and of speech persisted throughout Milton's life.

The 'Sixth Prolusion' offers an early view of Milton's negotiation between his worldly ambition and his need to dedicate himself in chaste fidelity to God: a negotiation he later expressed so coherently in his sonnet. Milton does not describe explicitly the importance of self-dedication in his University performance, as he does in his sonnet. A too genuine humility is, after all, anathema to his project. However, he nonetheless denounces his peers for self-interest and stupidity. In doing so, he also makes it known that he is not so presumptuous as to claim for himself unqualified greatness: 'But indeed as to any such nick-name as "Lord" or "Lady" I utterly reject and repudiate it; for, gentlemen, it is only in your courts and on your platforms that I have any ambition to lord it' (99). Milton is above all titles because he denies himself any claim to them unless in a purely formal capacity. We have seen, in the sonnet, how he seeks first to achieve greatness if it is to be denied in subjection and dedication to God. The young poet recognises that he aspires to greatness in courts and on platforms, but reduces the significance of those sites by suggesting that beneath their strictly superficial and public function, lies a self whose real sentiment and actions are of true moral importance. His own greatness is dependent upon his denial of the worldly greatness embodied by titles. This is a rebellious rejection of authority that is at once a denial of the feminine title with which his peers address him and a claim to the moral superiority of those who have 'no ambition to lord it'.

In its negotiation between the contrary aims of inoffensively fulfilling generic expectations while subtly critiquing the moral stance of those by whom the genre is most valued, Milton's University oration was excellent preparation for his bold intervention in the royal genre. When in 1634 he came to describe the chaste adventurer in the person of Alice Egerton, Milton was able to draw on his own experience of chastity as a battle against pride, physical impurity and ill-refined language. For Milton, chastity was crucial to moral strength. It is through her 'well governed' and 'wise appetite' that the Lady of Milton's masque fosters the chaste proliferation and propagation of the self. Here, as elsewhere in his corpus, Milton asserts that furtherance and production are in fact only possible through diligent care and discipline of the self's resources. The Lady chooses her words carefully while her opponents are, like those to whom Milton performed his University oration, 'unlettered', 'jocund', 'gamesome', and 'ill-managed' (172–4). She exemplifies Milton's view that if the self is not tempered and restrained, it will not flourish in the appropriate manner. The virtue and fertility, so joyfully detailed at the conclusion of the masque, shows that the Lady's temperance allows for the growth of something more valuable than that which could be produced by the instinctive indulgence of the appetites. The tendency to such indulgence, and the burden of venal dissipation that results from it, characterises the suffering Milton ascribes to all the unchaste persons in his corpus: persons who, by partaking of pleasure readily, are unable to produce anything good or worthy by it. Like Satan, they must ultimately recoil back unto themselves. Or like the souls described by the Elder Brother in the masque, they let defilement into their 'inward parts' until 'clotted by contagion', they embody and imbrute. Chaste restraint is in fact the supreme cultivation, indulgence is dissipation.

For Milton, this moral opposition is specific to the human abilities of language and reason:[13] the qualities that marked his ascendancy over his collegiate audience. As Christopher Kendrick has observed, Milton's chastity 'served as a support' for his 'poetic aspiration'.[14] Comus, who knows nothing of divine dedication, offers 'false rules pranked in reason's garb' (759). His misuse of language and reason confirm what the Lady intuited early in the masque: that he 'thanks the gods amiss' (208). A manly fidelity to God requires a constant struggle with the self, and the fruit of such a struggle, fit for divine dedication, is the right, proper, and good use of language and reasoning: evidence of a well-governed self and a wise

---

[13] For a discussion of the divinity of language as human agency, see Leonard Mustazza, *'Such Prompt Eloquence': Language as Agency and Character in Milton's Epics* (London: Associated University Presses, 1988).

[14] Christopher Kendrick, 'Milton and Sexuality: A Symptomatic Reading of Comus', in *Re-Membering Milton: Essays in the Texts and Traditions*, p. 48.

application of the self's resources. In the sonnet, Milton denied the need for poetic repute while at the same time establishing his reputation. In the masque, he asserts that good, plain language marks the truly chaste masque (where the royal masque relies on spectacle) even while Milton himself allows his observers to relish the heights of baroque ornamentation in Comus' effeminate language. This is most evident in Comus' debate with the Lady, but his moral health, relative to hers, is revealed much earlier through their use of language. Comus reports that he saw the Lady's brothers 'under a green mantling vine ... Plucking ripe clusters from the tender shoots, ... I took it for a faery vision ... I worshipt'. He is 'over-exquisite' in his speech (359) but the Lady (good, plain speaker) stops his excess: 'Gentle villager / What readiest way would bring me to that place?' (294–305).

Not unlike the speaker in the Prolusion, the Lady when trapped in Comus' throne, physically and sexually vulnerable, is forced to rely on her linguistic skill if she is to assert the 'hidden strength', the 'sacred' 'steel' of chastity that the elder brother believed would protect her from all assailants. Thus, the word – the chaste word – becomes the supreme masculine force, privileged over traditionally masculine martial skills as over the more visually spectacular form of the masque at court. In Milton's masque, the masculine word becomes a divine force: the 'he' lodged in the Lady's breast is figured masculine because it is 'holy'. Milton would later elaborate on this construction in *Paradise Lost*. There, the struggle with the self is the truly heroic act, while the actual (celestial) battle – the use of arms – is shown to be less important, both through its de-emphasised placement in the recapitulation and through the hyperbolic terms in which it is dramatised. The epic conception of winning the kingdom, which the celestial battle in *Paradise Lost* references, is less relevant for Milton. The real kingdom to be won is the kingdom of God. When one's faithfulness to God fails, that kingdom is lost. The real battle, therefore, is with the self: a battle to maintain obedience to God. In *Paradise Lost*, the loss of this obedience is catastrophic, while the loss of the battle is almost meaningless. Indeed, in Milton's masque, the only martial figure is the angel of chastity.

When the Lady first perceives her danger, she has a vision of chastity as the 'hovering angel girt in golden wings' (214), the same chaste 'quivered nymph' which her brother describes as 'clad in complete steel', armed with 'arrows keen', who traces all the world unharmed and victorious. This powerful angel, who spreads her 'sacred rays of chastity' without 'pride' or 'presumption' is so 'saintly' and powerful that she brings with her 'a thousand liveried angels' to drive off each 'thing of sin and guilt'

(421–56). We can perhaps hear in this scriptural reference an echo of Milton's self-defence against his more conventionally masculine peers in the Prolusion. Before his crucifixion, Christ chastised the disciple who drew his sword to protect his master against his assailants. Christ reminded him that were it God's will, twelve legions of angels would come to his protection.[15] Traditional masculine victories are again recuperated through chastity. The truly heroic, and truly masculine, act becomes the considered use, and dedication to God, of one's faculties of language and reason. Physical action is so immaterial it rarely features at all in the lives of Milton's chaste characters. The Attendant Spirit advises the Lady's two brothers to put their swords away: 'Farr other arms and other weapons must / Be those that quell the might of hellish charms' (612–13). Conversely, the often very bodily assailants of the Prolusion, the masque, *Paradise Lost*, and *Samson Agonistes*, are distinctly effeminate. Eve, Comus, Satan, Delilah, are all licentious, wanton, and deceitful in physical and feminine terms: serpentine, bent, Bacchic, knotted, painted, intemperate, their arguments cunning and obscured by their physical presence. Whereas the Lady of Comus, Samson, Abdiel, and, to a large extent, Adam are all upright, sure, unbending, firm, steadfast, temperate, and their speech is clear and un-calculated.

The speaker in 'How Soon Hath Time' is ultimately chastised by reminding himself to whom his works must be dedicated. He learns to navigate the territory between his own enjoyment of, and triumph over, the work he cultivates, and the realisation that the product of his cultivation is ultimately under the sovereignty of God. This requires passing from manly self-government to feminine supplication without risking the charge of effeminacy. In order to do this, Milton re-interprets the presumption and wickedness of individual poetic greatness as a weakness coded effeminately. Conversely, supplication and divine dedication – a good that is achieved through struggle – becomes manly and upright. He codes chaste goodness as a virile masculine struggle and self-oriented pride as unchaste and effeminate weakness. Satan's charismatic masculine stature, his epic heroism, is undermined by his serpentine, intemperate, and covetous effeminacy; beneath Eve's effeminate licentiousness, she is artistically adept, rational, and ultimately the source 'by her Seed' of man's deliverance; and Milton himself, in the 'Sixth Prolusion', can be a woman because he is not an ass (516).

---

[15] Matthew 26: 52–3.

Spiritual combat and courtly celebration: the throne in 'A Maske' and *A Maske*

While it fulfils the demands of the royal genre,[16] Milton's masque celebrates the interior struggle for chastity as a process of greater moral weight than the means of achieving virtue popularised by the Caroline masque: monastic piety, ritualised devotion, ornament, wonder, and chaste female fertility. Milton's masque is 'a victory of personal integrity over public conventions'[17] and a criticism of the court's ephemeral celebrations.[18] It is an early articulation of Milton's growing sense that 'the only space over which political power cannot exert its ravenous claims is the inward space of the self. Where Herbert struggled to make these spaces available to his God, Milton struggled to hide them from his king'.[19] Crucially, Milton's masque achieves this vision of interiority through a sophisticated depiction of the chaste adventurer learning personal virtue from an attitude of political rebellion: it asserts that true chastity is individuating, while the court's cult of chastity is nothing but an external and empty show, frivolous, effeminate, and morally bankrupt.

My reading of Milton's masque situates his thinking on chastity as a masculine and individuating virtue, at once defiant on the earthly plane and supplicating to heaven, within the context of his rhetorical struggle in the 'Sixth Prolusion' and his thinking about the growing tradition of thrones depicted as chaste or unchaste. Milton's developing understanding of his vocation as a poet meant he worked through the different mediums and social demands of both the performed and printed versions of his masque

---

[16] Maryann Cale McGuire, *Milton's Puritan Masque* (Athens: The University of Georgia Press, 1983); David Norbrook, 'The Reformation of the Masque' in David Lindley (ed.), *The Court Masque* (Manchester: Manchester University Press, 1984), pp. 94–110; Peter Walls, 'Comus: The Court Masque Questioned', in John Caldwell, Edward Olleson and Susan Wollenberg (eds.), *The Well Enchanting Skill: Music, Poetry, and Drama in the Culture of the Renaissance, Essays in Honour of F. W. Sternfield* (Oxford: Clarendon Press, 1990), pp. 107–13; Ann Baynes Coiro, 'Anonymous Milton, or, A Maske Masked', *English Literary History* 71 (2004), pp. 609–29; Heather Dubrow, 'The Masquing of Genre in Comus', *Milton Studies* 44 (2005), pp. 62–83; Barbara K. Lewalski, 'Milton's Comus and the Politics of Masquing', in David Bevington and Peter Holbrook (eds.), *The Politics of the Stuart Court Masque* (Cambridge: Cambridge University Press, 1998), pp. 296–315; Martin Butler, 'The Masque of Blackness and Stuart Court Culture' in Garrett A. Sullivan, Jr, Patrick Cheney, and Andrew Hadfield (eds.), *Early Modern English Drama: A Critical Companion* (Oxford: Oxford University Press, 2006), pp. 152–63; Kate D. Levin, 'Coming of Age on Stage: The Pedagogical Masque in Seventeenth-Century England', *George Herbert Journal* 29 (2005), pp. 114–30.

[17] Norbrook, *Poetry and Politics in the English Renaissance*, p. 252.

[18] Maryann C. McGuire, *Milton's Puritan Masque* (Athens: Univ. of Georgia Press, 1983), p. 131.

[19] Michael Schoenfeldt, *Bodies and Selves in Early Modern England: Physiology and Inwardness in Spenser, Shakespeare, Herbert, and Milton*, p. 166.

in order to embed within his vision of spiritual combat a moral comparison between his personal chaste struggle against authority and pride and the claims to virtue being made through the court's cult of chastity. That is, in Milton's treatment of the masque genre as both performance and printed text, we can see a model for the opposition that would emerge more widely throughout the 1630s and 1640s between the kind of chastity celebrated on stage and at court and that articulated in prose pamphlets and sermons. Scholars have for some decades debated the degree of control Milton had over the two versions of his masque.[20] This chapter is concerned with the different versions of chastity made possible by the two generic forms in themselves and so does not assert that Milton had definitive control over the staging of the masque or the cuts made to the performed text. When it came to the performed masque, the young Milton participated in all the expected forms of collaboration that attended early modern dramatic practice (indeed, he may even have given his script over to Henry Lawes almost entirely). However, as Milton's poetic reputation grew, so did his sense of authority over his self-presentation. By 1645, when the masque text was published as part of Milton's larger corpus, his control over the text's construction was far greater than it had been in the 1630s. The re-inclusion in the 1645 publication of those sections that were omitted from performance can be seen as an editorial decision very much within Milton's authority.

The form of spiritual adventure in which Milton invested tested one's virtue through encounters with authority. For Milton, moral formation took place within the tension between a proper resistance of the worldly, including worldly authority, and the resistance of that effeminate and self-certain pride which rebellion could incite in the spiritual adventurer – precisely that pride which his defensive and self-protecting attack on his University peers produced in himself in the 'Sixth Prolusion'. This reality is evident in both the 1634 Bridgewater Manuscript of the performed masque and its subsequent print version of 1637.[21] However, the first ('A Maske') and the second (*A Maske*) offered both the observers at Ludlow Castle and, a few years later, the readers of the printed version,

---

[20] Ann Baynes Coiro, 'Anonymous Milton, or, A Maske Masked', *ELH* 71 (2004), pp. 609–29; Stephen B. Dobranski, *Milton, Authorship, and the Book Trade* (Cambridge: Cambridge University Press, 1999); Jonathan Goldberg, 'Dating Milton' in Elizabeth D. Harvey and Katherine Eisamann Maus (eds.) *Soliciting Interpretation: Literary Theory and Seventeenth-Century English Poetry* (Chicago: University of Chicago Press, 1990).

[21] S. E. Sprott, *A Masque: The Earlier Versions* (Toronto: University of Toronto Press, 1973); Cedric Brown, *John Milton's Aristocratic Entertainments* (Cambridge: Cambridge University Press, 1985).

two separate visions of moral and spiritual formation, which, though their structure was essentially the same, were nuanced in such a way as to produce differing narratives of chastity and the spiritual fruits gained by those who strive for it. Most of these differences were contingent upon the two mediums' generic requirements: where the printed version is more introspective, descriptively detailed, and requires readers to visualise internally its more finely wrought verbal imagery, the other was realised through spectacle, sense and movement, and spatial positioning: all elements whose precise details at the time of staging we can only speculate over now. Stemming from the two texts' generic conditions are their more meaningful differences. As a depiction of combat between chastity and tyranny, the printed version invited individual readers to enter into a spiritual and moral battle with both their own prideful fallenness and with a form of tyrannical earthly authority that was very broadly defined, a process which clearly identified the individual as an entity separable from a range of earthly authorities. The performed masque, however, was a communal and largely private, celebratory, and aristocratic text in which the Protestant Egerton family were praised for possessing a virtuous form of authority that had not been sullied by the unchaste stain of tyranny. It was thus neither individuating nor critical of earthly authority except in its most corrupted forms.

The difference between the two visions of chaste spiritual combat is exemplified by Comus in State. In 'A Maske', Comus first entered 'with a charming rod in one hand, his glasse in the other, with him a rout of Monsters . . . their apparell glistring'. 'They come in making a riotous and unruly noise, with Torches in their hands' (100). Comus' court, throne, regalia, and entourage amount to a parody of stately power both royal and ecclesial. Although the parody would have been more visually evident in the Ludlow performance than it was to later readers, for whom it was mentioned once in a stage direction and never seen visually, it was ultimately more conservative in performance. Where the printed text invited readers to see in Comus the corruption inherent in all forms of courtliness, in 'A Maske' it is the Protestant Egerton family and the ancient seat of which they have recently taken possession against which Comus' corruption is measured. Rather than embodying the irredeemable perversion at the heart of all courts, Comus was, in performance, merely found wanting as a perversion of that proper courtliness embodied by the Egertons. The printed text instead contains a long passage, presumably omitted from the performance text both because it slowed dramatic pace and was rendered unnecessary by the masque's visual parody of state.

But also because it was only appropriate to the printed text's particular description of spiritual combat. It is the passage in which Comus, compelling the Lady to become his queen, describes the pleasure of court life:

> List, lady; be not coy, and be not cozened
> With that same vaunted name, Virginity.
> Beauty is Nature's coin; must not be hoarded,
> But must be current; and the good thereof
> Consists in mutual and partaken bliss,
> Unsavoury in the enjoyment of itself.
> If you let slip time, like a neglected rose
> It withers on the stalk with languished head.
> Beauty is Nature's brag, and must be shown
> In courts, at feasts, and high solemnities,
> Where most may wonder at the workmanship.
> It is for homely features to keep home;
> They had their name thence: coarse complexions
> And cheeks of sorry grain will serve to ply
> The sampler, and to tease the huswife's wool.
> What need of vermeil-tinctured lip for that,
> Love-darting eyes, or tresses like the morn?
> There was another meaning in these gifts;
> Think what, and be advised; you are but young yet.
> (771–89)

Comus reveals his corruption by allying 'courts and feasts and high solemnities' with fleshly indulgence, dissolute display, prideful beauty, and flirtation. For readers, Comus is the only figure of courtly authority within the text and his arguments could have easily been interpreted as evidence that courtliness in general is corrupted and corrupting. In the performed masque, in which the passage was omitted, Comus did not and could not berate the Lady for failing to display her treasures in courts, feasts, and high solemnities since that is precisely what Alice Egerton was doing. Instead, the courtly dissolution which the Lady must resist was more narrowly defined as the inversion of those truly chaste courtly virtues for which the masque praised her and her family.

In 'A Maske', the battle between chastity and tyranny was largely visual and made innovative use of the early seventeenth-century tradition of chaste throne imagery. I have demonstrated how the capacity for thrones to figure virtuous or venal leadership generated a number of stage and print instances in which pairs or sets of thrones were depicted in comparison: *Novembris Monstrum*'s chaste Elizabethan and unchaste Roman thrones and its triptych of Bacchus', Pan's and Phocas' unchaste thrones;

Penthea's apparently chaste martyr's throne flanked by those of her oppressive and murdering lovers in *The Broken Heart*; even Ford's more subtle evocation of the barber's chair and Throne of State in one single image, which drew on each chair's capacity to cause both chastity and unchastity, sound and broken bodies, true and corrupt leadership. At Ludlow Castle's masque, the opposing thrones were that of Comus, centre-stage, and of Lord and Lady Egerton, for whom the masque was performed. As John Demaray observes, 'Comus and the [Earl of Bridgewater] are the two authority figures in direct opposition. And just as Comus reigns surrounded by his rabble from his palace located at the stage end of the performance space, so too the peer reigns, surrounded on three sides by aristocrats ... from a raised chair at the opposite end of the space'.[22] What Demaray reads as the thrones of Satan and God, I am reading as the thrones of unchastity and chastity.

The virtuous seat of chaste leadership looked across the masquing space at the gross unchastity with which the trappings of courtly life could poison humanity. The Peer inhabited the central viewing position, most like that of the State in a royal masque, where he was praised for maintaining virtue in his household. He and Lady Egerton were the 'Noble Lord and Lady bright' who at the conclusion of the masque received from the Attendant Spirit their 'Three fair branches' who, bearing a 'crown of deathless praise', had 'triumph[ed] in victorious dance / O're sensual folly and intemperance' (925–34). The children's triumph was also a model for the Earl's own triumph over adversity: he 'A noble peer of mickle trust and power / Has in his charge, with temper'd awe to guide / An old and haughty nation proud in Arms' (54–6). The 'sober' Castlehaven family were neither the 'lewdly-pampered' gluttons and 'mincing dryades' of a dissolute court nor the 'unlettered hinds' over whom they had come to govern. Instead, they were an example of 'moderate', 'holy', and 'goodly' courtly values exercised with due humility, moral and intellectual sophistication, and chastity (736;740;922;205;739;737;927).

By balancing Comus with the Throne of the peer, 'A Maske' followed the royal form of the genre, in which the Throne of State overpowers the threat posed by the anti-masque. However, although Milton's depiction of Comus as a dissolute anti-masque was in keeping with the demands of the royal genre, building his vision of unchastity from an inverse use of the props of state was not. Two Jacobean court masques incorporated a second

---

[22] John G. Demaray, 'The Thrones of Satan and God: Backgrounds to Divine Opposition in *Paradise Lost*', in *The Huntington Library Quarterly* 31 (1967), pp. 21–33, 26.

throne but neither were constructed as moral oppositions to the Throne of State. The Throne of Beauty in Jonson's *The Maske of Beauty* (1608) was universally held to be a 'miracle' of engineering. Surrounded by cupids and spinning in a series of directions so that it produced sparks of light like a cut jewel, the throne was a brilliant tribute to Anne of Denmark's crucial place in the 'motion of the world'.[23] In Daniel's *Tethys Festival* (1610), the throne on stage spun in a watery world of bare-breasted nymphs: it was a tribute to Anne's rule 'within the large extent / of [Tethys'] waves and watery government'.[24] Both of these second thrones reflected the Throne of State rather than opposing it. In the Caroline masques of the 1630s, no stage throne rivals the power and virtue of the Throne of State, though in Townshend's *Tempe Restored* (1631), Circe momentarily sits in State to observe the anti-masque before departing when the vale of Tempe returns to the court and the sovereignty of Divine Beauty and Heroic Virtue (the monarchs) is once again asserted. Milton not only introduced a second throne into his masque, he made the competition between the two central to the masque's moral and dramatic combat. During the final dances, the Lady would have moved 'between the opposite centers of power of Comus and the peer'.[25] From the moment Comus entered with his diabolical props of state to the Lady's final movement from Comus' corrupt throne to the virtuous seat of her Father, Milton's splitting of the centre of authority into two polarised positions invited comparisons between the Egertons and the most corrupt form of courtliness, thereby complimenting the Egertons on their more rigorous and more temperate realisation of stately virtue.

Even more than in his mother's masques, the Throne of State in Charles' royal performances was crucial to the action; it was the state that, though static and emblematic, enacted the masque's triumph over the anti-masque. The Throne played a central role visually and ideologically: its power was asserted through its ability to subdue evil and resistance without actually participating in the action. Further, in the Caroline masque, the Throne of State symbolically and actually contained and was co-terminous with the royal body: it was the seat of married chastity from which radiated the Crown's sanctity, authority, and virtue. In Milton's masque, the function of the throne is exactly the opposite: it ensnares the Lady's chastity. In demonstrating the capacity for the throne to embody such

---

[23] See Tomlinson, *Women on Stage*, p. 29.   [24] David Lindley, *Court Masques*, p. 59, line 208–9.
[25] Demaray, 'The Thrones of Satan and God', p. 27.

an opposing moral function as that claimed for the throne at court, Milton in one sense agrees with the royal masque's assertion that the throne and the body are co-terminous. A number of critics have posed the question of whether the 'gums of gluttenous heat' (867) are produced by the Throne or by the Lady.[26] The answer is: both. Just as in court masques the chaste throne embodies the chaste monarch, so in the Lady's trial, the unchaste throne embodies the – momentarily – unchaste body. In the Caroline masque, the virtue of the monarchs and the divinity of the throne are co-determining, the one fitting naturally and constantly to the other. In Milton's masque, even the most chaste maiden's body can be altered when entrapped by an unchaste throne. And, presumably, the opposite is true: the chaste Egerton throne would be corrupted if Comus were to take it from them. Importantly, Milton's masque relocates the seat of the virtues away from the Throne and places it instead in the heart and will of Alice Egerton, and by extension, that of her family. When the 'freedom' of the Lady's 'mind' is cast as the true seat of chastity, the physical throne is left to signify those unchaste appetites by which the 'corporal rind' is 'immanacled' but which the virtuous adventurer, learning self-mastery, can overcome (665–8).

Trapped within Comus' throne, the Lady is tempted by those delights offered at court. By resisting them, she demonstrates that those in the audience who are associated with her through social and familial ties have a more nuanced understanding of chastity's moral requirements. Through the Lady's resistance, the masque complemented the whole company by the implicit comparison between themselves and those who participate in the monarchs' masques of chastity at court without understanding the true moral demands of the virtue. The Egertons were no strangers at court, and their children knew court masquing well, having performed in *Tempe Restored* (1632) and *Coelum Britannicum* (1634). Where the court masques asserted that the monarchs' authoritative chastity radiated easily from their persons, reforming and sanctifying all their subjects, Milton's masque instead depicts real chastity as a difficult but crucial moral struggle fought only by those individuals who are called 'by due steps to aspire / To lay their just hands on that golden key / That opes the palace of eternity' (37).

---

[26] William Shullenberger, 'Milton's Lady and Lady Milton: Chastity, Prophecy and Gender in *A Maske Presented at Ludlow Castle*', in Claude J. Summers (ed.), *Fault Lines and Controversies in the Study of Seventeenth-Century English Literature* (Columbia: University of Missouri Press, 2002); Debora Shuger, '"Gums of Glutinous Heat"and the Stream of Consciousness: The Theology of Milton's Maske', *Representations* 60 (1997), pp. 1–21. See also Catherine Gimelli-Martin (ed.), *Milton and Gender* (Cambridge: Cambridge University Press, 2004).

The Egertons and their guests are, like Milton, able to participate in the joy of the royal genre without being drawn into the trap of believing, as Comus does, that chastity is a wasteful storing up of sensual goods, or, as the court masques could be construed as arguing, that chastity is merely a facet of Henrietta Maria's beauty. However, by staging the reformation of sensual, courtly pleasures through the redirection of them away from the self and towards the glorification of God, Milton's masque in fact makes the same claim as *The Temple of Love*. It is in the manner by which the arts and sensual pleasures are reformed that the two performances and their attendant political and religious outlooks differ. Henrietta Maria's masque reformed courtly arts through chastity by making them more Catholic in tone: confining their enjoyment to strictly chastened hetero-social relations, celebrating their place within community and Marian worship, and bending them to beautified devotions and a lavish glorification of God. Milton's masque, however, chastened courtly arts through the Lady's personal struggle to make the best use of her talents and to resist the lure of tyrannical ambition, venal pleasure, excessive and effeminate display, and, most importantly, the supreme and most effeminating sin: pride.

Most fundamental to the rhetoric of anti-court controversialists' depiction of unchaste thrones was the fearful warning against the tyranny of princes, whose pride, running to unchaste excess, infected the Throne of State. In parliamentary justifications of regicide, to which Milton would become a key contributor, this argument later proved very valuable. Charles' opponents often claimed that they sought to protect the purity of the Crown against the King's personal weaknesses, his unjust neglect of Parliament, his erroneous perception of his own power, and his failure to stay faithful to his contracts. In Milton's masque, the Lady is tempted towards just such an unchaste pride when she is seated in Comus' throne. Comus uses all his courtly 'glozing' to woo the Lady, not just to drink his 'spirits of balm' and become monstrous, but because he wants her to be his queen (161). He is tempting her to tyranny, the kind of tyranny depicted by a corrupt throne, liquified by unchastity, in the works I have explored. While the Lady's brothers are comforting themselves by recalling their sister's likeness to Diana, the 'Fair silver-shafted Queen for ever chaste', the 'queen oth' Woods' (442–6), Comus is trying to convince the Lady to taste his 'treasonous offer' and become the queen of his diabolical court where she could sit in state and live a life of 'soft delicacy' (702, 681). Comus brings to the Egerton's revels 'feasting', 'midnight shout, and revelry,/ Tipsy dance, and jollity'. He calls the Earl's guests to braid their locks with rosy twine 'dropping odours, dropping wine'. He shuns 'Rigour' and

'Advise', 'Strick Age and Severity' (102–9). His dance and call to pleasure are a most attractive invitation to enjoy youthful and seemingly innocent rural pleasures. But the Attendant Spirit has forwarned that his world is in fact a 'brutish', 'miserable', and monstrous 'sensual sty' (70–7). The Lady possesses chastity, the 'golden key / That opes the palace of eternity' (13–14), and is thus able to recognise Comus' 'riot' and 'ill managed merriment' when she hears it, just as the unchaste Comus knows her 'chaste footing' when he hears her approach (172, 146). The unchaste throne into which Comus traps the Lady stands amid the 'stately palace, set out with all manner of deliciousness' (680). Comus seeks to make the Lady his queen by drawing her Into the very seat where 'a king must be adored like a demigod, with a dissolute and haughty court about him, of vast expense and luxury, masques and revels, to the debauching of our prime gentry'.[27]

The masque's anti-court criticisms were not only politically-inflected but can be seen as engaging also with local ecclesiological and theological problems. Milton's depiction of Comus' effeminate court is also a nod to anti-Laudian writing. Milton may have loved beauty and been attentive to due reverence but he was careful to delineate the beauty of chaste, refined speech and 'footing' from that of the self-indulgent physical display to which court masquing and high-Church ceremony were both at risk of descending. Blair Hoxby notes that 'in his stately palace, Comus is Cavalier poet, a reveling courtier and a Laudian prelate supervising a morris dance'.[28] That the unchaste throne in which the Lady is trapped is also a bishop's chair, and that she must resist the lure of Comus' erroneous worship, is evidenced not only by the fact that the Lady is offered a 'charmed' and 'banefull cup' but because she intuits immediately that Comus and his rabble 'thank the gods amiss' (74;528;208). They are 'loose' and 'unlettered' country rioters who, with 'swill'd insolence' indulge in the 'ill-managed merriment' endorsed by the Book of Sports, but their dance is also noted for its 'duck' and 'nod': two terms whose pejorative use were becoming routine in anti-Laudian caricature of gestural worship (205;209;203;918).

Milton's criticism of the court in the performed masque was subtle but nonetheless took issue with the kind of chastity being celebrated by the Caroline cult. His redefinition of chastity in the performed masque was in

---

[27] *The Ready and Easy Way*, CPW 7:360.
[28] Blair Hoxby, 'The Wisdom of Their Feet: Meaningful Dance in Milton and the Stuart Masque, *ELR* (2007), pp. 74–99, 89.

line with both his own developing ideas of chastity and that view of the virtue possibly also held by the Protestant Egertons. But the performed masque was still very much in keeping with the form: 'A Maske' celebrated the family's virtue and delighted in the pleasure and spectacle fitting for the occasion. It was in the printed version of the masque that Milton was able to explore more fully that oppositional model of the virtue being increasingly espoused by court critics in prose pamphlets and sermons. In the printed *A Maske*, Milton drew the line between chastity and tyranny quite differently than in the Bridgewater Manuscript. In the omitted speech, quoted earlier, Comus argues that chastity is a storing up of those goods that should properly be shared, a point he makes through various figures: the hoarding of coin, the unseen beauty, the unplucked rose, flesh that has not known 'mutual' 'bliss'. His position is a fitting one for the Lady to put her opposing argument, drawn from the 'Sixth Prolusion' and 'How Soon Hath Time', that chastity is instead productive, a rendering of the self's best qualities through moral, spiritual, and intellectual effort. Just as he did in his 'Sixth Prolusion', Milton describes chastity as a denial of fleshly pleasure and ambition, and the cultivation of the self's best qualities in order to dedicate their fruits to God. With only one throne to resist in the printed version of the masque, the individuating cultivation of the self Milton offered his readers was played out in their own intellectual resistance to an authority defined very generally.

Where in *The Temple of Love* it is the Throne of State that affects the reformation of dissolute appetites and directs its subjects to God, in Milton's masque, the throne is a trap, as capable of liquid contamination, of watery unchastity, as were those depicted by so many critics of the court. In his printed text, Milton presents a single throne as the unchaste site of moral and spiritual trial. In so doing, he locates the chaste throne at once in heaven and in each human heart. Milton achieves this displacement of chastity away from the royal throne in the very first lines of the masque. The Attendant Spirit introduces the occasion by referring to Jove's court, whose majesty is unmatched and which is the only true source of power and virtue (1–37), from which the world's 'several government[s]' are allowed by God's grace alone to wield their 'little tridents' (48, 50). No masque throne, Milton announces, can match the throne in heaven. He then goes on to emphasise that a throne more chaste than any royal throne can be found in each of his readers: those who by their 'due steps' (or as Milton put it in 'How Soon Hath Time', 'strict measure') prove that they are mindful of the 'crown that virtue gives' are numbered 'amongst the enthroned gods on sainted seats' (32–4). This displacement of chastity from the courtly throne onto both God's heavenly throne and the thrones in each human heart was present also for the performed masque but its significance would have been hugely overshadowed by the visual feat that pitted the Egerton throne against Comus' seat of courtly corruption. In *A Maske*, the Lady no longer signifies her family's virtue but rather embodies the individual spiritual combat to which each reader is invited to participate.

Made up of words on the page, Milton's printed text also emphasises the degree to which his heroine discredits the genre's sensual delights in favour of individual self-articulation. *A Maske* describes the individuating acquisition of chastity as that denial of authority which makes supreme use of the medium to which Milton's prodigious talent disposed him: language, the same talent by which he differentiated himself from his unchaste University peers in the 'Sixth Prolusion'. This emphasis is particularly strong in the printed version of the masque, not only because it lacked the spectacle of the performance but because it contained the passage, omitted from the performance text, in which the Lady denounces Comus' 'words' while vehemently asserting the chastity of her own:

>   Shall I go on?
> Or have I said enow? To him that dares
> Arm his profane tongue with contemptuous words
> Against the sun-clad power of chastity
> Fain would I something say;—yet to what end?
> Thou hast nor ear, nor soul, to apprehend
> The sublime notion and high mystery
> That must be uttered to unfold the sage
> And serious doctrine of Virginity;
> And thou art worthy that thou shouldest not know
> More happiness than this thy present lot.
> Enjoy your dear wit, and gay rhetoric,
> That hath so well been taught her dazzling fence;
> Thou art not fit to hear thyself convinced.
> Yet, should I try, the uncontrolled worth
> Of this pure cause would kindle my rapt spirits
> To such a flame of sacred vehemence
> That dumb things would be moved to sympathise,
> And the brute Earth would lend her nerves, and shake,
> Till all thy magic structures, reared so high,
> Were shattered into heaps o'er thy false head.
>   (813–33)

Clearly audible are the echoes of Milton's damning portrayal of his 'effeminate' University peers and his assertion of his own chaste 'virility'.

Comus may possess 'wit' and 'gay rhetoric', where Milton's University audience were 'bungling grammarians', but both are effeminate and morally immature 'brothellers'. In his youth, Milton distinguished himself by comparing his moral refinement and exceptional articulacy to the brute strength of his oppressors, re-coding feminine refinement and the correct dedication of cultivated language and reason to God as properly masculine and chaste. In *A Maske*, the Lady compares the 'sage' and 'serious doctrine' of her 'pure', 'sun-clad' chastity and the 'high mystery' and 'sacred vehemence' of her language to Comus' sensual indulgence, profanities, and his 'magic structures' which, though 'dazzling', are merely a 'false' veneer which with one word from her will shatter and fall from their great heights. In both the Lady's speech and Milton's 'Sixth Prolusion', the triumphant qualities of chastity are the same, but by the mid-1630s, the unchaste and effeminate opposition is no longer a 'prize fighter' but a courtly dissolute.

One of the remarkable qualities of the speech above, and one which has attracted significant attention from those recent scholars interested in revising the long-standing view of Milton's anti-feminism, is the tremendous rhetorical power of the Lady's self-assertion.[29] What I am about to propose complicates this crucial observation but does not contradict it. One of the speech's most important functions was only relevant to the printed *A Maske*, to its particular description of spiritual combat, and was arguably to this end added by Milton just before 1637. The passage is absent from both the Trinity Manuscript (Milton's early notes) and the Bridgewater manuscript, so it was most likely not removed prior to performance and then reinserted for print, but was rather added some time between performance and printing, when Milton was consolidating the work for the printed version's particular audience and purpose. I have argued that the challenge for the chaste adventurer in Milton's early work was to resist authority and venal pleasure but not, in the process, to fall into pride. In the 'Shall I go on?' speech, the Lady's bold assertion of her chastity contains within it the hint of excessive self-certainty, which is at its most explicit when she damns Comus to his evil, declaring that he is not 'worthy' to 'know / More happiness than this thy present lot'. Milton knew very well God's capacity to call sinners back from error and that to think otherwise was to deny God's nature just as Milton himself would have pridefully denied him had he persisted in 'How Soon Hath Time' to

---

[29] See especially the work of William Shullenberger: 'Milton's Lady and Lady Milton'; 'The Profession of Virginity in A Maske Presented at Ludlow Castle', in *Milton and Gender* and *Lady in the Labyrinth* (Associated University Presses, 2008).

wish for the blossom of his talents for his own sake and not for the sake of his 'task master'. The Lady may be trapped and assaulted but her predicament, though lamentable, in no way alters the abiding truth of God's mercy. Her pride, however understandable, remains erroneous. In wishing damnation on her persecutor, the very chastity she seeks to assert slips away from her. By invoking chastity as a violent threat, the Lady may come closer to winning the battle with her adversary (though Comus in fact reacts to her threat with greater physical force) but she loses the more important and more difficult struggle with the self. Where before her Shakespeare's chaste exemplars – Hermione, Imogen, Marina, Isabella, Desdemona – retain, even strengthen, their chastity and their chaste influence on others while defending themselves against assault, the Lady falters by declaring that her assailant is not 'fit to hear [him]self convinced'.

Seated in an unchaste throne and denouncing Comus so definitively, the Lady may in fact play the tyrant. Arguably, it is this momentary fall from virtue that produces the 'gums of gluttenous heat'. If we place the masque's throne within the literary, dramatic, and controversialist tradition of depicting unchaste thrones as watery and fleshly, then the question which has long plagued critics about the nature of the gums can be posed more specifically as: what is the unchastity that causes the throne's material change to take place? Perhaps there is no cause other than Comus himself: his chair is unchaste before the Lady is trapped within it and she is merely tainted by his tyranny, erroneous worship and gluttony. While this conclusion might suit the celebratory occasion of the performed masque, it is out of keeping with Milton's treatment of chastity throughout his writing, since it does not grant the Lady any internal transformation but merely the retention of the chastity she already possessed before her trial. Instead, the Lady, like Milton himself in his earlier work and like Adam and Eve in *Paradise Lost*, actually falls, momentarily, into the greatest of errors. Pride is, after all, the error which the unchaste and 'clotted' throne embodies most often in the tradition detailed in previous chapters. The Lady falls into pride by wishing to see Comus and his rabble remain perpetually in their sensual sty, by believing them beyond redemption. When finally able to assert his superiority over his persecutors in the 'Sixth Prolusion', Milton himself sank into pride and was only checked by a humility which, in its immaturity, remained a veiled attack: 'I have no ambition to lord it'.

By the 1630s, Milton's greater maturity can be detected in the seriousness with which he treats the Lady's error. Her own slip into tyranny renders her more spiritually vulnerable than she is physically vulnerable to

Comus' threatened violence. This is perhaps a novel recasting of the Classical heroines' belief in death-before-unchastity. For Milton's Lady, pride is a crime as unchaste, even more unchaste, than physical despoliation. Milton makes clear that, so morally weakened, the Lady must rely on God's grace. Having been marked by the same fleshly matter that marked so many unchaste thrones in the literary depictions of tyrants, the Lady is rescued from her pride, her 'gums', by the grace of God (in the form of Sabrina and the Attendant Spirit) and by her loyal brothers, inadequate though they are in their assault on Comus. That she, like all chaste adventurers, needs God's grace for spiritual combat is also made clear when she specifically calls on the theological virtues to assist her, among which Milton places chastity. The Lady's vivid vision of the personified virtues and the desert of sin from which they can protect her is the second extended passage not included in the performance text and thus of particular relevance to Milton's individual readers. The Lady calls upon her own conscience and the three virtues in order to protect her against the 'thousand fantasies' which 'throng' her memory 'of calling shapes, and beckning shadows dire, / And ayrie tongues, that syllable mens names / On Sands, and Shoars, and desert Wildernesses' (220–35). The sin against which Jesus struggled in the desert was pride. It is, above all others, the sin that would 'syllable mens names', calling them to seek the inordinate power by which they might denounce their opponents and ensure their own names are immortalised by fame.

In performance, 'A Maske' was only able to emphasise the importance of avoiding pride through its subtle distinction between two thrones and their respective approaches to and uses of courtly values, thus complementing the Egertons on their virtuous avoidance of courtly dissolution. In this context, the Lady's 'Shall I go on?' speech, and the pride it exemplifies, would have been unnecessary and counter-productive. Milton did not want to warn the Egertons against damning the errors of courtly dissolution because his masque subtly invited them to do just that. In *A Maske*, the battle against pride takes place within each reader where, because the capacity for disdain is far greater in the individual human heart than it is in the communal identity of a stately family, the struggle is more complex and demanding. In Milton's view, the individual heart is also therefore the site of the greatest salvation since it is where the most truthful and difficult battle is played out, a battle least compromised by the demands of compliment and occasion. In *A Maske*, no second throne is required to define the trial of chastity and Milton can emphasise more clearly what was for him the true spiritual hierarchy: one that incorporated God's throne in heaven and the many thrones in each heart or 'mind'. To depict *A Maske*'s theology of sin, only one Throne of State was required and its sole function was to embody those forces of earthly unchastity and ungodly self-reliance that each man must resist as he walks on his own path away from effeminacy and towards his 'sainted seat'.

How did Milton respond to the two versions of his masque? Did he think that the sponsored performance, however brilliantly it launched his reputation, compromised that vision which he sought to re-articulate in *A Maske*? Perhaps the epigraph which Milton attached to the 1637 *A Maske* is useful here. It is taken from Virgil's second Eclogue: 'Eheu quid volui misero mihi! floribus austrum / Perditus' ('Alas! what have I done to my miserable self? I have let the south wind ruin my flowers'). John Shawcross reads the epigraph as part of Milton's relationship with Diodati, an argument to which the Second Eclogue as a whole does lend itself.[30] But what if the flowers, gathered lovingly by Corydon, are the buds and blossoms of which Milton speaks in 'How Soon Hath Time', and the stormy south wind the compromising occasion of an aristocratic masque? Milton's first high-profile commission posed a very similar problem as did the requirements of the 'Sixth Prolusion': in both, his chance to take his place in the world of reputation depended on his writing in the genre so enjoyed by those figures whom he at once wanted to be approved by and wanted to denounce. In this context, it is worth considering whether the epigraph signified Milton's anxieties that, by allowing the flowers of his poetic flourishing to be spread on the rough winds of a genre so associated with values of which he was suspicious, he had brought about their ruin. The epigraph could merely be in keeping with the conventions of gentlemanly authorial disownment, in which Milton and Lewes fully participate throughout the prologue to the 1637 edition. If so, the south wind that ruined Milton's work is merely the printing press and the public eye. But the prologue surely sufficiently fulfils the convention, leaving Milton's epigraph to pursue the point rather fastidiously.

If we instead read the reference to Corydon's flowers, wasted on an uninterested Alexis, as a figure for Milton's offering of his 'blossoms' to his sponsors, then the epigraph becomes an announcement to those readers of the 1637 edition capable of so interpreting it that the real fruits of his work have been ruined by the demands of the occasion. In its acknowledgement that true chastity, which requires a rigorous individuating anatomy of

---

[30] John Shawcross, *John Milton: The Self and the World* (Lexington: University Press of Kentucky, 1993), p. 55.

pride, could not be realised in the Egerton celebration, *A Maske* is also therefore a very subtle criticism of the occasion for which 'A Maske' was written and, to a certain extent, of 'A Maske' itself. However, the printed masque's humble and self-accusatory acknowledgment of the human tendency to pride, most rigorous in its 'Shall I go on?' speech and its invocation of the divine virtues, is conversely part of the text's claims to moral superiority. *A Maske*'s individual chaste adventurer is not only morally ascendent over the masques at court (which do not make any such acknowledgment of failure on the part of their royal chaste exemplars) but even over the Egerton masque, which could not assert as firmly as Milton would have liked the lure of unchaste pride – an error which threatens the spiritual adventurer even, especially, when they are defending themselves against unchaste assault.

With *A Maske*, Milton announced the moral sophistication of the poet, his ability to pursue chastity through the resistance of worldly authority but, crucially, his ability also to resist his own tendency to that effeminate pride which most asserted itself when questioning authority. When we compare 'A Maske' and *A Maske*, we see that Milton in fact sets up three visions of chastity. The first is that of Comus, who cannot see his own tyranny and effeminate dissolution, who believes the best and most true use of the self and the world's resources is to indulge in them as much as one can so as not to waste them and make bastards of nature's children. In 'A Maske', the Egerton family are celebrated for their ability to possess a temperate worldly authority without slipping into Comus' errors. Through its performance, the family can witness themselves as masquers able to enjoy the pleasures of dance, music, banqueting, and display with proper restraint and an understanding of chastity more developed than that of Comus and the supporters of the cult of chastity. But in *A Maske*, Milton offers a vision of the chaste individual, whose virtue is modelled on his own life and spiritual combat, which, while it is clearly superior to that of Comus, is also subtly shown to be superior to that of the Egerton family. The chaste poet can interrogate his own internal unchaste impulses more thoroughly than is possible in the public mediums through which figures of authority are identified and complimented. Indeed, *A Maske* narrates the individuating processes of a poetry that is identified against those communal celebrations in which a too-rigorous self-criticism would be impossible. This does not, however, mean that Milton was openly criticising the Egertons or, indeed, that he was in any way celebrating the common man. Each of his three visions of chastity applauds courtly virtue but he is careful to locate the individual as the site in which courtly virtues can best flower. Where the Egertons realised chastity more fully and properly than Comus, Milton himself realised it more fully and properly than the Egertons.

How can Milton's reworking of chastity be understood as responding not just to the vision of the virtue offered in the Caroline masques but to the seventeenth-century tradition of chastity which I have been detailing? Does his masque respond to the vision of chastity laid out in Shakespearean tragicomedy? While Milton scholars have looked to Spenser as one source of *A Maske*'s chastity, certain elements of the masque do reveal that Milton was also thinking about Shakespeare, or at least those aspects of his tragicomedies which formed the basis of the Caroline cult of chastity. *The Winter's Tale*'s statue scene enacted an affective experience of wonder coded feminine and built from the apprehension of Marian acts of chaste creation – Paulina's creation of the statue itself, Hermione's 'begetting' of the holy spirit in her reanimation. This presentation of statuesque wonder and female fertility as the realisation of chastity went on to inform the culture of Caroline masquing, in which all participants joined in the celebration of the monarchs' triumphant tableaux of chaste fertility. The relative chastity of statuesque wonder and female fertility are subjects which Milton's masque also treats. In a significant departure from the wondrous statuary in the final tableaux of both *The Winter's Tale* and Caroline masques, Milton makes the Lady's enrapture 'in stony fetters fixt and motionless' the very means by which Comus ensnares her in his unchaste throne, her 'nerves' 'chain'd up in alabaster' until she is 'a statue' (856–9). The Lady only discovers her true chastity, spiritual bliss, and fertility when she is released from the statuesque. Where in *The Winter's Tale*, statuesque and affective wonder are the product of chastity as a spiritual and emotional reunion and regeneration built from images of female fertility, Milton's masque sees the Lady's transfixion as anathema to the fertility of chaste spiritual bliss promised to her at the conclusion of the masque. Crucially, her future fertility is only celebrated in the 1637 printed version of the masque and is omitted from the performed version. It is tempting to read a certain defiance in this: the fertility of spiritual bliss is something for the individualised moral combatant, not for the family of masquers to whom the promise of a secure future bloodline would seem more conventionally appropriate.

Milton's celebration of the Lady's fertility with reference to Cupid and Psyche in the printed version is further evidence of the 1637 masque's more pointed criticism of court taste than the 1634 performance. In her triumph against unchaste effeminacy, the Lady at the conclusion of the printed masque embodies the union of Cupid and Psyche, from whose 'eternal' and 'unspotted' love, youth, and joy are born (1054–61). David Norbrook notes that the Psyche and Cupid myth was a conventional allegory for the union of the soul with heavenly love. Popular at the Caroline court as one more sign of mystical union which could be mapped onto the monarchs' marriage, the allegory also, Norbrook argues, had apocalyptic associations 'to which Milton delicately pointed'. For Calvinists, Psyche had become a symbol of the true, visible Church, wandering in the wilderness, as the Lady 'wand[ers] in labours long' (1056). Against the Court's depictions of Henrietta Maria as the embodiment of the true temple, Milton's masque posits the Lady as the truly chaste Church undergoing trial in obscurity. Milton's argument to readers of his masque that the Lady is finally reunited with Cupid is, Norbrook argues, a sign that through their trial and wandering, the souls of the godly are united with Christ. This image of blissful spiritual union is a direct rejection of those heavenly unions celebrated in court masques. 'The traditional epithalamic imagery with which Milton celebrated the union was', Norbrook notes, 'a repudiation of asceticism'. Importantly, Norbrook reads the masque's final union as a celebration of spiritual bliss between the elect and God that is not only marital but which strongly implies 'sexual joy, and the joy of poetic composition'.[31] The manly struggle with pride which I have been detailing is in the printed masque the source of spiritual and poetic fertility. It is distinctly un-Marian and unassociated with monastic chastity or a devotion built from statuesque wonder. Despite the marital and sexual tone of Milton's depiction of spiritual bliss, references to female biological creation and the piety of monasticism – both cornerstones of the Caroline cult of chastity – are distinctly absent from his masque's vision of the sanctity produced by chastity.

In another quibble over the definition of chaste 'wandering' and trial, Milton elsewhere took issue with the association between devotion and acts of female, biological creation and his views can be taken as further evidence of his rejection of the vision of chastity first articulated in *The Winter's Tale*. Those who preferred plain religion objected to the view of childbirth as a trial, and to the ceremony of churching in particular, on the grounds of its ritualism and superstition, but also its irreverence. In his *Apology for Smectymnuus* (1642) Milton scoffed at the churching of women on the basis that the ceremony was built around the reading of Psalm 121, which promises that God will deliver the Jewish people as they come out of

---

[31] Norbrook, *Poetry and Politics*, pp. 251–2.

the wilderness and into Canaan. He rejected the suggestion that the labouring woman had 'been travailing not in her bed but in the deserts of arabia'.[32] The reference to a bed here is telling. Since early modern births more commonly took place on or against a chair, Milton's reference to a mother's travails in her bed evokes the sexual act rather than labour. We have seen how the two acts were fundamentally linked in early modern thinking on sexuality and childbirth, but Milton's desire to rescue God's people from their association in the churching ritual with the trials of biological birth is best fulfilled by elevating the one and diminishing the other. He therefore removed childbirth from the litany of genuine Christian trials by suggesting that it is too unchaste to be included.

Milton is careful to claim for his version of masculine, intellectual and individuating moral combat the fruits of spiritual union and poetic 'issue', while rejecting those elements so central to the Caroline cult of chastity and its vision of spiritual bliss: the processes of biological and female fertility, asceticism, and the pious, collective, and affective celebration of statuesque tableaux. Milton's assertion of his own version of chastity over that celebrated at court was subtle in his masque but it would grow more robust as his career progressed. Equally, his re-coding of chastity within the more individualised processes of manuscript reading was a crucial step on the way towards his co-religionists' definitive rejection of tragicomedy with the closure of the theatres.

---

[32] Keith Thomas, *Religion and the Decline of Magic*, p. 68; *CPW*, I: 939.

Conclusion

For some decades, scholars have recognised how crucial Elizabeth I's chastity was to her political moment and the degree to which her embodiment of the virtue grew out of and exploited the literary tropes of Petrarchism and romance. To a large extent, the great flowering of English literature under Elizabeth I can be attributed to her willingness to cast herself as Petrarch's Laura, withholding money and titles, and to keep her literary courtiers in competition with each other for her favour. The capacity for chastity to function at the intersection of politics and literature should therefore come as no surprise to us. This book has argued that it is in fact the first decades of the seventeenth century that offer the greatest and most problematic moment for our understanding of early modern chastity as a phenomenon at once moral, political, cultural, and textual.

In the decades following Elizabeth I's death, pamphlets concerned with defining the nature of the emerging Protestant nation and its conception of the visible Church relied heavily on what were clearly very affecting images of breached nuptial bonds between individuals and Christ, individuals and the Church, England and Christ, Christ and the King, or Christ and the true Church. In its anxiety to distinguish between the true Church as the chaste bride of Christ and the Roman Church as the Whore of Babylon, this body of writing tells us much about how early moderns thought about and feared institutional schism – even while, perhaps especially while, they were in the process of bringing it about. By making full use of the image of unchastity as a breached vessel, all sides in the debate over the nature of the visible Church accused their opponents of reducing the Crown, Church, and Christ to broken bodies whose precious fluids mingled erroneously.

The early modern vision of institutional bodies bound together in nuptial bonds whose chastity needed to be protected did not stop at discussions of the visible Church. It was also a favourite in arguments about the relationship between the Crown, Parliament, and people, and it was in this context that memorialising Elizabeth's virginity became particularly useful. In the 1630s and 1640s, Elizabeth was held up by Parliamentarians as an example of a monarch whose desire for Church reform was only surpassed in merit by her ability to marry herself to both her Parliament and her people. Where to many, Charles' chaste relationship with his Parliament or people was compromised by his marriage to a foreign Catholic and his allegiance to Popish bishops, Elizabeth's chastity was remembered as certain and complete. Elizabethan images of the Virgin Queen's body as a sound container were recalled by Parliamentarians and, combined with humoral imagery, used to argue that a monarch in loving chaste union with her Parliament was a chaste vessel for the nation's blood or a 'true gate' that could both shut out unwanted influences from abroad and open up the flow of grace between heaven and earth.

This nostalgic and inward-looking view of chastity as something that can be deployed in the service of policing boundaries is a version of the virtue that Shakespeare gives to Leontes. But *The Winter's Tale* ultimately demands that Leontes be reformed from such a limited and self-protecting view of chastity. In this, the play's vision of chastity is in many ways in keeping with the Caroline cult of chastity that would emerge in the 1620s. Henrietta Maria brought with her from France a strong tradition of courtly chaste imagery which she and Charles confidently deployed throughout their reign in order to assert the sanctity, and sanctifying influence, of their marriage and the new court culture that surrounded it. Presenting Henrietta Maria as a saint or monarch of chastity, court performances argued that the Queen's influence on the King and his subjects was beneficent and reforming. The proto-Catholic taste for chastity in the piety and artistic culture of Henrietta Maria's supporters in the 1630s was informed by St Francois de Sales' Counter-Reformation spirituality and markedly feminine in its passion for devotions to the mother of God and its aesthetic and spiritual investment in women who took vows of chastity or who identified closely with the virtue. The dramatic genres most associated with this courtly and feminised attitude in the 1630s were the royal masque and tragicomedy, not simply because their tone matched the personal style of Henrietta Maria and the Salesian devotional temperament she introduced at court but because both actual issue and psychological and social rebirth were central to the genre in ways that feminised the chaste and providential workings of God.

In his own masque, Milton re-imagined the courtly genre's vision of the divine will and its language of issue in order to re-gender chastity as masculine, while arguing for a Protestant and individualist pursuit of virtue that was at once a spiritual combat and a political rebellion.

Milton's response to the changing religious and cultural landscape of the 1630s reveals his anxiety over the court's Laudian and Catholic appropriation of chastity's rhetorical force and its monopoly, within both its favoured devotional practices and its dramatic performances, on feminised descriptions of the divine will. He was not alone in this: the pro-Parliamentarian and Puritan writers whose pamphlets and sermons this book has treated were all concerned with the court's vision of cultural and spiritual reform. They made full use of their chosen genre's capacity to arraign and attack and to identify and speak to the individual souls of readers and listeners. In this way, the prose pamphlet worked against the communal vision of tragicomedy and masque. Those working in the genre often exploited its implicit individualism by using it to re-interpret the court's inclusive, pietised and feminine version of chastity as a sullying or prostituting of the Church and nation.

This competition between opposing genres is one that is best illustrated through the corpus of Milton since throughout his career he worked in almost every form available to him. When Milton re-gendered chastity in his 1634 masque, he channelled the genre's images of fertility and rebirth into his argument for the development of an individualised, politicised, and masculine chastity that could valiantly resist the effeminate and courtly culture of chastity in which Marian devotions and Salesian piety flourished. Milton knew that by laying claim to chastity and controlling its definition and interpretation, the battle for political influence could be won: by the 1630s, chastity had become a key conceptual site on which the revolutionary linguistic, political, devotional, and aesthetic shifts which propelled the Reformation were played out.

By the 1640s, chastity had become a virtue so central to distinctions between virtue and vice, between the saved and the damned, that the language and imagery associated with it was one of the most prevalent and affective forms of argumentation throughout the pamphlet wars. By mapping out the importance of chastity from the death of Elizabeth I to the beheading of Charles I, this book has sought to reveal how the same virtue that could protect the body from infection and a marriage from dissolution could eventually help to topple a government and undo a King.

Bibliography

Primary texts

Abbott, George. *An exposition vpon the prophet Ionah Contained in certaine sermons, preached in S. Maries church in Oxford.* London, 1600.

Abbot, Robert. *A triall of our church-forsakers. Or A meditation tending to still the passions of unquiet Brownists* . . . London, 1639.

Adams, Thomas. *Englands sicknes, comparatively conferred with Israels diuided into two sermons* . . . London, 1615.

The happiness of the Church: or a description of those spiritual prerogatives wherewith Christ hath endowed her . . . London, 1619.

Ainsworth, Henry. *An animadversion to Mr Richard Clyftons advertisement* . . . London, 1613.

Covnterpoyson considerations touching the poynts in difference between the godly ministers and people of the Church of England, and the seduced brethren of the separation . . . London, 1642.

Almond, Oliver. *The vncasing of heresie, or, The anatomie of protestancie* . . . London, 1623.

Andrewes, Lancelot. *Sermons by the Right Honorable and Reverend Father in God, Lancelot Andrewes, late Lord Bishop of Winchester. Published by His Majesties speciall command.* London, 1629.

Anonymous. *Novembris Monstrum.* London, 1641.

The great eclipse of the sun, or Charles his waine over-clouded. London, 1644.

The most strange and wonderful apparition. London, 1645.

The Scots Scouts discoveries. London, 1642.

Lachrymae Londinenses: or, Londons lamentations and teares for Gods heauie visitation of the plague of pestilence . . . London, 1626.

Bacon, Nathaniel. *The continuation of an historicall discourse of the Government of England.* London, 1650.

Baillie, Robert. *A dissuasive from the errours of the time wherein the tenets of the principall sects* . . . London, 1645.

Bastwicke, John. *The Letany of John Bastwicke.* Leiden, 1637.

Baxter, Richard. *The saints everlasting rest, or, A treatise of the blessed state of the saints in their enjoyment of God in glory* . . . London, 1650.

Bell, Thomas. *The Catholique triumph conteyning, a reply to the pretensed answere of B.C. (a masked Iesuite,), lately published against the Tryall of the New Religion* ... London, 1610.
Birch, Thomas et al. *The court and times of Charles I*. London: Henry Colburn, 1848.
Bourgeois, Louise. *Observations diverses sur la stérilité, perte de fruict, foecundité, accouchements, maladies des femmes et des enfantss nouveaux niz*. Paris, 1617.
Bradshaw, Ellis. *An husbandmans harrow to pull down the ridges of the presbyteriall government and to smooth, a little, the independent ... containing divers new and unanswerable arguments* ... London, 1649.
Brinsley, John. *The araignment of the present schism of new separation in old England. Together with a serious recommendation of church-unity and uniformity* ... London, 1646.
Burgess, Cornelius. *A sermon preached to the honourable house of commons* ... London, 1641.
Burton, Henry. *Conformitie's deformity*. London, 1646.
Burton, Robert. *Anatomy of melancholy*. London, 1621.
Carew, Thomas. *The Poems of Thomas Carew and his Masque Coelum Britannicum* edited by Rhodes Dunlap. Oxford: Clarendon Press, 1964.
Charles I. *His Majesties answer to the petition which accompanied the Declaration of the House of Commons*. London, 1641.
   His Majesties declaration to all his loving subjects. London, 1641.
Cosin, John. *A collection of private devotions: in the practice of the ancient church*. London, 1627.
Cowley, Abraham. *Verses, written upon several occasions*. London, 1663.
Davenant, William. *The Dramatic Works of Sir William D'avenant*. 5 Vols. edited by J. Maidment and W.H. Logan. New York: Russell and Russell, 1872.
Davies, John. *Nosce teipsum this oracle expounded in two elegies, 1. Of humane knowledge, 2. Of the soule of man, and the immortalitie thereof*. London, 1599.
de Sales, Francois. *A Treatise of the Love of God*. London, 1630.
   Introduction to a Devout Life translated by Michael Day. London: J. M. Dent & Sons, 1961.
Dunlop, Rhodes (ed.). *The Poems of Thomas Carew and his Masque Coelum Britannicum*. Oxford: Clarendon Press, 1964.
Fletcher, John. *The Faithful Shepherdess*, 1609.
Ford, John. *The Broken Heart* edited by T.J.B. Spencer. Manchester: Manchester University Press, 1980.
   The Nondramatic Works of John Ford edited by Judith M. Kennedy et al. New York: Center for Medieval and Renaissance Studies, 1991.
   Tis Pity She's a Whore and Other Plays edited by Marion Lomax. Oxford: Oxford University Press, 1995.
Gilbert, William. *On the Magnet*. London, 1600.
Guarani, Giovanni Battista. *Il Pastor Fido, Tragicommedia Pastorale ... con un compendio di poesia*. Venice, 1602.
Guillemeau, Jacques. *The Happy Delivery of Women*. London, 1612.
   The Nursing of Children. London, 1612.

Halle, J. *An Historicall Expostulation*. London: Percy Society, 1844.
Harvey, William. *De Motu Cordis. In The Anatomical Exercises of Dr. William Harvey*. Ed. G. Keynes ed. London: The Nonesuch Press, 1928.
The Anatomical Lectures of William Harvey. Prelectiones anatomie universalis. De musculis edited and translated by Gweneth Whitteridge. Edinburgh and London: E. & S. Livingstone, 1964.
Houssaye, M. *Le Cardinal de Bérulle et le Cardinal de Richelieu, 1625–1628*. Paris, 1875.
Jonstonus, Johannes. *The Idea of Practical Physick, in Twelve Books* translated by Nicholas Culpeper. London, 1657.
King, Henry. *A deep groane, fetch'd at the funerall of that incomparable and glorious monarch, Charles the First, King of Great Britaine, France and Ireland . . .* London, 1649.
Knox, John. *The First Blast of the Trumpet against the Monstruous Regiment of Women*. London, 1558.
Laud, William. *A sermon preached on Monday, the sixth of February, at Westminster at the opening of the Parliament. By the Bishop of St. David's*. London, 1625.
'Concerning the Clergy'. *Articles to be inquired of in the metropoliticall visitation of the most reverend father, William, by Gods providence, Lord Arch-bishop of Canterbury*. London, 1635.
Lindley, David, (ed). *Court Masques*. Oxford: Oxford University, 1959.
Loe, William. *Vox clamantis. Mark 1. 3 A stil voice, to the three thrice-honourable estates of Parliament: and in them, to all the soules of this our nation, of what state or condition soeuer they be*. London, 1621.
Melanchthon, Philip. *De Anima*. London, 1540.
Middleton, Thomas. *The Ghost of Lucrece*. London, 1600.
Milton, John. *A Masque: The Earlier Versions* edited by S.E. Sprott. Toronto: University of Toronto Press, 1973.
Complete Prose Works of John Milton edited by Don Wolfe et al. 8 Vols. New Haven: Yale University Press, 1953–82.
Private Correspondence and Academic Exercises translated by Phyllis B. Tillyard. Cambridge: Cambridge University Press, 1932.
The Complete Poetry of John Milton edited by John Shawcross. New York: Anchor Books, 1971.
Montagu, Walter. *The Shepherd's Paradise*. Malone Society Reprints, Vol. 159 edited by Sarah Poynting. Oxford: Oxford University Press, 1997.
Norden, John. *The Mirror of Honor*. London, 1597.
Overbury, Sir Thomas. *Works*. edited by E. F. Rimbault. London: J. R. Smith, 1856.
Parliament of England and Wales, *A remonstrance of the state of the kingdome of England*. London, 1641.
Prynne, William. *A quench-coale. Or A briefe disquisition and inquirie, in vvhat place of the church or chancell the Lords-table ought to be situated, especially when the Sacrament is administered*. London, 1637.
Canterburies Doome. London, 1646.

Histriomastix. The players scourge, or, actors tragaedie, divided into two parts . . . London, 1633.
   The Soveraigne Power of Parliaments and Kingdomes. London, 1643.
   Truth Triumphing over Falsehood. London, 1645.
Reuff, James. *The Expert Midwife*. London, 1637.
Scott, Thomas. *Vox Regis*. London, 1642.
Shakespeare, William. *Shakespeare's Poems* edited by Katherine Duncan-Jones and H. R. Woudhuysen. London: Arden, 2007.
   The Winter's Tale. edited by Stephen Orgel. Oxford: Oxford University Press, 1996.
Southwell, Robert. *Marie Magdalens funeral teares*. London, 1591.
   Saint Peters complaint with other poems. London, 1595.
Spenser, Edmund. *The Faerie Queene*. Revised 2nd Edition edited by A.C. Hamilton. London: Longman, 2007.
Stubbs, Philip. *Anatomy of Abuses*. London, 1583.
Vanbrugh, John. *The Provoked Wife* edited by Antony Coleman. Manchester: Manchester University Press, 1982.

Secondary texts

Achinstein, Sharon. 'Women on Top in the Pamphlet Literature of the English Revolution'. *Women's Studies* 24, 1994, 131–63.
Albion, Gordon. *Charles I and the Court of Rome: A Study in Seventeenth-Century Diplomacy*. London: Burns, Oates & Washbourne, 1935.
Atherton, Ian and Sanders, Julie (eds). *The 1630s: Interdisciplinary Essays on Culture and Politics in the Caroline Period*. Manchester: Manchester University Press, 2006.
Badir, Patricia and Yachnin, Paul. *Shakespeare and the Cultures of Performance*. Aldershot: Ashgate, 2008.
Bailey, Rebecca A. *Staging the Old Faith: Queen Henrietta Maria and the Theatre of Caroline England, 1625–42*. Manchester: Manchester University Press, 2009.
Baker, Joanne. 'Female Monasticism and Family Strategy: The Guises and Saint Pierre de Reims'. *Sixteenth Century Journal* 28, 1977, 1091–1108.
Bartholomeusz, Dennis. *The Winter's Tale in Performance in England and America, 1611–1976*. Cambridge: Cambridge University Press, 1982.
Barber, C.L. and Wheeler, Richard. *The Whole Journey: Shakespeare's Power of Development*. Berkeley: University of California Press, 1986.
Barbour, Reid. 'John Ford and Resolve'. *Studies in Philology* 86, 1989, 341–66.
Bate, Jonathan. *Shakespeare and Ovid*. Oxford: Oxford University Press, 1993.
Bates, Catherine. *The Rhetoric of Courtship in Elizabethan Language and Literature*. Cambridge: Cambridge University Press, 1992.
Bellamy, Elizabeth J. 'Waiting for Hymen: Literary History as "Symptom" in Spenser and Milton', *English Literary History* 64:2, 1997, 391–414.

Bellany, A. *The Politics of Court Scandal in Early Modern England: News Culture and the Overbury Affair, 1603–1660*. Cambridge and New York: Cambridge University Press, 2002.
Berry, Philippa. *Of Chastity and Power: Elizabethan Literature and the Unmarried Queen*. London: Routledge, 1989.
Bevington, David and Holbrook, Peter, (eds). *The Politics of the Stuart Court Masque*. Cambridge: Cambridge University Press, 1998.
Billing, Christian. 'Modelling the Anatomy Theatre and the Indoor Hall Theatre: Dissection on the Stages of Early Modern London'. *Early Modern Literary Studies* 13, 2004, 1–17.
Blakemore, Colin and Jennett, Sheila, (eds). *The Oxford Companion to the Body*. Oxford University Press, 2001.
Boehrer, Bruce. '"Nice Philosophy": *'Tis Pity She's a Whore* and the Two Books of God'. *Studies in English Literature, 1500–1900*. 24, 1984, 355–71.
Breasted, Barbara. 'Comus and the Castlehaven Scandal'. *Milton Studies* 3, 1971, 201–24.
Briggs, Robin. *Early Modern France 1560–1715*. Oxford: Oxford University Press, 1977.
Britland, Karen. *Drama at the Courts of Queen Henrietta Maria*. Cambridge: Cambridge University Press, 2006.
Broomhall, Susan. *Women and Religion in Sixteenth-Century France*. Basingstoke: Palgrave Macmillan, 2005.
Brown, Cedric. *John Milton's Aristocratic Entertainments*. Cambridge: Cambridge University Press, 1985.
Brundage, James A. *Law, Sex and Christian Society*. Chicago: University of Chicago Press, 1987.
Butler, Martin. *Theatre and Crisis 1632–1642*. Cambridge: Cambridge University Press, 1984.
Bynam, Caroline Walker. *Holy Feast and Holy Fast: The Religious Significance of Food to Medieval Women*. Berkeley: University of California Press, 1986.
Caldwell, John et al. (eds). *The Well Enchanting Skill: Music, Poetry, and Drama in the Culture of the Renaissance, Essays in Honour of F. W. Sternfield*. Oxford: Clarendon Press, 1990.
Callaghan, Dymphna. *The Impact of Feminism in English Renaissance Studies*. Basingstoke: Palgrave Macmillan, 2007.
Campbell, Gordon and Corns, Thomas. *John Milton: Life, Work, and Thought*. Oxford: Oxford University Press, 2008.
Carlin, Claire L. (ed). *Imagining Contagion in Early Modern Europe*. Basingstoke: Palgrave Macmillan, 2005.
Carlson, Eric Josef. *Marriage and the English Reformation*. Oxford: Blackwell, 1994.
Carney, Sophie. Unpublished doctoral thesis 'The Queen's House at Greenwich: The Material Cultures of the Courts of Queen Anna of Denmark and Queen Henrietta Maria, 1603–1669'. Roehampton University, 2012.
Chedgzoy, Kate. 'The Cultural Geographies of Early Modern Women's Writings: Journeys across Spaces and Times', *Literature Compass* 3/4, 2006, 884–95.

Cheney, Patrick et al. (eds). *Early Modern English Drama: A Critical Companion.* Oxford: Oxford University Press, 2006.
Clarke, Elizabeth. *Politics, Religion and the Song of Songs.* Basingstoke: Palgrave Macmillan, 2011.
Clerico, Terri. 'The Politics of Blood: John Ford's *'Tis Pity She's a Whore'*. *English Literary Rennaissance* 22:3, 1992, 405–34.
Clifton, Robin. 'The Popular Fear of Catholics during the English Revolution'. *Past & Present* 52, 1971, 23–55.
Clubb, L. G. *Italian Drama in Shakespeare's Time.* New Haven: Yale University Press, 1989.
Cohn, Samuel K. Jr., *Cultures of Plague: Medical Thinking at the End of the Renaissance.* Oxford: Oxford University Press, 2010.
Coiro, Ann Baynes. 'Anonymous Milton, or, A Maske Masked'. *English Literary History* 71, 2004, 609–29.
Coletti, Teresa. *Mary Magdalene and the Drama of the Saints.* Philadelphia: University of Pennsylvania Press, 2004.
Colie, Rosalie. *The Resources of Kind: Genre Theory in the Renaissance.* Berkeley: University of California Press, 1973.
Collinson, Patrick. *The Birthpangs of Protestant England: Religion and Cultural Change in the Sixteenth and Seventeenth Centuries.* New York: Macmillan, 1988.
Connolly, Annaliese F. and Hopkins, Lisa. *Goddesses and Queens: The Iconography of Elizabeth I.* Manchester: Manchester University Press, 2007.
Cosgrove, Denis and Daniels, Stephen (eds). *The Iconography of Landcape: Essays on Symbolic Representation, Design and the Use of Past Environments.* Cambridge: Cambridge University Press, 1989.
Crang, Mike. *Cultural Geography.* London: Routledge, 2002.
Crawford, Julie. *Marvelous Protestantism: Monstrous Births in Post-Reformation England.* Baltimore: John Hopkins University Press, 2005.
Creaser, John. 'Milton's Comus: The Irrelevance of the Castlehaven Scandal'. *Milton Quarterly* 4, 1987, 25–34.
Cressy, David. *Birth, Marriage, and Death: Ritual, Religion, and the Life-Cycle in Stuart and Tudor England.* Oxford: Oxford University Press, 1997.
Curtright, Travis and Smith, Stephen W. *Shakespeare's Last Plays: Essays in Literature and Politics.* New York: Lexington, 2002.
Cust, Richard and Hughes, Anne. *Conflict in Early Stuart England.* London: Longman, 1989.
Davies, Joan. 'The Montmorencys and the Abbey of Sainte Trinité, Caen: Politics, Profit and Reform'. *Journal of Ecclesiastical History* 53, 2002, 665–85.
Dawson, Lesel. *Lovesickness and Gender in Early Modern English Literature.* Oxford: Oxford University Press, 2008.
Degenhardt, Jane and Williamson, Elizabeth (eds). *Religion and Drama in Early Modern England.* Aldershot: Ashgate, 2011.
Demaray, John G. 'The Thrones of Satan and God: Backgrounds to Divine Opposition in *Paradise Lost*'. *The Huntington Library Quarterly* 31, 1967, 21–33.

Dillon, Janette. *Theatre, Court and City, 1595–1610: Drama and Social Space in London*. Cambridge: Cambridge University Press, 2000.
  The Language of Space in Court Performance 1400–1625. Cambridge: Cambridge University Press, 2010.
Dixon, Mimi Still. '"Thys Body of Mary": "Femynyte" and "Inward Mythe" in the Digby Mary Magdalene'. *Mediaevalia* 18, 1995, 221–44.
Dobranski, Stephen B. *Milton, Authorship, and the Book Trade*. Cambridge: Cambridge University Press, 1999.
Dolan, Frances E. 'Gender and the "Lost" Spaces of Catholicism'. *Journal of Interdisciplinary History* 32:4, 2002, 641–65.
  Marriage and Violence: The Early Modern Legacy. Philadelphia: University of Pennsylvania Press, 2008.
  'Taking the Pencil out of God's Hand: Art, Nature, and the Face-Painting Debate in Early Modern England'. *Modern Language Association* 108, 1993, 224–39.
  Whores of Babylon: Catholicism, Gender, and Seventeenth-Century Print Culture. Ithaca: Cornell University Press, 1999.
Donnison, Leah. *Midwives and Medical Men*. New Barnet: Historian Publishers, 1988.
Doran, Susan and Freeman, Thomas S. *The Myth of Elizabeth*. Basingstoke: Palgrave Macmillan, 2003.
Dubrow, Heather. *Echoes of Desire: English Petrarchism and its Counter-discourses*. Ithaca: Cornell University Press, 1995.
  'The Masquing of Genre in Comus'. *Milton Studies* 44, 2005, 62–83.
Duff, David (ed). *Modern Genre Theory*. Harlow: Pearson Education Limited, 2000.
Dunn, P.M. 'The Chamberlen Family (1560–1728) and Obstetric Forceps'. *Archives of Disease in Childhood: The Journal of the British Paediatric Association: Fetal and Neonatal Edition* 81.3, 1999, 232–34.
Eggert, Katherine. *Showing Like a Queen: Female Authority and Literary Experiment in Spenser, Shakespeare, and Milton*. Philadelphia: University of Pennsylvania Press, 2000.
Enterline, Lynn. '"You speak a language that I under stand not": The Rhetoric of Animation in *The Winter's Tale*'. *Shakespeare Quarterly* 48, 1997, 17–44.
Erickson, Peter. *Patriarchal Structures in Shakespeare's Drama*. Berkeley: University of California Press, 1985.
Esche, Edward J. (ed). *Shakespeare and his Contemporaries in Performance*. Aldershot: Ashgate, 2000.
Evans, R.J.W. and Marr, Alexander. *Curiosity and Wonder from the Renaissance to the Enlightenment*. Aldershot: Ashgate, 2006.
Fallon, M. *Milton's Peculiar Grace*. Ithaca and London: Cornell University Press, 2007.
Fantoni, Marcello (ed). *The Politics of Space: European Courts 1500–1750*. Roma: Balzoni, 2009.
Farr, Dorothy M. *John Ford and Caroline Theatre*. London: Macmillan, 1979.

Ferguson, Margaret W. et al. (eds). *Rewriting the Renaissance: Discourses of Sexual Difference in Early Modern Europe*. Chicago and London: University of Chicago Press, 1986.

Ferry, Anne. *The 'Inward' Language: Sonnets of Wyatt, Sidney, Shakespeare, Donne*. Chicago: University of Chicago, 1983.

Ffolliot, Sheila. 'The Italian "Training" of Catherine de Medici: Portraits as Dynastic Narrative'. *The Court Historian* 10, 2005, 36–54.

Fincham, Kenneth and Tyacke, Nicholas. *Altars Restored: The Changing Face of English Religious Worship, 1547–c.1700*. Oxford: Oxford University Press, 2007.

Fincham, Kenneth (ed). *The Early Stuart Church, 1603–1642*. Basingstoke: Macmillan, 1993.

Fletcher, Angus. *The Transcendental Masque: An Essay on Milton's Comus*. London: Ithaca, 1971.

Fletcher, Anthony. *Gender, Sex, and Subordination in England 1500–1800*. New Haven: Yale University Press, 1988.

Floyd-Wilson, Mary and Sullivan, Garrett, (eds). *Environment and Embodiment in Early Modern England*. Basingstoke: Palgrave Macmillan, 2007.

Fowler, Alistair. *Kinds of Literature*. Cambridge, Mass.: Harvard University Press, 1982.

Frye, Susan. *Elizabeth I: The Competition for Representation*. Oxford: Oxford University Press, 1993.

Gertsman, Elina (ed). *Visualising Medieval Performance: Perspectives, Histories, Contexts*. Aldershot: Ashgate. 2008.

Gillespie, Katharine. 'Anna Trapnel's Window on the Word: The Domestic Sphere of Public Dissent in Seventeenth-Century Nonconformity'. *Bunyan Studies* 7, 1997, 49–72.

Gilman, Ernest B. *Plague Writing in Early Modern England*. Chicago and London: University of Chicago Press, 2009.

Gimelli-Martin, Catherine (ed). *Milton and Gender*. Cambridge: Cambridge University Press, 2004.

Gordon, Andrew and Klein, Bernard (eds). *Literature, Mapping and the Politics of Space in Early Modern Britain*. Cambridge: Cambridge University Press, 2001.

Gouk, Penelope and Hills, Helen (eds). *Representing Emotion: New Connections in the Histories of Art, Music and Medicine*. Aldershot: Ashgate, 2005.

Gowing, Laura. *Domestic Dangers: Women, Words, and Sex in Early Modern London*. Oxford: Clarendon Press, 1996.

  'Secret Births and Infanticide in Seventeenth-Century England'. *Past & Present* 156, 1997.

Grantley, Darryll. '*The Winter's Tale* and Early Religious Drama'. *Comparative Drama* 20, 1986, 17–37.

Greenblatt, Stephen. *Renaissance Self-Fashioning*. Chicago: Chicago University Press, 1980.

Gregerson, Linda. *The Reformation of the Subject: Spenser, Milton, and the English Protestant Epic*. Cambridge: Cambridge University Press, 1995.

Griffey, Erin (ed). *Henrietta Maria: Piety, Politics and Patronage*. Aldershot: Ashgate, 2008.

Griffiths, Paul and Jenner, Mark (eds). *Londinopolis: Essays in the Cultural and Social History of Early Modern London*. Manchester: Manchester University Press, 2000.

Gross, Daniel. *The Secret History of Emotion: From Aristotle's Rhetoric to Modern Brain Science*. Chicago and London: University of Chicago Press, 2006.

Groves, Beatrice. *Texts and Traditions: Religion in Shakespeare, 1592–1604*. Oxford: Clarendon Press, 2007.

Haigh, Christopher. 'The English Reformation: A Premature Birth, a Difficult Labour and a Sickly Child'. *Historical Journal* 33, 1990, 449–59.

Hamilton, Donna and Strier, Richard (eds). *Religion, Literature and Politics in Post-Reformation England 1540–1688*. Cambridge: Cambridge University Press, 1996.

Hale, David George. *The Body Politic*. The Hague: Mouton, 1971.

Harline, Craig. *The Burdens of Sister Margaret*. New York: Doubleday, 1994.

Harris, Jonathan Gill. *Foreign Bodies and the Body Politic*. Cambridge: Cambridge University Press, 1998.

Harrison, Stephan (ed). *Patterned Ground: Entanglements of Nature and Culture*. London: Reaktion Books, 2004.

Harvey, Elizabeth D. (ed). *Sensible Flesh: On Touch in Early Modern Culture*. Philadelphia: University of Pennsylvania Press, 2003.

Harvey, Elizabeth D. and Eisamann Maus, Katherine (ed). *Soliciting Interpretation: Literary Theory and Seventeenth-Century English Poetry* Chicago: University of Chicago Press, 1990.

Haselkorn, Anne M. and Travitsky, Betty S. *The Renaissance Englishwoman in Print: Counterbalancing the Canon*. Boston: University of Massachusetts Press, 1990.

Healy, Margaret. *Fictions of Disease in Early Modern England: Bodies, Plagues, and Politics*. New York: Palgrave, 2001.

Helgerson, Richard. *Forms of Nationhood: The Elizabethan Writing of England*. Chicago and London: University of Chicago Press, 1992.

Helly, Dorothy O. and Reverby, Susan M. (eds). *Gendered Domains: Re-thinking Public and Private in Women's History*. Ithaca: Cornell University Press, 1992.

Henderson, Diana E. *Passion Made Public: Elizabethan Lyric, Gender, and Performance*. Urbana: University of Illinois Press, 1995.

Henke, Robert. *Pastoral Transformations: Italian Tragicomedy and Shakespeare's Late Plays*. Newark: University of Delaware Press, 1997.

Herrick, Marvin. *Tragicomedy: Its Origin and Development in Italy, France, and England*. Urbana: University of Illinois Press, 1955.

Herrup, Cynthia. *A House in Gross Disorder*. Oxford: Oxford University Press, 1999.

Hibbard, Caroline. *Charles I and the Popish Plot*. Chapel Hill: University of North Carolina Press, 1983.

'Translating Royalty: Henrietta Maria and the Transition from Princess to Queen'. *Court Historian* 10, 2005, 15–29.

Hill, Christopher. 'William Harvey and the Idea of Monarchy'. *Past and Present* 27, 1964, 54–72.
Hillman, David. *Shakespeare's Entrails*. Basingstoke: Palgrave Macmillan, 2007.
Hillman, David and Mazzio, Carla (eds). *The Body in Parts: Fantasies of Corporality in Early Modern Europe*. London: Routledge, 1997.
Hindle, Steve. 'The Shaming of Margaret Knowsley: Gossip, Gender, and the Experience of Authority in Early Modern England'. *Continuity and Change* 9, 1994, 391–419.
Holland, Peter and Scolnicov, Hanna. *Reading Plays: Interpretation and Reception*. Cambridge: Cambridge University Press, 1991.
Hopkins, Lisa. *John Ford's Political Theatre*. Manchester: Manchester University Press, 1994.
  'Knowing Their Loves: Knowledge, Ignorance, and Blindness in '*Tis Pity She's a Whore*'. *Renaissance Forum* 3, 1998, 1–14.
Houlbrooke, Ralph. *The English Family 1450–1700*. London: Blackwell, 1986.
Howard, Jean. *Theatre of a City: The Places of London Comedy 1595–1610*. Philadelphia: University of Pennsylvania Press, 2008.
Hoxby, Blair. '"The Wisdom of Their Feet": Meaningful Dance in Milton and the Stuart Masque'. *English Literary Review* 37, 2007, 74–99.
Huebert, Ronald. *John Ford: Baroque English Dramatist*. Montreal and London: McGill-Queen's University Press, 1977.
Jardine, Lisa. *Still Harping on Daughters: Women and Drama in the Age of Shakespeare*. Brighton: Harvester, 1983.
Jed, Stephanie. *Chaste Thinking: The Rape of Lucretia and the Birth of Humanism*. New York: John Wiley & Sons, 1989.
Jensen, Phebe. 'Singing Psalms to Horn-pipes: Festivity, Iconoclasm, and Catholicism in *The Winter's Tale*'. *Shakespeare Quarterly* 55.3, 2004, 279–306.
Kahn, Coppélia and Schwartz, Murray M. (eds). *Representing Shakespeare: New Psychoanalytic Essays*. Baltimore: Johns Hopkins University Press, 1980.
Kahn, Victoria (ed). *Politics and the Passions 1500–1850*. Princeton: Princeton University Press, 2006.
Kaula, David. 'Autolycus' Trumpery'. *Studies in English Literature, 1500–1900*. 16:2, 1976, 287–303.
Kay, Sarah and Rubin, Miri (eds). *Framing Medieval Bodies*. Manchester: Manchester University Press, 1994.
Keller, Eve. *Generating Bodies and Gendered Selves: The Rhetoric of Reproduction in Early Modern England*. Seattle and London: University of Washington Press, 2007.
Kiernan, M. (ed). *The Advancement of Learning*. Oxford: Oxford University Press, 2000.
Klestinec, Cynthia. 'Civility, Comportment, and the Anatomy Theater: Girolamo Fabrici and His Medical Students in Renaissance Padua', *Renaissance Quarterly* 60:2, 2007, 434–63.
Knapp, Jeffrey. *Shakespeare's Tribe: Church, Nation, and Theater in Renaissance England*. Chicago: University of Chicago Press, 2002.

Knoppers, Laura Lunger. *Politicising Domesticity from Henrietta Maria to Milton's Eve*. Cambridge: Cambridge University Press. 2011.
Korda, Natasha. *Shakespeare's Domestic Economies: Gender and Property in Early Modern England*. Philadelphia: University of Pennsylvania Press, 2002.
Kroll, Richard. *Restoration Drama and 'the Circle of Commerce'*. Cambridge: Cambridge University Press, 2007.
Krook, Dorothea. *Elements of Tragedy*. New Haven: Yale University Press, 1969.
Landau, Aaron. '"No Settled Senses of the World can Match the Pleasure of that Madness": The Politics of Unreason in *The Winter's Tale*'. *Cahiers Élizabéthains* 64, 2003, 29–42.
Lander, Bonnie. 'Interpreting the Person: Tradition, Conflict, and *Cymbeline*'s Imogen,' *Shakespeare Quarterly* 59:2, 2008, 156–84.
Langer, Susanne. *Feeling and Form*. New York: Charles Scribner's Sons, 1953.
Laoutaris, Chris. *Shakespearean Maternities*. Edinburgh: Edinburgh University Press, 2008.
Lawrence, Ralph J. *Sacramental Interpretation of Ephesians 5:32 from Peter Lombard to the Council of Trent*. Washington: Catholic University of America Press, 1963.
LeFanu, W.R. 'Huguenot Refugee Doctors in England'. *Proceedings of the Huguenot Society of Great Britain and Ireland* 19, 1955, 113–27.
Lefebvre, Henri. *The Production of Space*. Translated by Donald Nicholson Smith. Oxford: Blackwell, 1991.
Lehfeldt, E.A. 'Discipline, Vocation, and Patronage: Spanish Religious Women in the Tridentine Microclimate'. *Sixteenth Century Journal* 30, 1999, 1009–30.
Lesser, Zachary. 'Tragical-Comical-Pastoral-Colonial: Economic Sovereignty, Globalisation, and the Form of Tragicomedy'. *English Literary History* 74.4, 2007, 881–908.
Levi, Anthony. *French Moralists: The Theory of the Passions, 1585–1649*. Oxford: Clarendon Press, 1964.
Levin, Kate. 'Coming of Age on Stage: The Pedagogical Masque in Seventeenth-Century England', *George Herbert Journal* 29, 2005, 114–30.
Lieb, Michael. 'Milton and Kenotic Christology: Its Literary Bearing'. *English Literary History* 37, 1970. 342–62.
  Milton and the Culture of Violence. London: Cornell University Press, 1994.
Lindley, David (ed). *The Court Masque*. Manchester: Manchester University Press, 1984.
Lupton, Julia Reinhard. *Afterlives of the Saints: Hagiography, Typology, and Renaissance Literature*. California: Stanford University Press, 1996.
Macfarlane, Alan. *Marriage and Love in England: Modes of Reproduction 1300–1840*. Oxford: Blackwell, 1986.
Mackin, Theodore. *Marriage in the Catholic Church: Divorce and Remarriage*. New York: Paulist Press, 1984.
Maguire, Nancy K. (ed). *Renaissance Tragicomedy: Explorations in Genre and Politics*. New York: AMS Press, 1987, 217–240.
Mahood, M. M. *Bit Parts in Shakespeare's Plays*. Cambridge: Cambridge University Press, 1992.

Marcus, Leah S. 'The Milieu of Milton's Comus: Judicial Reform at Ludlow and the Problem of Sexual Assault', *Criticism* 25, 1983, 293–327.
  The Politics of Mirth: Jonson, Herrick, Milton, Marvell, and the Defense of Old Holiday Pastimes. Chicago: The University of Chicago Press, 1986.
Marotti, Arthur F. (ed.) *Catholic Culture in Early Modern England*. Indiana: University of Notre Dame Press, 2007.
  ed. *Catholicism and Anti-Catholicism in Early Modern English Texts*. Basingstoke: Macmillan, 1999.
  Religious Ideology and Cultural Fantasy: Catholic and Anti-Catholic Discourses in Early Modern England. Indiana: University of Notre Dame Press, 2005.
Marshall, Cynthia. 'Bodies in the Audience'. *Shakespeare Studies* 29, 2001, 51–7.
  'Dualism and the Hope of Reunion'. *Soundings* 69.3, 1986, 295–309.
  Shattering the Self: Violence, Subjectivity, and Early Modern Texts. Baltimore: Johns Hopkins University Press, 2002.
Martos, Joseph. *Doors to the Sacred: A Historical Introduction of the Sacraments in the Catholic Church*. New York: Image Books, 1982.
Maus, Katharine Eisaman. *Inwardness and Theater in the English Renaissance*. Chicago and London: University of Chicago Press, 1995.
McEachern, Claire. '"A whore at the first blush seemeth only a woman": John Bale's Image of Both Churches and the Terms of Religious Difference in the Early English Reformation'. *Journal of Medieval and Renaissance Studies* 25, 1995, 245–69.
  The Poetics of English Nationhood, 1590–1612. Cambridge: Cambridge University Press, 1996.
McGuire, Maryann C. *Milton's Puritan Masque*. Athens: University of Georgia Press, 1983.
McLaren, Dorothy (ed). *Women as Mothers in Pre-Industrial England*. London: Routledge, 1990.
McManus, Clare. *Women and Culture at the Courts of the Stuart Queens*. Basingstoke: Palgrave Macmillan, 2003.
  Women on the Renaissance Stage. Manchester: Manchester University Press, 2002.
McMullan, Gordon and Hope, Jonathon (eds). *The Politics of Tragicomedy*. London: Routledge, 1992.
McRae, Andrew. *Literature and Domestic Travel in Early Modern England*. Cambridge: Cambridge University Press, 2009.
Merritt, J.F. *The Social World of Early Modern Westminster: Abbey, Court and Community, 1525–1640*. Manchester: Manchester University Press, 2005.
Mikalachki, Jodi. *The Legacy of Boadicea: Gender and Nation in Early Modern England*. London: Routledge, 1998.
Miller, John. *Popery and Politics in England, 1660–1688*. Cambridge: Cambridge University Press, 1973.
Milton, Antony. *Catholic and Reformed: The Roman and Protestant Churches in English Protestant Thought, 1600–1640*. Cambridge: Cambridge University Press, 1995.

Monsarrat, Gilles D. *Light From the Porch: Stoicism and English Renaissance Literature*. Paris: Didier-Érudition, 1984.
Montrose, Louis Adrian. '"The Place of a Brother" in *As You Like It*: Social Process and Comic Form,' *Shakespeare Quarterly* 32, 1981, 28–54.
  The Subject of Elizabeth: Authority, Gender, and Representation. Chicago and London: University of Chicago Press, 2006.
Mukherji, Subha and Lyne, Raphael (eds). *Early Modern Tragicomedy*. Woodbridge: D. S. Brewer, 2007.
Mustazza, Leonard. *'Such Prompt Eloquence": Language as Agency and Character in Milton's Epics*. London: Associated University Presses, 1988.
Naphy, William G. *Plagues, Poisons and Potions: Plague-Spreading Conspiracies in the Western Alps 1530–1640*. Manchester: Manchester University Press, 2002.
Neill, Michael (ed). *John Ford: Critical Re-Visions*. Cambridge: Cambridge University Press, 1988.
Norbrook, David. *Poetry and Politics in the English Renaissance*. Oxford: Oxford University Press, 2002.
Nunn, Hillary. *Staging Anatomies*. Aldershot: Ashgate, 2005.
Nyquist, Mary and Ferguson, Margaret W. (eds). *Re-Membering Milton: Essays in the Texts and Traditions*. New York: Methuen, 1987.
O'Connell, Michael. *The Idolatrous Eye: Iconoclasm and Theatre in Early Modern England*. Oxford: Oxford University Press, 2000.
Orgel, Stephen. *The Illusion of Power: Political Theatre in the English Renaissance*. Berkeley: University of California Press, 1975.
  The Jonsonian Masque. Cambridge, Mass.: Harvard University Press, 1965.
  (with Roy Strong) *Inigo Jones: the Theatre of the Stuart Court*. Berkeley: University of California Press, 1973.
Orlin, Lena Cowen (ed). *Material London ca. 1600*. Philadelphia: University of Pennsylvania Press, 2000.
  (ed). 'Women on the Threshold'. *Shakespeare Studies* 25, 1997, 50–8.
Orrell, John. *The Theatres of Inigo Jones and John Webb*. Cambridge: Cambridge University Press, 1985.
Parker, Patricia. *Literary Fat Ladies: Rhetoric, Gender, Property*. London: Methuen, 1987.
Parry, Graham. *Glory, Laud and Honour*. Rochester: Boydell Press, 2008.
  The Golden Age Restor'd: The Culture of the Stuart Court, 1603–42. Manchester: Manchester University Press, 1981.
Paster, Gail Kern. *Humoring the Body*. Chicago: Chicago University Press, 2004.
  ed. *Reading the Early Modern Passions: Essays in the Cultural History of Emotion*. Philadelphia: University of Pennsylvania Press, 2004.
  The Body Embarrassed: Drama and Disciplines of Shame in Early Modern England. Ithaca: Cornell University Press, 1993.
Paxson, James J. and Selinsgrove, Cynthia Gravlee. *Desiring Discourse: The Literature of Love, Ovid Through Chaucer*. London: Associated University Presses, 1998.

Pearson, Jacqueline. *Tragedy and Tragicomedy in the Plays of John Webster*. Manchester: Manchester University Press, 1980.
Plowden, Alison. *Henrietta Maria: Charles I's Indomitable Queen*. Stroud: Sutton Publishing, 2001.
Pollard, Tanya. *Drugs and Theatre in Early Modern England*. Oxford: Oxford University Press, 2005.
Prioleau, William H. 'The Chamberlen Family and Introduction of Obstetrical Instruments'. *Proceedings of the Huguenot Society of Great Britain and Ireland* 27.5, 2002, 705–14.
Prior, Mary. *Women in English Society, 1500–1800*. New York: Methuen & Co, 1985.
Purkiss, Diane. 'Women's Stories of Witchcraft in Early Modern England: The House, the Body, the Child'. *Gender and History* 7:3, 1995, 408–432.
Quilligan, Maureen. *Milton's Spenser: The Politics of Reading*. Ithaca: Cornell University Press, 1983.
Radcliffe, Walter. *Milestone in Midwifery*. Bristol: John Wright & Sons, 1967.
The Secret Instrument. London: Heinemann, 1947.
Reiss, Timothy. *Mirages of the Self: Patterns of Personhood in Ancient and Early Modern Europe*. California: Stanford University Press, 2003.
Reynolds, Brian and West, William. *Rematerialising Shakespeare*. Basingstoke: Palgrave Macmillan, 2005.
Ridden, G.M. (ed). *Freedom and the English Revolution: Essays in History and Literature*. Manchester: Manchester University Press, 1986.
Rist, Thomas. *Shakespeare's Romances and the Politics of Counter-Reformation*. Lampeter: The Edwin Meller Press, 1999.
Rogers, John. *The Matter of Revolution: Science, Poetry, and Politics in the Age of Milton*. Ithaca: Cornell University Press, 1996.
Rose, Mary Beth (ed). *Women in the Middle Ages and the Renaissance*. Syracuse: Syracuse University Press, 1986, 135–72.
The Expense of Spirit: Love and Sexuality in English Renaissance Drama. Ithaca: Cornell University Press, 1995.
Russell, C. (ed). *The Origins of the English Civil War*. London: Macmillan, 1973.
Ryan, Kiernan (ed). *Shakespeare: The Last Plays*. London: Longman, 1999.
Sanders, Julie. *The Cultural Geography of Early Modern Drama, 1620–1650*. Cambridge: Cambridge University Press, 2011.
Sawday, Jonathan. *The Body Emblazoned: Dissection and the Human Body in Renaissance Culture*. London: Routledge, 1996.
Schaff, Philip. *Nicene and Post-Nicene Fathers*, First Series, Vol. 8. Buffalo, New York: Christian Literature Publishing Co., 1888.
Schalkwyk, David. '"A Lady's 'Verily' is as Potent as a Lord's": Women, Word and Witchcraft in *The Winter's Tale*'. *English Literary Renaissance* 22, 1992, 242–72.
Scheingorn, Pamela. *The Easter Sepulchre in England*. Kalamazoo: Medieval Institute Publications, 1987.
Schneider, Frederico. *Pastoral Drama and Healing in Early Modern Italy*. Aldershot: Ashgate, 2010.

Schoenfeldt, Michael C. *Bodies and Selves in Early Modern England: Physiology and Inwardness in Spenser, Shakespeare, Herbert, and Milton.* Cambridge: Cambridge University Press, 1999.

Schwoerer, Lois (ed). *The Revolution of 1688–1689: Changing Perspectives.* Cambridge: Cambridge University Press, 1992.

Schwyzer, Philip. 'Purity and Danger on the West Bank of the Severn: The Cultural Geography of *A Masque Presented at Ludlow Castle, 1634*'. *Representations* 60, 1997, 22–48.

Sedgwick, Eve Kosofsky. *Between Men: English Literature and Male Homosocial Desire.* NewYork: Columbia University Press, 1993.

Selleck, Nancy. *The Interpersonal Idiom in Shakespeare, Donne and Early Modern Culture.* Basingstoke: Palgrave Macmillan, 2008.

Sennett, Richard. *Flesh and Stone: The Body and the City in Western Civilisation.* London: Norton, 2003.

Shanley, Mary L. 'Marriage Contract and Social Contract in Seventeenth Century English Political Thought'. *Western Political Quarterly* 32, 1979, 79–91.

Sharpe, Kevin. *Criticism and Compliment: The Politics of Literature in the England of Charles I.* Cambridge: Cambridge University Press, 1987.

John Milton: The Self and the World. Lexington: University Press of Kentucky, 1993.

Shawcross, Jonathan. *John Milton: The Self and the World.* Lexington: University of Press of Kentucky, 1993.

Shell, Alison. *Catholicism, Controversy and the English Literary Imagination 1558–1660.* Cambridge: Cambridge University Press, 1999.

Shakespeare and Religion. London: A & C Black, 2010.

Shuger, Debora. '"Gums of Glutinous Heat" and the Stream of Consciousness: The Theology of Milton's Maske'. *Representations* 60, 1997, 1–21.

Shullenberger, William. *Lady in the Labyrinth.* New Jersey: Associated University Presses, 2008.

Siraisi, Nancy G. *Medieval and Early Renaissance Medicine: An Introduction to Knowledge and Practice.* Chicago and London: University of Chicago Press, 1990.

Slack, Paul. *The Impact of Plague in Tudor and Stuart England.* London: Routledge, 1985.

Slights, William. 'Bodies of Text and Textualized Bodies in *Sejanus* and *Coriolanus*'. *Medieval and Renaissance Drama in England* 5. New York: AMS Press, 1991.

Smallwood, Robert (ed). *Players of Shakespeare 5.* Cambridge: Cambridge University Press, 2006.

Smith, Emma. 'Richard II's Yorkist Editors', *Shakespeare Survey 63.* Cambridge: Cambridge University Press, 2010.

Smuts, Malcolm. *Court Culture and the Origins of a Royalist Tradition in Early Stuart England.* Philadelphia: University of Pennsylvania Press, 1999.

'Religion, European Politics and Henrietta Maria's Circle, 1625–41'. *Henrietta Maria: Piety, Politics and Patronage.* Aldershot: Ashgate, 2008, 13–38.

Smyth, Adam. '"Shreds of holinesse": George Herbert, Little Gidding, and Cutting Up Texts in Early Modern England', *ELR* 42, 452–81.
Snyder, Susan. *Shakespeare: A Wayward Journey*. Newark: University of Delaware Press, 2002.
Sokol, B.J. '"Tilted Lees", Dragons, Haemony, Menarche, Spirit, and Matter in Comus', *The Review of English Studies, New Series*, 41, 1990, 309–24.
Spiller, Elizabeth. *Science, Reading and Renaissance Literature*. Cambridge: Cambridge University Press, 2004.
Stanivukovic, Goran V. (ed). *Ovid and the Renaissance Body*. Toronto: Toronto University Press, 2001.
Starkey, David (ed). *The English Court: From the War of the Roses to the Civil War*. London: Longman, 1987.
Stern, Tiffany. *Making Shakespeare: From Page to Stage*. London: Routledge, 2004.
Stone, Lawrence. *The Family, Sex and Marriage in England 1500–1800*. New York: Harper & Row, 1977.
Strasser, Ulrike. *State of Virginity: Gender, Religion and Politics in an Early Modern Catholic State*. Ann Arbor, Mich.: University of Michigan Press, 2004.
Strong, Roy. *Gloriana: The Portraits of Queen Elizabeth*. London: Thames and Hudson, 1987.
The Cult of Elizabeth. Oakland: University of California Press, 1977.
Sugg, Richard. *Murder After Death*. London and Ithaca: Cornell University Press, 2007, 111–29.
Sullivan, Garret A. Jr. *The Drama of Landscape: Land, Property and Social Relations on the Early Modern Stage*. Redwood City, Calif.: Stanford University Press, 1999.
Summers, Claude J. (ed). *Fault Lines and Controversies in the Study of Seventeenth-Century English Literature*. Columbia: University of Missouri Press, 2002.
Sutton, James. *Materialising Space at an Early Modern Prodigy House: The Cecils at Theobalds, 1564–1607*. Aldershot: Ashgate, 2004.
Sutton, John. *Philosophy and Memory Traces: Descartes to Connectionism*. Cambridge: Cambridge University Press, 1998.
Tadmor, Naomi. 'Women and Wives: The Language of Marriage in Early Modern English Biblical Translations'. *History Workshop Journal* 62, 2006, 1–27.
Thirsk, Joan. 'Younger Sons in the Seventeenth Century'. *History* 54, 1969, 358–377.
Thomas, Catherine. 'Chaste Bodies and Poisonous Desires in Milton's Mask'. *Studies in English Literature* 46. 2006, 435–59.
Thomas, Keith. *Religion and the Decline of Magic*. New York: Scribner, 1971.
Thompson, Ann and John O. *Shakespeare: Meaning and Metaphor*. Sussex: Harvest Press, 1987.
Thorne, Alison. *Shakespeare's Romances*. Basingstoke: Palgrave Macmillan, 2003.
Thurley, Simon. *Somerset House: The Palace of England's Queens 1551–1692*. London: Topographical Society, 1999.

The Royal Palaces of Tudor England: A Social and Architectural History. New Haven and London: Yale University Press, 1993.
'The Stuart Kings, Oliver Cromwell and the Chapel Royal 1618–1685'. *Architectural History* 45, 2002, 238–74.
Tilley, Christopher. *A Phenomenology of Landscape: Places, Paths and Monuments*. Oxford: Berg, 1994.
The Materiality of Stone: Explorations in Landscape Phenomenology. Oxford: Berg, 2004.
Tomlinson, Sophie. *Women on Stage in Stuart Drama*. Cambridge: Cambridge University Press, 2006.
Totaro, Rebecca and Gilman, Ernest B. *Representing the Plague in Early Modern England*. London: Routledge, 2011.
Traub, Valerie. 'Jewels, Statues, and Corpses: Containment of Female Erotic Power in Shakespeare's Plays'. *Shakespeare Studies* 20, 1987, 215–38.
Turner, James Grantham. *One Flesh: Paradisal Marriage and Sexual Relations in the Age of Milton*. Oxford: Clarendon Press, 1987.
The Politics of Landscape: Rural Scene and Society in English Poetry, 1630–1660. Cambridge, Mass.: Harvard University Press, 1979.
Tylus, Jane. *A History of Literary Criticism in the Italian Renaissance*. Chicago: Chicago University Press, 2004.
Van Elk, Martine. '"Our praises are our wages": Courtly Exchange, Social Mobility, and Female Speech'. *The Winter's Tale*. *Philological Quarterly* 79.4, 2000, 429–58.
Vanita, Ruth. 'Mariological Memory in *The Winter's Tale* and *Henry VIII*'. *Studies in English Literature, 1500–1900* 40:2, 2000, 311–37.
Vaught, Jennifer C. (ed). *Rhetorics of Bodily Disease and Health in Medieval and Early Modern England*. Aldershot: Ashgate, 2010.
Veevers, Erica. *Images of Love and Religion*. Cambridge: Cambridge University Press, 1989.
Walker, Greg. 'Playing by the Book: Early Tudor Drama and the Printed Text'. *The Politics of Performance in Early Renaissance Drama*. Cambridge: Cambridge University Press, 1998.
Walker, Julia M. *The Elizabeth Icon, 1603–2003*. Basingstoke: Palgrave Macmillian, 2004.
Walker, S.F. *A Cure for Love: A Generic Study of the Pastoral Idyll*. New York: Garland, 1987.
Wall, Wendy. *The Imprint of Gender: Authorship and Publication in the English Renaissance*. Ithaca and London: Cornell University Press, 1993.
Walsham, Alexandra. '"The Fatall Vesper': Providentialism and Anti-Popery in Late Jacobean London'. *Past & Present* 144, 1994, 36–87.
Watkins, John. *Representing Elizabeth in Stuart England: Literature, History, Sovereignty*. Cambridge: Cambridge University Press, 2002.
Wear, Andrew. *Knowledge and Practice in English Medicine, 1550–1680*. Cambridge: Cambridge University Press, 2000.

Wedgwood, Cicely Veronica. *The King's Peace 1637–1641*. London: Collins, 1955.
Weinstein, Donald and Bell, Rudolph M. *Saints and Society: The Two Worlds of Western Christendom 1000–1700*. Chicago: University of Chicago Press, 1982.
Weitz, Nancy. 'Chastity, Rape, and Ideology in the Castlehaven Testimonies and Milton's Ludlow Mask', *Milton Studies* 32, 1995, 153–68.
Whitehead, Barbara (ed). *Women's Education in Early Modern Europe*. London: Garland, 1999.
Whitteridge, Gwyneth. *William Harvey and the Circulation of the Blood*. London: Macdonald, 1971.
Williamson, Elizabeth. *The Materiality of Religion in Early Modern English Drama*. Aldershot: Ashgate, 2009.
Wilson, Adrian. *The Making of Man-Wifery*. London: UCL Press, 1995.
Wilson, Dudley. *Signs and Portents: Monstrous Births from the Middle-Ages to the Enlightenment*. London: Routledge, 1993.
Wilson, John Dover. *Life in Shakespeare's England: A Book of Elizabethan Prose*. New York: Cosimo, 2008.
Witte, John Jr. *From Sacrament to Contract: Marriage, Religion, and Law in the Western Tradition*. Louisville: Westminster John Know Press, 1997.
Woodbridge, Linda. 'Palisading the Elizabethan Body Politics'. *Texas Studies in Literature and Language* 33:3, 1991, 327–54.
Wright, Stephen. "Loe, William (d. 1645)," in *Oxford Dictionary of National Biography*, online ed., Lawrence Goldman, Oxford: OUP www.oxforddnb.com/view/article/16927 (accessed October 11, 2011).
Wright, Thomas. *Circulation: William Harvey's Revolutionary Idea*. London: Chatto & Windus, 2012.
Wymer, Roland. *Suicide and Despair in the Jacobean Drama*. Sussex: Harvester Press, 1986.
Yates, Frances Amelia. *Astraea: The Imperial Theme in the Sixteenth Century*. London: Routledge & Kegan Paul, 1975.
  Elizabethan Neoplatonism Reconsidered: Spenser and Francesco Giorgi. London: The Society for Renaissance Studies, 1977.
Zimmerman, Susan (ed). *Shakespeare's Tragedies*. Basingstoke: Palgrave Macmillan, 1998.

Index

Abbot, Robert
  A triall of our church-forsakers, 52
Adams, Thomas
  Englands sicknes, 50
  The Happiness of the Church, 129
adultery, 1–2, 8, 10, 14, 20–1, 25, 28, 52, 61, 63, 105–6, 114, 131
Ainsworth, Henry
  An animadversion to Mr Richard Clyftons advertisement, 52
  Covnterpoyson considerations touching the poynts in difference, 52–3
Almond, Oliver
  The vncasing of heresie, or, The anatomie of protestancie, 51
architectural space, 11, 14–19, 33–45, 128

Bacon, Nathaniel
  The Continuation of an Historicall Discourse of the Government of England, 26–7
Baillie, Robert
  A dissuasive from the errours of the time wherein the tenets of the principall sects, 51
birthing chair, 102–3, 130, 136–7, 139
blood, 5, 9, 12–13, 19–20, 30, 47–8, 59, 61–3, 67, 69, 71–2, 77, 85, 87–8, 91, 95–7, 99–100, 113, 132, 135, 139, 173
Brinsley, John
  The araignment of the present schism of new separation in old England, 51
Burgess, Cornelius
  A Sermon preached to the honourable house of commons, 21, 50

Carew, Thomas
  Coelum Britannicum, 29
Carlomaria tradition, 29, 111
Castlehaven trial, 6, 9, 88–93
Chamberlen family, 133–6

Charles I, 2–3, 6, 8–9, 21–33, 39–40, 44, 81, 85–94, 96, 100–3, 108–9, 111–13, 123–5, 127–8, 131, 138–9, 173–4
chastity *See also* unchastity
  as communal integrity, 50–4, 73, 78–9, 81
  as legitimate unions, 21–30
  as sluicing, 46–54
contamination, 14–15, 21, 33, 44–5, 49, 83, 86, 142, 162
Cosin, John
  A collection of private devotions, 116–17
Cowley, Abraham
  Coy Nature, 98

Davenant, William
  The Temple of Love, 41, 123–6, 160, 162
de Sales, Francois, 108, 112
disease, 11, 14–18, 21, 23, 26, 32–4, 36–7, 39, 41, 43–5, 47–51, 54, 60, 68, 81, 87, 129

Elizabeth I, 1–3, 13, 21, 25–8, 33–4, 37, 46, 50, 86, 117, 172–4
emblem, 8, 46, 63–4, 83, 124, 128

Fletcher, Phineas
  The Locusts, 20
Ford, John, 45
  Christes Bloodie Sweat, 59–60, 73, 81
  The Broken Heart, 8, 57–61, 69–70, 73–81, 93–7
  'Tis Pity She's a Whore, 8, 56, 61–4, 67–8, 70–3, 95

Harington, John
  The Metamorphoses of Ajax, 16
Harvey, William, 69–70, 85, 97–102
Henrietta Maria
  births, 128–37
  containment of, 34–6
  masques and performances, 41–2, 55–6, 120–8, 137

Henrietta Maria (cont.)
spirituality and religious observances of, 34–6, 38–43, 109–28
Henry VIII, 24

James I/VI, 14, 85–6, 111, 122
John Bastwicke
The Continuation of an Historicall Discourse of the Government of England, 24

Laud, William (Archbishop of Canterbury), 8, 23–4, 26, 30, 58, 81, 84, 86, 117, 120
leakiness, 7, 11, 13, 33, 37, 45, 47, 49–50, 53, 68, 106–7
Little Gidding community, 117

marriage, 6, 8, 11–12, 15, 21–34, 37, 45, 49, 61, 70, 74, 77, 86, 88, 95, 104, 108, 111, 114, 128–30, 136, 170, 173–4
Mary Tudor, Queen of England, 24, 27–8
Middleton, Thomas
The Ghost of Lucrece, 19
midwife/midwives, 6, 13–14, 24, 104, 130–1, 133–6
Milton, John
Comus, 140–1, 149–71
How Soon Hath Time, 143–4, 152, 162, 164, 167
Paradise Lost, 63, 146
The Sixth Prolusion, 146–9
Montagu, Walter
The Shepherds' Paradise, 12, 28, 41–2, 120–4, 137

penitence, 3–4, 53–4, 57, 60, 71–81, 95
Petition of Right, 23, 27
phlebotomy, 8, 69, 95, 97
plague, 8, 11, 15, 31, 33–45, 127

pregnancy, 5, 15, 39, 104, 106, 131–3, 135
privy/privies, 8, 12, 16–17, 33
Prynne, William, 23–4, 26, 40, 113–15, 120

Reuff, James
The Expert Midwife, 131–2

schism, 3, 20, 31, 50–1, 54, 81, 124, 172
Shakespeare, William
Pericles, 104
The Winter's Tale, 2, 4, 8, 10–15, 103–8
sieve, 14, 46

The Grand Remonstrance, 31
Thomas, Scott
Vox Regis, 25
Throne of State, 5–6, 9, 81, 83–5, 88–9, 101–3, 137–40, 157–60, 162, 167
tragicomedy, 2, 4, 7–8, 54–6, 83, 132, 138, 169, 171, 173

unchastity *See also* chastity
as idolatry, 21–2, 28, 30, 50
as sluicing, 10–21, 33–44
as tyranny and power, 82–102
as tyranny and pride, 46–9, 53–5, 64–81, 141–71

Vestal Virgins, 14, 46
Virgin Mary, 27–8, 43, 86, 110, 118
virginity, 2, 27, 118, 156, 163, 173
virginity test, 13
visible Church, 4, 23, 50–1, 53, 124, 126, 170, 172

Whore of Babylon, 3, 21–2, 24, 26, 84, 113, 172
witch, 13–14, 16, 84, 131